# ACADEMIC
# FREEDOM
# AND
# ACADEMIC
# ANARCHY

# ACADEMIC FREEDOM AND ACADEMIC ANARCHY

by Sidney Hook
*Professor of Philosophy*
*New York University*

COWLES BOOK COMPANY, INC.
NEW YORK

SBN 402-12211-9

Library of Congress Catalog Card Number 79-90060

Cowles Book Company, Inc.
A subsidiary of Cowles Communications, Inc.

Published simultaneously in Canada by
    General Publishing Company, Ltd., 30 Lesmill Road,
    Don Mills, Toronto, Ontario

Printed in the United States of America

First Edition

To

Edward J. Rozek—

Embattled fighter for free men, free society,
and the free university against fascism,
communism, and totalitarian liberalism

# CONTENTS

# PREFACE

It is not hard to predict that from the vantage point of the year 2000, if not earlier, the last decade in American education will appear as the most bizarre in its history. The college and university system of the nation is being transformed, both in its curriculum and organization, not to further the genuine educational growth of students but primarily to meet the challenge and threats of student unrest and disruption. The criterion for educational reform is openly proclaimed: How to restore peace to the campus? How to end educational chaos?

The history of American higher education has been a history of change. Programs have been proposed and evaluated on the basis of controlled observation of the different effects of viable alternatives. Although practice has sometimes lagged behind profession, until now the customary justification of curricular revisions has been in terms of educational consequences—experienced or anticipated. These are measured by the degree of interest and mastery students achieved in coping with intellectual problems; and by their sensitivity to ideas, patterns of forms, colors, and action. They were never judged by effectiveness in establishing or reestablishing law and order on our campus.

How different the scene is today! From one end of the country to another, the major problems that are agitating faculties and administrations are not, What is the best education for modern men and women?—a question that should be of perennial concern to educators—but, What must be done to put an end to disruption; to prevent the outbreak of violence and the threats of violence from disorganizing the academic community? It has been naively assumed that the answer to the latter question constitutes an answer to the former, whereas at best it can only be a necessary condition to an adequate answer.

Those who desire to orient the curriculum only to present-day concerns would do well to ponder Oscar Wilde's remark: "He to whom the present is the only thing that is present, knows nothing of the age in which he lives." The only considerations that would justify orienting the curriculum to the problems of campus pacification would be convincing evidence that campus disorders have been mainly caused by the dissatisfaction of students with their educational experience. If students had actually felt that the educational curriculum was outmoded, irrelevant to the great problems and issues of the world, that it was intellectually inferior or degrading, that they were being deprived of their educational birthright by incompetent teachers—something might be said for suspecting that a causal connection existed between a poor or inadequate education and student disruption.

The existence of student malaise is not disputed. But there is no evidence that it has expressed itself in dissatisfaction with college and university curricula, no evidence that students have dissented from or petitioned and protested against their curricular fare in vain. Only if this had been the case, would it lend any plausibility to the hypothesis that student outbreaks of violence will be obviated by enlightened educational reforms.

Every informed observer, however, knows that the major outbreaks of violence and disruption on American campuses have had nothing or little to do with the curricular organizational setup in the American university. To imagine, therefore, that curricular and administrative reforms will contain this violence and disruption is farfetched. It is to bank on an improbable conjunction of unrelated phenomena. It is comparable to advocating as a curb on arson the construction of better houses. But if the causes of arson are not the houses people live in but some injustice in the community or some terrible incident, like the assassination of a charismatic leader or the direction of foreign policy, the better-constructed houses will be burned down, too.

There may be situations in which the housing is so bad that those suffering from it are willing to destroy it rather than endure it further. Under such circumstances, in addition to other humane reasons for constructing better housing, the desire to prevent further arson is a legitimate supporting ground for the construction of better homes. But if the arson is the result of some deeper political strategy, how will better housing put a stop to it? There is always a valid reason for offering better housing as there is for providing better schooling, but the reason for such improvement has nothing to do with its efficacy in preventing arson in the one case or forcible occupation of the university in the other.

When tempers run high, garden cities are in just as great danger from fire as are slums, and activist students who invade and take over college and university centers are initially indifferent for the most part to what is taught or how. By their own account, they are trying to punish or move the larger society outside the university.

The stormy years of student uprising have resulted in both a failure of nerve and an eclipse of intelligence among many of those who have traditionally been entrusted with the guidance of our educational enterprise. The commonplace truths about the weight of evidence, responsible assertion, striving for objectivity, and fairness in controversy sound today like wild paradoxes. Nothing is too extreme to be said or believed. Some of these amazing phenomena have been documented and analyzed in the body of this book. It would require an encyclopedia of absurdity to do justice to the varieties of doctrines and practices that have been urged as panaceas for campus peace. Actually if peace were the only desideratum, a massive dose of serenity pills in student diet would do the trick. Some proposed remedies are more amusing than dangerous, like the hope placed in the effect of unlimited premarital intercourse in producing stupefaction or quiescence among undergraduates.

Perhaps the most radical of all proposals is to make a curriculum, so to speak, of the phenomenon of the student revolt itself. Men and women of mature years have been so impressed by some students' assertion that they learned more about life by disrupting the university than from all their peacefully conducted classes within it, that they have refused to condemn student disruption on educational grounds. A few have even gone so far as to propose that state universities offer courses in guerrilla warfare in order to facilitate "meaningful" social change. The state is expected to underwrite activities directed against its own survival. When courses of this kind are exposed for what they are, the invariable cry is sounded that academic freedom is being endangered, with the loudest outcries coming from those who denounce it as a "bourgeois illusion," and whose actions against scholars and teachers with whom they disagree testify to their complete disbelief in it.

One unintended by-product of student disruption—unintended in that it was not on any program of student demands, negotiable or nonnegotiable—has been a greater concern about the art of teaching on the part of colleges, something that was shamefully neglected, in some places pridefully. Good teaching is something that is owed to students not in order to keep them pacified but in order to educate them properly. If there is adequate moral and political justification for rebellion, the best teaching in the world could not and should not abort it—indeed, it would in all likelihood indirectly encourage it. Hopefully teaching will improve in our colleges in the next few years. But like other improvements, it did not require mass violence and lawlessness to bring it about. To justify student disruption because it has resulted in some good is like justifying arson because it has led to more efficient methods of putting fires out. The reforms could have been achieved at a far lesser cost.

In the period ahead, the serious arguments about education will take place not between revolting students and concerned educators—for the revolting students unfortunately have so far refused to engage in sustained argument—but between the faculty allies and apologists for student disruption and their critical colleagues. The necessity for continued interest in, and criticism of, teaching techniques goes without saying. But it is a far cry from some recent condemnations of all current modes of teaching, good or bad, as irrelevant, as too intellectual, as too much removed from "life."

My own conclusion about teaching is that its chief weakness is that it is not intellectual and imaginative enough. Those who mistakenly identify the use of the intellect with "intellectualism" seem somewhat fearful that the passionate pursuit of ideas might divert student activities from their current tasks. And it very well might, for no full-time activist can acquire a liberal-arts education of a depth and breadth commensurate with his talents, for the simple reason that there are not enough hours left in the day for study and reflection after the caucuses, meetings, demonstrations, and news conferences are over.

One school of critics denigrates much of what is taught in our colleges as merely preparation for achievement on "verbal-rational" tests; as if such tests were in no way a measure of achievement of rationality, and as if they could not have diagnostic value for the student himself. The choice should be not between tests and no tests but between those that are punitive and those that have a genuine educational value.

Worst of all, among the educational effusions of those who seek to provide a rationale for student irrationalism and "anti-intellectualism" is the confusion between education as a process wherein the flow of experience becomes a basis for anticipating and coping with the future in a more or less adequate fashion that does not require formal schooling or classrooms or teachers; and education as schooling, by means of the disciplines of organized subject matter, rational method, and voluntary participation in the experience of learning.

Some critics of our modern educational system—in which we are trying to educate everybody—appalled by the difficulties of providing the appropriate schooling required for the growth of all individuals, have discovered the fact that it is not necessary to go to school to acquire an education, and have made a virtue of it. Their wisdom reduces to the insight that not everybody requires the *same* schooling.

Their foolishness consists in their denying the fact that everybody can profit from *some* schooling, if it is related to individual needs and capacities. Many individuals have been autodidacts. But it is the height of absurdity to convert what was a limitation or deprivation into a privilege. It is like making a virtue of the necessity of having to work one's way through college. Having done so out of necessity, I can see no sense in doing so where there is no necessity—unless the work is specifically related to what one is studying or is part of public service along lines William James suggested.

Today, where the "street" or "gang" or "trade" or "farm" becomes the only "school" one knows, except for rare and lucky persons, the individual becomes limited if not brutalized. There are things that human beings should know about nature, society, and themselves that they will never learn from the haphazard succession of events in their adventitious experiences, or at the very least, that they can learn much better, more quickly, and at lesser cost through schooling with the help of competent teachers.

It may be argued that bad schooling at any level is worse than none but to prefer none to better schooling is willful nonsense. When it is realized that we are concerned with the education of many millions, the responsibility of such recommendations becomes obvious. It is like arguing for the virtues of education by log-cabin firelight on the basis of Lincoln's early years. Hardly more plausible is the view that any subject can be adequately mastered in later life when the need for it arises in one's experience. This is not true even for the elementary skills of arithmetic and spelling, and for many subjects that require a background of prior knowledge. There is also the habit or capacity of learning to learn that must be strengthened in the early years.

Not far removed from this negativism is the celebration of new ways of acquiring an education off the campus—away from libraries, away from the give and take of classroom discussions or seminars, away from teachers. One modern Rousseau has discovered it is more efficacious and rewarding to meet at a swimming pool than to hold his class in a classroom. It is true that a lively and successful meeting of any normal group can be held almost anywhere and under almost any set of circumstances—even at a swimming pool! The real question is whether more than one successful session can be so held, whether the consecutive and cumulative development of subject matter and the mastery of a discipline can be achieved in this way. Swimming can best be taught at a swimming pool but not symbolic logic or physics, history or economics.

From the same source we learn that "not only ordinary classrooms but ordinary clothes put distance between people and hinder learning." It is left somewhat uncertain whether learning is hindered least when no clothes or extraordinary clothes are worn. It all depends, of course, on what is to be learned. A former disciple of Dewey who has outgrown his master teaches philosophy by reading from notes assorted at random while behind him equally random pictures flash on three screens simultaneously to the accompaniment of desultory snatches of sound-track music, from Bach to Cage. One may grant that if anything significant can be learned this way, classrooms and colleges can be largely dispensed with. But there is no independent evidence that anything significant is learned this way.

A much more dangerous confusion is the view that knowledge and ideas are inert unless they lead to action while they are being learned, unless they facilitate immersion in life experiences. According to the activists' maxim, unless students are prepared to put their bodies on the line—indeed their very lives—for their beliefs, they are not truly serious. This is romantic nonsense and substitutes role-playing for reflection and analysis.

No problem of learning is ever settled by putting one's body on the line. Laboratory practice, field work, clinical experience—it goes without saying that these are very helpful in learning, sometimes essential. But commitment to action in a good cause is no substitute for learning. We learn by doing but not all doing leads to learning. To interpret the pragmatic principle that thought and action are related, as if the action necessarily had to be something practical or useful or convenient or progressive, is to convert it into a slogan of philistinism and social uplift.

Particularly baneful is the view that understanding ideas in the social sciences must involve activity on behalf of good causes—that to study trade unionism or relief one must become a trade-union organizer or welfare worker, or that to study employment trends one must go into the factory. No one can complete his education this way because one activity precludes many others. Karl Marx never spent a day of his life in a factory, but he studied the factory system and its applications in the light of ideas whose truth or falsity depended not on his own personal experiences but on the empirical, historical evidence.

The relationship between education and experience, and schooling and experience, is much more complex than is implied by those who simply tell us that the test of a student's education is "the way he lives." The test of a student's education is whether he has acquired a basic literacy in certain skills and knowledge, and a sensitivity to the values of a humane and civilized culture; whether he can meet the problems he has been educated to meet; whether it enables him to find a center or basis around which to organize in a significant way his experiences.

The function of a college education is not to teach a person

"how to live." He can live without it. It is to give him perspective—insight into ideas, trends, values, and an ability to
live with himself. A man may be a well-educated classics
scholar or engineer or social worker or physician and die a
drunken failure for reasons that have nothing to do with his
education. The way a man earns a living is, of course, very
likely to be related to his education and in a good society it
should be related; but the way a man earns his living is not
or should not be the whole of the way he lives.

The reaction to student disruption has ignored the extent to
which student behavior has been influenced by ideas—unsound
ideas—despite the current student fetishism of action. Force
and violence may be contained by courageous faculty action,
and in the extremities of disaster, by courts and civil authorities. But in the long run they can best be met by confronting
the ideas that inspire them with better ideas, by patiently and
persistently exposing the mythologies and discredited idealo-
gies whose slogans and rhetoric they repeat. The mixture of
"vulgar Marxism," "anarchism," and "elitism" is no less explosive for being confusedly held and accompanied by anti-
intellectualistic bias.

Most discussions of student unrest treat the students as if
they were not reponsible for their actions; as if their beliefs
and attributes were merely incidental to a pattern of compulsive behavior whose sources are to be found elsewhere. This
does not account for the fact that the overwhelming number
of students do not engage in disruption.

I do not see how education as distinct from training is possible, without the assumption that most students can respond
to ideas and that they are responsible in large measure for
their actions. Although it is possible that they may continue
to turn a deaf ear to criticisms of their position and a blind
eye to ideals continuous with the liberal and humanist tradition from Socrates to John Dewey, the effort must be made
until they see reason. Whether they see reason or not, what
their teachers say and do must exemplify it.

It is this positive educational philosophy that underlies all the criticisms of the subsequent chapters. It unifies discussions written at different times on different facets of the educational crisis and published in part in various periodicals.

SIDNEY HOOK

*South Wardsboro, Vermont*
*September, 1969*

# CHAPTER ONE

# THE CURRENT SCENE

Five years ago, when the news of the Berkeley rebellion at the University of California was still fresh, had anyone predicted that a Presidential paper would be issued on campus disruption and violence, he would have been regarded as an irresponsible alarmist. Particularly mordant in their criticism would have been those who are today claiming that student unrest is the natural consequence of the failure of university education to be "relevant," or to make long overdue curricular changes, or to restructure its entire system.

The plain truth is that what has happened has taken everyone by surprise, and not least some of the student leaders themselves, whose wildest expectations, discounting their rhetoric, have been surpassed by reality. I can make this admission without embarrassment since at the time of the Berkeley revolution I predicted that a turning point had been reached in the history of higher American education.

My anticipations, however, fell far short of the event. In the thirties, as a Council member of the American Association of University Professors, I had raised the question of the role of the faculty in determining university policy and the most effective methods of realizing it, but few were the faculty members—aside from professional educators scorned by their liberal-arts colleagues—who were concerned.

More than twenty years ago, in my *Education for Modern Man*, arguing against Dr. Robert Hutchins' proposals for a "timeless" education that would be the same everywhere for all men, I outlined in detail a liberal-arts education relevant to modern man that would take as its point of departure the great social problems of our time. Nonetheless, although I still believe in the validity of the positions I have taken with respect to the reform of the university, I would never dream of relating the failure to adopt these or similar educational proposals to student disruption and rebellion.

The unexpectedness of the academic storms of the last few years testifies not only to the complexity of social phenomena —which is an old story by now—but to the rapidity of social developments. Large-scale events may now occur without preliminary or preparatory signs to indicate what storms are brewing. In the past, rumblings of discontent, and sometimes premature outbursts of resentment or violence by frustrated groups, enabled one to chart the areas of social life in which tensions were building up to the explosive point.

This is no longer true. The riots of the French students in 1968 triggered off social disturbances that no analyst of social affairs came near anticipating. Yet they could have resulted in a full-scale revolutionary action. It is extremely unlikely that student activism, even if it intensifies, can have anything like a similar effect in the United States. Nonetheless, the cumulative effects of sustained disruptions could provoke within a relatively short period of time strong measures of social reaction that would sweep away many of the liberal gains of the last half century.

No one understands fully why social events move today at such an unprecedented pace. It is obvious that developments in the field of communications have an important influence. News of dramatic happenings anywhere can be transmitted with the velocity of light to the far corners of the earth. Such news, upon meeting a prepared consciousness, may ignite it into action. The prepared consciousness will be found among groups aware of the ways in which today's world—despite its divisions—constitutes a community of auditors and of the extent to which men are fellow creatures in a common destiny.

In addition, because of the political history of recent years in which small nations and dictators have successfully defied major powers, the attitude has developed in some revolutionary quarters that anything is possible and therefore anything may be attempted. After all, who knows what the limits of action are, without trying? If Cohen-Bendit could almost bring down De Gaulle in a country that boasted of its relative stability, why can't Tom Hayden dream of leading a great popular crusade in a country whose cities threaten to burst into flames every summer? Whether or not these considerations are valid, it is hardly contestable that youthful rebellion, more particularly student rebellion, in the United States is an altogether different phenomenon from student rebellions of the past. No one would have thought of characterizing the expressions of youthful spirit and high jinks in the past as "rebellion."

Some commentators, and even some politicians, desirous of ingratiating themselves with the young, have referred to current youthful activism as a healthy, even if slightly more exuberant, expression of traditional youthful idealism. They are fortunate the American public has such a short memory of the predictions made by columnists and of the mindless inanities perpetrated by political-speech writers. But since they, as well as others, may genuinely be convinced that what we are witnessing today is a continuation of normal youthful restiveness, aggravated by the hysterical overreactions of some educators and administrators, we cannot dismiss this point of view.

Let us then ask: What is different today about the widespread disaffection of university youth? Before answering this question, we should put in perspective a phenomenon that is very puzzling to the educational layman or intelligent citizen not intimately aware of campus realities—the disparity between the small numbers of activist students involved and the magnitude of their influence and capacity for disorganization.

To say that 2 percent of the student population of the United States are militants or activists is to overstate the truth. If so, how is it possible for them to produce so much chaos, to bring universities to "a grinding halt," to convert so many campuses into battlefields—not of ideas and books, but of students against faculty and administration, and students against the police? Were 2 percent of the working force of a factory to go out on strike, it would be a failure, and no amount of violence could retrieve it. How can two or even 1 percent of the student body be so much more successful?

The answer flows from the difference between the factory or industrial plant and the university, and points up the vulnerability of the latter to any kind of violence. In an industrial plant a strike cannot be successful unless a large body of the workers support it; and it will always fail if a substantial number of the workers march through the picket lines.

In a university, if students declare "a strike," all they need do is to take control of some vital structure or center, the paralysis of which over a prolonged period of time effectively prevents the university from functioning. I place the term "strike" in quotes because it does not have to take the form of a declaration that the militant students will stay away from class, and an invitation to fellow students to follow suit. The "strike" is, in effect, an action that disorganizes the university. Once the students insist on any nonnegotiable demand, the "strike" cannot be broken except either by capitulation or by invoking sanctions, physical and educational, which the university administrators are usually ill-prepared to do.

On occasions when administrations have been goaded into summoning the police, because of the demoralization produced by prolonged occupation of university buildings or because of threatened acts of vandalism and violence, student militants have issued calls for a boycott of all classes. Where no attempts have been made to coerce or intimidate other students from attending classes, such strikes have usually failed —except where police intervention has resulted in evoking sympathy in the general student body.

The nature of a student strike is quite different from an industrial strike. In a student strike the victims are the students themselves. They cannot inflict any harm upon their teachers comparable to the losses imposed by strikers on employers. That is why a student strike in the form of a boycott of classes cannot be prevented and should not be penalized if and when it occurs. Students, as a rule, should be free not to attend their classes if they do not wish to do so. Where such absence is prolonged, most parents who are defraying the substantial costs of tuition would naturally prefer their children "to strike" at home.

Aware of this, student strike leaders must not only encourage their followers to absent themselves from class, they must prevent other students who do not wish to strike from attending class. The chief method employed is to close down the university by seizing classroom buildings or administrative centers. It is this intolerable interference by coercion, or threats of coercion, with the freedom of students who wish to continue their education that makes student strikes occasions for riot and/or dangerous sabotage. The security forces of a university are very few in number, and are usually retired or superannuated employees from other fields who are more qualified to direct traffic than to restrain excited youths. They cannot cope with even a mere handful of rampaging students prepared to go all the way to impose their will on fellow students and the campus community. This explains why a few resolute students prepared to seize and hold buildings, and to withstand efforts to dislodge them can cause so much difficulty for the university.

The spectacle of the police clearing a campus building or area always arouses the hostility of a considerable number of students and faculty members who, until then, had been unsympathetic to the goals and methods of the student activists. The paradoxical fact is that the student violence, even if deplored, does not stir them to the same pitch of fury as the use of violence to prevent the exercise or further spread of violence. They either make common cause with the victims of police action or organize themselves independently to mediate between the rebels and the administration and/or faculty.

Many of them would rather see the university closed down than remain open by means of a forceful defense against those who have resorted to force. This suits the book of campus militants, who bank upon the pressure of the student body and faculty on the administration to reopen, even at the cost of capitulation to the rebels and amnesty for all their acts of lawlessness.

This, in broad outline, and with many details and qualifications necessarily omitted, explains how a small group of students can tie up a large university. Those unfamiliar with events may be tempted to suggest that there is always the alternative of simply ignoring the students' lawless action. This may be possible if the students have seized the religious center where the chaplain can parley with them or some outlying annex where little goes on. It is not possible to ignore for long the illegal possession of other buildings housing classrooms, laboratories, or administrative offices. Even if it were, students would escalate their lawlessness to a point where it could not be ignored.

We return to the question of the ways in which student disaffections of the past differ from those of the present. We may distinguish five generic differences:

1. In the past student protests were directed against *specific* abuses, real or fancied. The occasion may have been the barring of a controversial figure from the campus, an attempt to censor a salacious issue of a student magazine, or the dismissal of a teacher who had won a popular following among students but who had failed to convince his professional colleagues that he had qualified for tenure. Or, the protest might have been over the dullness or unwholesomeness of the food, the absence of beer, or the illiberality of the rules governing visitation hours in the dormitories of coeducational colleges.

Today, although agitation may begin over such issues, they are quickly related to much broader ones that involve not only the university but the outside community, and often national policy. The cooperation of the universities in reporting student standing to draft boards; admission policies with respect to minorities; conscription; the war in Vietnam; the character of student recruitment and faculty research— these are some of the typical themes of student agitation and disaffection today.

In the past most of these questions would have been considered of no special concern to students, although their interest in these subjects would have been welcomed as broadening their outlook. The making of programmatic *demands* upon the community and university would have been considered a matter beyond student competence or authority to be left to the ordinary political democratic process. It would have been obvious that the universities as such do not and cannot initiate or terminate national policies any group finds objectionable.

2. In the past, reactions to grievances were spontaneous. They would boil up in the course of a few days and have a limited life span. After a short time, the campus would return to the normal process of teaching and learning and extracurricular diversion.

Today, many of the reactions to campus grievances are organized either in the sense that some national group has a program for agitation on all campuses, and dispatches individuals to different campuses to encourage and mastermind student discontent; or some group of militants on the local campus draws up a schedule of complaints to keep the academic pot boiling. These activities are often related but it may be helpful to distinguish between them.

During the thirties there were youth groups affiliated with the Socialist and Communist parties. But in the main they were active only where there already existed young Socialists and young Communists on campuses who organized chapters. Few were the emissaries sent to campuses to organize cells, and the great majority of such efforts proved abortive.

Today, both among Negro and white students, representatives of national organizations are at work on many campuses. The best known are Students for a Democratic Society (SDS);

Students Non-Violent Coordinating Committee (SNCC)*; the Peace and Freedom Party; the Congress of Racial Equality (CORE); the National Student Association; the Progressive Labor Movement; and a half-dozen organizations that have developed around one or another phase of the opposition to the Vietnam War. Their function, often proclaimed, is to help radicalize the American student body by directly linking campus issues to the great social and political issues of the time. They differ among themselves, sometimes fiercely, but they are united by a common determination to destroy the existing social and political system by violence if necessary.

Even where these representatives of national groups are not active, on almost every campus of the country there is a small local group of independent activists. Their members reflect the *Zeitgeist* to the extent of wishing to wake up their campus and bring it into the mainstream of student activism, whose doings fascinate the press and television.

I have often been consulted by such groups during my visits to college and university campuses to analyze the general situation in the country. With varying degrees of wistfulness over being left out of the action or with frank envy of what was occurring elsewhere, I would be asked to suggest a few possible grievances around which to organize student protest. The tempo of events elsewhere had created a positive hunger for the excitement of confrontation tactics in a small but active minority. Hardly any college is immune from the infection.

There is nothing surprising about this. Nor does it indicate that on the other campuses genuine grievances are missing. Human beings are imitative animals and even more so when they are members of groups than when they are alone. There was an element of psychic imitation during the goldfish-swallowing, tree-sitting, marathon-dance craze of the twenties, too. But these were merely forms of exhibitionism that had only nuisance value when ignored. But today's students do not want to be ignored. They would be extremely frus-

---

* Symptomatic of recent developments, the term, "non-violent," has been dropped from the name of the organization.

trated if they were. They know how to command attention. They have a will to provoke confrontation with the administration, faculty, or civil authority.

This will to confrontation sometimes takes strange forms. At one well-known liberal-arts college in the Midwest, after I had checked off a list of possible grievances with some student leaders, who despairingly told me that they didn't apply to the local situation, a committee awaited my departure to inform me that they had finally hit upon a real issue around which they hoped to organize a demonstration. They were going to demand that the college library be open all night—instead of shutting down at midnight and opening at 8:00 A.M.

For a moment, in a glow of pleasant surprise, I thought that this revealed a surging even if delayed passion for scholarship. But a few inquiries elicited the information that there had been no mass demand for the service; that none of the leaders of the group were themselves interested in using the library during these unearthly hours and didn't know for sure how many would avail themselves of the opportunity. Nor had any inquiries been made to see if resources were at hand to defray the expense of three library shifts.

My amusement turned to shock when I learned that although there was a Faculty-Student Library Committee, the request was not going to be presented to its members because, said the spokesman, "First, they'll appoint a subcommittee to consider the proposal and that'll take months. Who knows, they may end up by adopting it, and where will that leave us? This way we can have our sit-in right away!"

And they did!

At another banner-bright liberal institution with pacifist antecedents the campus had been rocked by a series of stormy demonstrations, some of them in violent abridgement of the freedom of recruiters for industry and government. During a three-week period of relative calm, the campus newspaper reported that some students were organizing to protest the "mood of apathy" on the campus. In short, campus disorders today are organized as "spontaneous" in somewhat the same sense as the spontaneous demonstrations of the "socialist democracies."

3. In the past, student disaffection never raised issues concerning the nature, role, and organization of the university. It was directed to situations and actions *within* the university. More often than not, it was a plea for toleration of something new—or, at most, an agitation against some compulsory course.

Today in very large measure the very concept of the university, its organization and role, is under powerful assault. This attack almost always follows protests on other issues that have embroiled the academic community. Sometimes there is an explicit demand to reorganize the university in order to bring the faculty and students more directly into its governance. Frequently, specific demands are related to the necessity of restructuring the university. On any measures that affect the students, according to some claims, they should have a voice equal to any other. But according to some of the literature of the SDS, this is insufficient; students should have an equal vote on the same basis as the faculty. Nor are the principles and details of administrative policy regarded as beyond their competence.

One of the considerations obviously moving the students who were planning a sit-in to keep the college library open all night was the feeling that they should have as much power as others to determine the use of university space. The lowest form of academic life in the eyes of modern-day student insurgents consists of trustees or regents, regardless of their past services. They are judged by their economic association, not by their educational opinions and decisions; no secret is made, at least by radical students, of their belief that janitors have a more vital role to play in the university than those who today have the highest legal authority.

Actually it is difficult for most students to sustain a prolonged interest in purely educational questions, especially details of organizational structure that leave them largely unaffected. Only the insurgent student leaders have displayed a

strong concern with these questions after launching initial
demonstrations around issues altogether unrelated to internal
educational problems. That is why they have sought to
activate sections of the faculty, and tried to hitch their own
demands to those of the faculty, for which a much more
formidable case can be made.

The most distinctive aspect of the concern of insurgent
student leaders in educational matters, however, is the character of the educational philosophy behind it. We shall have
more to say about this in subsequent chapters, but suffice it
to say here that it is based upon a position completely at vari-
ance with the explicit and implicit educational assumptions of
the American or any other Western university system.

4. Student insurgents today contain a considerable number
of nonstudents who play a very active role in planning and
executing "creative disorders." During the academic year
1968-1969, the chief organizer for the SDS at N.Y.U. was
a nonstudent adult who was paid by the SDS with funds al-
lotted to it by the Student Organization, captured by militant
students in an election in which most of the other students did not participate. At Berkeley the role of outsiders
had always been quite marked. All this represents a great departure from the past, when students were proud to run their
own affairs without help from outsiders.

5. The final, and the most important, of all the differences
between past student disaffection and the present disorders is
that in the past students were rational both in their claims
and their methods of struggle. Today, there is a tendency
among intransigent student leaders to dismiss the whole concept of rational behavior as a middle-class prejudice. If one
feels himself to be in the right, to take any consideration of
consequences is to be "square." The weapons of struggle in
the past were argument, evidence, "the dictates of reason and
compassion." Today confrontation in any form is the
desired policy. Student activists have demonstrated quite
clearly that their paramount interest is in the effectiveness of

any confrontation—even though its attendant violence may run the gamut from bombings, beatings, and sabotage to arson, vandalism, and screaming obscenities.

My memories of student disaffection go back some fifty-odd years to a time when a small group of students in the Boys' High School of Brooklyn criticized the stand of the United States in World War I. We proposed a capital-gains tax to defray the war instead of Liberty Bonds, and objected to turning the classrooms into propaganda sessions in behalf of the war cause of the moment. At both the high school, and at the College of the City of New York in subsequent years, the disaffected students prided themselves upon their willingness and ability to present a reasoned case for their position. They would never dream of disturbing or breaking up meetings of students who disagreed with them, or the meetings of the speakers dispatched to the campus by the National Security League when word leaked out about the presence of "Young Bolsheviks," conjured up in the hysterical imaginings of faculty, the Board of Education, and the local press. It was our meetings that were often broken up and our noses bloodied by the defenders of the *status quo*.

There was a mixture of both naïveté and arrogance in our youthful assumption that violence was being used against us because our arguments were unanswerable, that we had the reason and the right of the ages on our side. But it was also a tribute to our faith in the power of reason. This assumption, however, was characteristic of all radical student groups, and explains their indifference to the direct-action philosophy of the Industrial Workers of the World (IWW).

Later, when Communist groups appeared on the campus, even during the thirties, the belief that historical evidence and argument pointed unmistakably to the need for social revolution was paraded by Communist partisans with a smugness and self-righteousness that became counterproductive. When violence was episodically used, it was in the factional disputes of the Communist movement or against Socialists as Stalin's criminally idiotic theory of "social fascism" made headway.

However, these incidents of violence were played down, sometimes denied, but never glorified.

The striking contrast between the reliance on argument in earlier American student movements and the assorted techniques of violence in the student movement today would be incredible were it not for the pictorial, televised, and documentary evidence that some groups among white and black students have deliberately adopted the tactics of guerrilla warfare, just short of the use of conventional firearms and sometimes beyond it, to impose educational demands—sometimes referred to as nonnegotiable—on the university community. An entire library of underground literature can be compiled to show how widespread, how serious, how radically novel the resort to violence has become.

As I write I have before me a copy of *Your Manual, Volume 1, No. 1*, published by "3" R News Service, Inc., San Francisco, California, and distributed on the campus of San Francisco State College, which was made available to me February 28, 1969, by Urban Whitaker, Professor of International Relations and Vice-President of Academic Affairs at that institution.

This is the college at which the offices of the editor of the *Gator*, the student newspaper, were invaded by students who disapproved of something he wrote, and beat him into unconsciousness. It is a campus whose classes have been disrupted by students, and whose professors have sometimes been forcibly prevented from teaching. It is the place where Professor John A. Bunzel and his family endured the torment of harassment and persecution—including an attempted bombing, slashing of the tires of his family car, and the painting of "Fascist Scab" on his automobile—because of his belief that a black-studies curriculum should present divergent points of view on racial questions and not be geared exclusively to the propagation of the separatist doctrines of militant black nationalists.[1]

[1] See the stories by Rosa Gustaitis in the *Washington Post* of February 27, 1969, and by Lawrence E. Davies in the *New York Times* of March 8, 1969.

*Your Manual* is a truly frightening document. It lists the basic equipment to bring to the campus for use against police, "the pigs" (detectives), and "the scabs" (nonstriking students). It goes on to enumerate "Supplies, Ordnance, and Logistics." I summarize some of the descriptions:

A. *Rocks and Bottles.*
   1. Supplying personnel
      How to bring rocks and bottles on campus and where to store them for later use.
   2. *Throwing Rocks and Bottles.*
      a. First at cameramen to drive them off so that no pictures can be taken.
      b. Then at scab students at windows.
      c. Where to throw in order to do the most damage.
      d. If no other targets are available, throw at scab cars.

B. *Red Pepper, Darts, Water Guns, etc.*
   1. Red pepper can be very effective "if thrown" downwind into horses' faces.
   2. Darts should be thrown at the horses' bodies.
   3. Water guns—Fill guns with regular household ammonia and squirt in horses' eyes and faces.
   4. Cherry bombs—To be effective they must have bb's and tacks glued onto the cherry bomb's surface.

C. *Ice Picks, Leather Punches, and Can Openers.*
   Used to best advantage on car tires of scab teachers, students, and administrators. Very good on plainclothes pigs, too.

D. *Sling Shots.*
   Buy at sports store, use marbles. Very good on windows, but can be used with relative safety at long distance against police. Highly recommended.

E. *Picket Signs.*
   A 1″ x 2″ or larger or broom or ax handle make very good clubs or at least defensive weapons to block clubbing pigs. If you wish, you may want to sharpen the end

of the club to have a more versatile weapon. Spears can be used to stab or club police.

F. *Steel Lead Pipe, Blackjacks, and Chains.*

G. *The Mace.*
   Varieties of missiles, some of which contain nails.

H. *Sugar.*
   To disable cars of scab students.

I. *Spray Paint for Those Artistically Inclined.*
   Spray on windshields and bodies of scab cars.

J. *Zippo Cigarette Lighter.*
   1. Can be used to ignite curtains, wastebaskets, and bulletin boards or paper towels in bathrooms.
   2. The use of lighter fluid increases effectiveness.

K. *Oven Cleaner in Aerosol.*
   Can be used as a weapon doing severe damage to any exposed skin of the enemy.

L. *Eggs, Tomatoes, and Ink Bottles.*
   Use fruit against enemy and ink against property.

Section III entitled "Bombs" begins with a warning against carelessness. Illustrations are provided to show how to manufacture various types of bombs. The following types of bombs are described in considerable detail as well as the most effective methods of using them.

A. Cherry bomb with armament.

B. Stink bomb.

C. Molotov cocktail.

D. Pipe bomb.

The final page lists coming attractions and feature articles of future issues. One is to be devoted to "our scholar in residence, John Bunzel." Another is on the "strategic planning of campus rallies." Still another deals with instructions for disabling a computer. I quote one peculiar item in full.

> *The Death List.* Many progressive thinkers of revolutionary theory believe assassination of pig leaders is one of the necessary variables for winning our struggle. Therefore, the editors of this journal (*Your Manual*)

have compiled a complete list of persons most likely to be assassinated and harassed (if you can't kill 'em, harass 'em).

So far this "Death List" has not been published.

In the light of the foregoing, it should not be cause for surprise that considerable difficulty has been encountered in getting faculty members to serve on the Disciplinary Action Panel of San Francisco State College or even to testify as witnesses. That literature of this kind could be distributed on the campus of even one college is evidence that there is qualitatively no connection between past student restiveness and present student disorders. That students could even entertain the notion of such actions would have been completely unthinkable even a few years ago. Not on all or even most campuses have actions like these been advocated.

Nonetheless, it is disquieting that not only at San Francisco State but at Berkeley, U.C.L.A., Cornell, and various state colleges, some of the techniques enumerated in this *vade mecum* of revolutionary campus warfare have been adopted. Nor are these phenomena restricted only to black students. Tom Hayden, one of the founders and leading spirits of the SDS, is prepared to go just as far in the process of confrontation as some of the leaders of the black militants. And unfortunately, he is not alone in his dedication.[2] The various factions among the revolutionary youth groups on campuses are beginning to differentiate themselves on the basis of commitment to a "soft" or "hard line" on the necessity of "armed revolution," "soft" meaning sometimes and "hard," always.

---

[2] cf. his article *Two, Three, Many Columbias* in *Ramparts*, June, 1968, and quoted in part on p. 260 of Appendix III.

CHAPTER TWO

# THE CAUSES OF TRANSITION

Granted that student activism is limited to a comparatively small number. What requires explanation is the success of the activists in attracting a large periphery of normally uninvolved students to their cause on crucial occasions of confrontation. After all, it was not so long ago that our publicists and influential organs of public opinion were deploring the so-called "silent generation" of the fifties and early sixties and declaring that the passivity of the students was a consequence of the demagogy of Senator Joseph McCarthy. What accounts for the change in student mood and manners?

As in most questions of social causation, the causes are complex and no one can plausibly claim to possess either a comprehensive or final understanding of the shift in the student climate of opinion. A few observations may be pertinent.

First of all, the "silent generation" was not more silent than most student generations of the past. The notion that "McCarthyism" had a serious intimidating effect on the universities is a myth. In fact, they were the centers of opposition and resistance to the cultural vigilantism of which McCarthy was the spokesman. Secondly, the events of the fifties—which included the brutal and sudden invasion of South Korea, the ruthless suppression of the workers' revolts in East Germany in 1953, and finally, the liquidation of the Hungarian freedom fighters at the time of the Hungarian Revolution in 1956—gave the Communist threat of expansion a grim presence that could not easily be dismissed. Thirdly, there were still a sufficient number of G.I.'s in the colleges and universities, which raised the average age of students and contributed to a seriousness of outlook that dampened student restiveness. Among the youth, there is no invariable correlation between intellectual achievement and emotional maturity.

The most important factor in arousing the student population of the country was the gradual but profound consequences of the Supreme Court's decision on desegregation in 1954 and the series of heroic actions by the Negro community in dramatic, *nonviolent* actions that touched the conscience of all Americans who took the ideals of democracy as more than idle rhetoric.

Students from campuses all over the country participated in demonstrations for civil rights, and in organizing, teaching, and serving in the civil-rights movement. Those who returned to their colleges and universities on the basis of their experience gravitated into positions of leadership in the multifarious groups that sprang up to further civil rights.

In the eyes of these young idealists the slowness of the progress made in achieving complete racial equality in education, politics, housing, and industry cancelled the great gains that had been made by legislative reforms and peaceful social protest. It tended to produce an unqualified demand for "Freedom Now" and other goals that were not immediately realizable, and led to extremism in actions of protest. If students encountered any seeming injustice or arbitrariness in university regulations, they tended to compare themselves to the oppressed Negroes in Mississippi and the administrative and faculty figures to the hooded gunmen and racist sheriffs who kept the Negroes in subjection.

The mood of protest among these activists became bitter with the onset of the Vietnam War and the impact of the draft. It must not be assumed, however, that it was American involvement in Vietnam that was the chief or sole cause of student rebelliousness. The mood was already there. At Berkeley the Vietnam issue was very peripheral even at the time of the final sit-in in December, 1964. But as the war escalated, it became focal to a point where activist leaders prevented those who tried to reply to criticisms of American policy from speaking.

The eloquent partisans of the Free Speech Movement consistently denied freedom of speech to anyone whose point of view did not coincide with theirs. What started as an ostensible discussion of the rights and wrongs of American policy degenerated during the space of a few years into a series of mob actions against any representative of the American government on the campuses of the country. Secretary of Defense McNamara was prevented from speaking at Harvard; General Wheeler, Chairman of the Joint Chiefs of Staff, was hooted and jeered and his meeting broken up at Brown University by students who rushed the platform, hurled the podium to the floor, and seized the microphone. At Stanford students showered Vice-President Humphrey with bags of urine and offal.

None other than Senator Eugene McCarthy, himself a former college professor, approved the action of students at the University of Wisconsin in preventing Secretary Orville Freeman from speaking, and encouraged students elsewhere to howl down spokesmen of the administration rather than to listen and reply to them.

However, meetings in behalf and in defense of the Vietcong and North Vietnam were conducted without any interference or interruption. Disciplinary action by administrations and faculties against student violence was rarely taken, and on the few occasions when proceedings were begun they were very prolonged and resulted in nominal punishments. There was really very little risk involved in the violent disregard of the elementary principles of courtesy, fair play, and public order.

It should also be noted that a few years earlier there had been cases of student hooliganism against speakers at meetings called to protest the American presence in Vietnam. Some of these disgraceful actions were not properly reported and denounced. But these incidents were isolated and episodic, and ceased altogether by the time the "teach-in" movement developed.

The "teach-ins" represented the last efforts at rational debate by student militants who resorted to progressively more violent "sit-ins," "mill-ins," "bitch-ins," "take-overs," and creative vandalisms against universities because of their real or alleged connection with the military establishment. Gradually the character of the antiwar movement and the student activists changed. Instead of protesting the presence of the United States in Vietnam by marching under the American flag, they publicly burned the American flag and paraded behind the Vietcong flag.

In the fall of 1968 I was roundly hissed by an audience of young misses in training for the role of Madame De Farge—in, of all places, Smith College—for suggesting that opponents of United States involvement in Vietnam would be more persuasive if they marched behind the American flag rather than the Vietcong flag. At the same meeting, a description of atrocities by the Vietcong against democrats who refused to accept their hegemony brought thunderous applause from the audience.

As George Woodcock, originally an enthusiastic supporter of the student revolt, sadly observed: "Antiwar demonstrators ceased—except in name—to live up to their overt intent; they became in reality war demonstrators in favor of the Vietcong, with its cold-blooded rule by terror."

Accompanying and intensifying these developments was a fascination among some student activist leaders with Castro, Ché Guevara, and even Ho-Chi-Minh, as well as other anti-American heroes of the moment. They replaced Martin Luther King as the charismatic spokesman of the liberation movement. Some of the student leaders journeyed to Havana and Prague, where they met representatives of the Vietcong.

This attitude of revolutionary romanticism, fed by official hand-outs and carefully conducted tours of great social achievements under the revolutionary dictatorships, encouraged the belief that the strategy of anticolonial warfare could be employed in the United States in order "to liberate" not only the black population but all other "oppressed" and "alienated" classes, among whom the students were regarded as the most important until the workers could be galvanized into action.

So far the preceding factors have undoubtedly helped to develop the revolutionary consciousness of student activist *leaders*. But they do not account for the following these leaders have attracted, for the shifting rank and file of their organizations, for their appeal to sympathetic participants in their demonstrations. What is there in the current psychology and mind-set of the American student body that makes it susceptible, even to the limited degree indicated, to the propaganda, both of word and "happening," of the radical militant leaders?

Most wholesale attempts to characterize the psychology of the present student generation, even when buttressed by elaborate charts and statistical tables, result in generalizations of limited validity. They do not hold for all student groupings. Far and away the best analyses of the psychology of that section of the present student generation periodically susceptible to the propaganda of the New Left (by no means a majority) seem to me to be those made by Professors Bruno Bettelheim and Lewis Feuer.*

Dr. Bettelheim's account is subtle, nuanced, and balanced. He stresses, among other factors, two things that I have confirmed in my own experiences with students. The first is the sense of guilt many have in virtue of the privileged status they enjoy under the draft. To make it easier to live with their acute consciousness of the fact that others of their age who are socially disadvantaged are running dangerous risks from which they are exempt, they exaggerate the moral guilt of their nation and its leaders in order to relieve their own burden

---

* Professor Bettelheim's analysis was presented before a Congressional subcommittee on higher education in the spring of 1969 and was extensively reprinted in the *Washington Post* of March 23, 1969. Professor Feuer's analysis appears in his *Conflict of Generation*, N.Y., Basic Books, 1969.

of responsibility. If they can make themselves believe that the United States is an aggressive imperialistic empire controlled by a capitalistic elite and therefore not worth defending, they can ease their sense of guilt, and deny that any substantial improvements have been made in the condition of the masses. Even those individuals to whose parents and grandparents the United States gave a haven from persecution shrugged off any obligation of national loyalty.

The second factor is the absence of any sense of mission or significance in their lives. Their education has failed to evoke in them a calling or vocation or an intellectual center around which to organize their experience. These lacks are compensated for by the excitements and temporary dedications that grow out of defiance of the Establishment.

Dr. Lewis Feuer, in a series of masterly studies, has stressed the generation conflict, the tendency of students to destroy the overriding father figure of childhood by turning against the values of institutions of the parental culture. There is undoubtedly a large measure of truth in this but it does not explain the specificities of the current student revolt. The gap between previous generations has been much greater and more embittered than the gap in our own times without resulting in such explosive denouements in the academy.

Never before in Western history has any generation of parents been so permissive, so close to their offspring, so involved in their lives, so eager to share vicariously their pleasures and pains. The objective conflicts between generations have been much more pronounced in the past, especially in America. With respect to culture, values, outlook, and sympathetic understanding, the behavior of the generations between 1900 and 1930 shows a greater contrast and more conscious conflict than the behavior of generations from 1930 to the present. A legitimate criticism of the contemporary generation of parents is not that they are too removed or detached but that they live the life of their children too much. The consequence is that parents often conceal their critical judgment of, or displeasure with, their offsprings' activities in cases where they cannot make over their own point of view to bring it in accord with that of the younger generation. I have taught and lived with student generations since 1919. For what they are worth, I submit some impressions of the current generation based upon careful observations of students in different parts of the country, friendly conversations, and reciprocal criticisms—impressions checked by consultations with colleagues in the various fields of the humanities, including the pure sciences.

Students today are less career-oriented and vocation-conscious than they have ever been in the twentieth century or since the days when attendance at college was mostly a status symbol for the offspring of the leisure class. They have little concern about how they will make a living. There is hardly any dread of unemployment. They are certain they will make out either with their parents' help or by some government grant. Even though more of them enter the graduate school than at any time in the past, they have less intellectual drive. They seem less intellectually excited by ideas than students of the past. More eccentric in appearance, diction, and life styles, they are less so in individual points of view, and are content with the conventional pieties of acceptance or with participation in *group* expressions of dissent. In the absence of genuine intellectual independence, dissent can become just as mechanical a reflex as assent.

Related to this diminished interest in a career or a calling or even a center of passionate concern for ideas around which to organize their experiences is a greater sense of immediacy. They seem to have adopted one of the early advertisement slogans as a principle with respect to satisfactions of aesthetic, sexual, and other needs—*Eventually, why not now?* The level of affluence seems higher than it has ever been. During short school vacations and even extended weekend holidays, scores of thousands of students will make their way to seaside, semitropical resorts, not so much to study as to play and gamble.

Modern students seem more contemporary minded than

their predecessors. They are devoid of a historical sense. It is as if they have never studied history or as if such study had never taken. Nothing in the past appears relevant to their current problems and concerns. References to Hitler and Stalin, whose shadows fell so darkly on the lives of their parents, mean hardly more to them than references to Caesar or Attila or Ghengis Khan. Even some of the leaders of the SDS have complained of the historical simplemindedness and indifference of their rank and file who can be relied upon to "turn out regularly for demonstrations."

Thus Carl Davidson, one of the vice-presidents of the SDS, after a coast-to-coast lecture and organizing tour, complains that most of its members are "anti-intellectual," unfamiliar even with the writings of C. Wright Mills, Bob Moses, and other prophets of the New Left. (*New Left Notes*, December 3, 1967).

Although this historical ignorance and indifference is not true of the leadership of the SDS, and not so true of the great mass of the students outside radical organizations, there is still a surprising unawareness of the history of radical thought and movements, its traditions, controversies, causes of success and failure—even when information on these matters bears relevantly on issues of present concern. Some evidence of this is provided by the curriculum of the so-called Free Universities established by radical organizations disenchanted with the allegedly "irrelevant" curriculum provided by the universities in which they are matriculated. Courses in Marxism are offered on the crudest propagandistic level and a century of Marxist scholarship is ignored or shunned on the ground that it is infected with imperialistic revisionisms.

Anti-intellectualism and the decline of the prestige of scholarship, and to some extent of scholarship itself, are in part attributable to the lowering of standards, both of admission and achievement, in some institutions. The consequences of this policy have been aggravated by the failure of universities to offer diversified curricula, within a common liberal-arts framework, to challenge the variety of capacities and interests among students, sure to be present when the doors of higher education are open to all who are willing and able to profit be continued education.

Despite the prevalence of anti-intellectualism, and perhaps partly because of it, the student population has become "moralistic." By "moralism" I mean an expression of moral concern that by its disregard of historical contexts and alternatives takes positions having consequences that undermine the likelihood of genuine moral advance. "Moralism" is the stance of God's or history's angry men who bring the world closer to hell than to the Heaven whose laws and felicities they proclaim.

The presence of moral concern by the young is an unqualified good. And in this respect the present generation of students cannot be faulted. On the contrary, for this they deserve the highest praise. Despite the detractors of current university education, this moral concern has been to a considerable degree inspired by their studies and their teachers. Regardless of the origin of this concern, there can be no doubt that awareness of the problems of war, race, housing, and poverty is to be preferred to indifference; and interest in the "mysteries" of politics preferred to interest in fashions, athletics, and the inanities of the social-gossip columns.

Of crucial importance is how this concern is expressed. Instead of seeking political solutions to these problems by hard and persistent work of organization, too many have been discouraged by their first political defeats and have become impatient and disenthralled with the political process. They tend to yield in their moods of quick impatience to solicitations to engage in direct action and confrontations to solve complex problems; to get quick results by tactics that sometimes border on and transcend the limits of legality in their threats of violence. When this provokes a backlash of fear at the first opportunity voters have to register their feelings, it is taken as overwhelming evidence of the futility of the normal democratic process as an instrument of social change. The predictions about the futility of political reforms become self-fulfilling prophecies. Resistance and revolution open up as the only alternatives available to those who would be serious. A mood of moralism now supervenes.

"Moralism" goes beyond the moral point of view. It recognizes only right or wrong, good or bad, and no degrees of evil. It is essentially unhistorical. If anything is good, it was always good; if anything is evil today, it was always evil. Political and social discrimination against black Americans is evil. What difference does it make if there is a Negro Senator, a Negro member of the Supreme Court, Negro mayors of large cities, elected Negro sheriffs in the South, a Civil Rights Voting Act on the law books with teeth in it—so long as the number of Negro office holders do not reflect the relative proportion of the blacks to the total population of the country? What difference does it make if there are laws penalizing racial discrimination in housing and employment, that the state laws forbidding racial miscegenation and the degrading legislative legacy of the post-Reconstrucion period have been struck down, if there is still widespread non-compliance?

It is here that the unhistorical attitude is reinforced by the tendency towards immediatism, and builds up a strong opposition—a violent scorn toward the politics of the lesser evil. The lesser evil is evil and an end on't! The consideration that the lesser evil in the given historical context is the greater good—that if it is rejected, the only likely alternative will be the greater evil—is dismissed as the prompting of cowardice and hypocrisy, disguised in liberal sophistry. In any situation there is only one solution from this point of view—the ideal solution. Those who deny its possibility are not idealists. They are opportunists who call themselves realists and serve the interests of the stand-patters. So run the pronouncements of the modern-day rebels.

Anyone who has argued with representatives of the New Left will convince himself of the depth and strength of this mood. The Declaration of Independence—a progressive and revolutionary document? Nonsense. It failed to condemn slavery! The Constitution—a remarkable if imperfect document (despite Gladstone)? Vicious nonsense! Garrison was right. It was "a compact with hell"—for it recognized slavery. Lincoln—a great emancipator? An obscene myth—he was prepared to sell out the whole program of freedom for Union! That all these documents represented compromises, the best mediations of conflicting interests that could be achieved in order to escape chaos, civil war, and defeat, does not mitigate their moral failure.

Well, then, what of the great charter of English liberties—the Magna Charta—with its discriminating provisions against women and Jews, and its defense of baronial privileges? The question answers itself. It is a legal relic of racist, antifeminist, and feudal prejudice. The past is judged by standards of justice of the present—standards that emerged only in virtue of the developments that today are condemned in the light of these standards!

"But," retort the idealists who were born yesterday, "if you admit, as you pretend to do, that slavery is immoral today, was it not immoral yesterday, and in 1776, and before that and wherever men arbitrarily imposed their will upon others?"

One inquires: "Would it follow from this that slavery was immoral even in the days when it was introduced as an alternative to the practice of decimating prisoners of war taken in battle?"

"Yes, that practice was evil, too."

"Which was the lesser evil, if these were the only historically viable alternatives at the time?"

The discussion is usually broken off before this point and rarely continues beyond it. To the eyes of those who were born yesterday, nature and art may reveal qualities and truths not discovered before; but to those who were born yesterday —and lack the perspective and maturity derived from experience—history and human affairs can be only dimly perceived, and what is perceived only very imperfectly understood.

At the moment I am not intent upon developing an argument but in describing a mood among students more in evidence today than at any time in the past. It would be a grave error, however, to treat the students as one homogeneous mass, and to fail to differentiate between the militant student leaders of the New Left on the one hand and the rank and file of their organizations and the sympathetic periphery on the other. What has been said so far about the mood and thought-ways of students who follow leaders does not apply without serious qualification to the articulate leadership. *They* are not anti-intellectual or unhistorical in defending their positions against criticisms but only in propagandizing it. Yet their mode of thinking has a characteristic stamp, too, that should be briefly identified in order to dsitinguish it from the democratic Old Left, which they have repudiated, as well as from the mainstream of the American liberal tradition from Jefferson to Dewey.

They would retort to the view that asserts that all great political choices are choices between the greater and lesser evil by pointing out that what appears to be a lesser evil may not actually be so; that, to use their favorite metaphor, the alleged lesser evil of reform as contrasted with revolution may be like applying a poultice where only surgery can save limb or life.

When the metaphor is replaced by a concrete problem of political choice, the empirical burden of proof must rest on them to show that what appears to be the lesser evil—say, certain desirable changes at a more moderate pace than "revolutionists" desire but at a smaller cost in human suffering—is not truly the lesser evil. This they are loath to do. But even if they were successful in showing that the *apparently* lesser evil was *actually* not the lesser evil, it is clear that despite themselves they do accept the principle of the lesser evil. For when the meaning and implications of the principle of the lesser evil are firmly grasped, only the obsessed can repudiate it.

The thinking of the leaders of student disaffection is marked by an impatience with the democratic process and *au fond* by a misunderstanding of the priority the democratic philosophy gives to process over product. The result is an uneasy acceptance of an elitism that would permit a revolutionary minority to impose its solutions on an unresponsive or recalcitrant majority in the name of democracy, and to deprive their opponents of the protection of the Bill of Rights while flaunting the banners and slogans of freedom. Direct action of an extraparliamentary kind is baptized "participatory democracy" in which the few control the many by inducing them to shout defiance at their elders and betters.

Impatience has soured the milk of idealism in the breasts of the student leaders. Encouraged by the ease with which the mass media of communication could be used to give their voices national resonance, they were soon frustrated by the uncanny capacity of the American political system to assimilate both criticism and critics. They could get a hearing but felt they could not influence events. The consequences have been the hardening of the temper of fanaticism, a recklessness that would force the pace of politicalization by violent confrontation, and a resort to tactics that could be precisely those urged by agent-provocateurs intent upon discrediting the movement of protest in the eyes of those not completely committed. But agent-provocateurs were not necessary to fan the frustrations and resentments of the student leaders into a blazing rage. Some of them had already proclaimed their acceptance of the tactics and techniques of guerrilla warfare.

What gives them confidence in their intransigent position?— Several things. First, a feeling that every defeat can be turned into a victory, if only the initiators of violence can appear as victims of an overreacting administration or police. In this, the organizers of student violence have been singularly successful. Second, even when they have not succeeded in winning converts from among the sympathizers with their plight, they seem to be buoyed up by a sense of heroism in defeat. The example of Castro and his band defying the most powerful nation in the world renews the flame of their hopes. Finally,

and perhaps most important, the memory of previously un-
imagined victories at Berkeley and Columbia, where a strategy
inspired by St. Just's revolutionary maxim "Audacity, audacity, and still more audacity!" carried the day, emboldens
them to launch desperate attacks in other institutions.

Baffled to explain the form and intensity of student disruption by specific educational grievances, even when these are
legitimate, some administrators and senior members of the
faculty have sought to find large social causes for the puzzling
phenomena. One could write a book on the multiple attempts
to describe what it is "the students are telling us" by their
violence and obscenity, and why. They are marked not only
by extreme divergence but by the renewed confirmations
they provide of the principle that there is no transfer of training from one field to another.

Those with nostrums for educational reform are convinced
that the failure of the university to abolish all departments,
to return to the classics, to impart religious education, to stress
esthetic experience, to minimize scientific and technologi-
cal subject matters or what not, is the real source of the
trouble. Others with strong feelings about social questions—
whether it be the dangers of too much governmental control
or too little, the posture of nuclear military defense, the pul-
lution of the atmosphere, the cold war, or the survival of the
human race—have convinced themselves that "unconsciously"
the students reflect the failure of society to resolve these
questions.

It is noteworthy that little effort is made to correlate "what
the students are really trying to communicate" by their actions
with what the students actually say before they act. It is
difficult to evaluate properly detailed reports about "an under-
lying uneasiness" among students that may be merely a pro-
jection of the uneasiness of the reporter. Nor is it explained
why the students behaved differently in previous periods
when the educational or social lacks that presumably cause
their present uneasiness were just as much in evidence.

The following chapters will explore some of the concepts

on everyone's lips that seem central to understanding what the issues are. I shall begin with a discussion of academic freedom because those who defend, as well as those who are critical of student activism, profess devotion to its principles.

# CHAPTER THREE

# ACADEMIC FREEDOM: "LEHRFREIHEIT"

One of the truly astonishing phenomena of American liberal thought is its inconsistent and unprincipled character. This is manifest in various ways. Depending upon whether a cause is considered "good" or "bad," "progressive" or "reactionary," ill-defined terms that are more often used as epithets of praise or abuse than of description, different positions are taken about the meaning and validity of civic and political rights.

When the Southern segregationists were riding high, liberals valiantly defended the principle that with respect to the possession, exercise, and defense of human rights, the administration of justice must be color-blind. No sooner did the temper of the country turn against segregation than some of the erstwhile leaders of the liberal cause began to insist that negative discrimination in *favor* of color was morally justified; that it was not enough to discriminate in favor of all who were especially distressed or disadvantaged—which would include a few whites among a vast number of blacks— but that color itself should become the criterion for good or "progressive" discrimination.

In effect, a distinction was recognized between "good" racism" and "bad racism," and it was denied that the victims of bad racism could themselves be guilty of it. Thus, after an interview over Channel 13 in New York City in which Rapp

Brown was given an opportunity to air his views in response to sympathetic questions, the master of ceremonies gravely announced: "In accordance with the request of Mr. Rapp Brown, this show has been televised by an all-black crew." In response to my inquiry whether, if Governor George Wallace had requested that an interview with him be televised by an all-white crew, his request would be granted, I was told: "Of course not! That would be racism!"

The same phenomenon was observable when liberals protested postwar repressive legislation. All guilt is personal, they properly said. No sooner was the black liberation movement in full swing than liberals began to speak of "collective guilt," and to extenuate dubious discriminatory provisions, positive and negative, in our educational system on the ground that the present generation of whites was morally guilty for the institution of slavery and its aftermath.

When the United States government groped its way, with many errors, toward an adequate security program, the liberal war cry "There is no guilt by association" contributed to the confusion by failing to distinguish between legal and moral guilt, and between degrees and quality of association—for example, between association by membership and by accidental proximity. Today even organs of liberal opinion editorially invoke the principle of guilt by association in opposing appointment of individuals to government positions because of their too close and recent association with members of the John Birch Association. If the meaning of "guilt by association" is fixed, and if such guilt warrants condemnation, then surely what is sauce for the red goose is sauce for the white goose.

There is some justification among critics of liberalism for their cynicism but it is misdirected. It is not the philosophy of liberalism that is compromised by the opportunistic applications of its principles but those ritualistic liberals who use liberal principles as political instruments to achieve some specific goal, discarding them just as soon as they become impediments in achieving other goals.

What is true of principles of political liberalism is also true of the principles of academic freedom. It is surprising to discover that these principles are elastic, too, and can be conveniently expanded and contracted for political purposes. This process of accommodation is often facilitated by a confusion that besets the whole question. It is necessary, therefore, to ask some simple but fundamental questions about "academic freedom."

What is academic freedom? Briefly put, it is the freedom of professionally qualified persons to inquire, discover, publish, and teach the truth as they see it in the field of their competence. It is subject to no control or authority except the control or authority of the rational methods by which truths or conclusions are sought and established in these disciplines.

So conceived, academic freedom is a comparatively recent acquisition in the United States. Actually it is less than a century old, and it was first introduced in a very tentative and precarious fashion at Johns Hopkins University. At the time it was an un-American import from Imperial Germany, a country then far removed from being a politically democratic state. Nonetheless, it was the first country in the history of the world to develop the theory and practice of "academic freedom" as this is understood today. At the time it was propounded and developed in Imperial Germany (at first in Prussia at the founding of the University of Berlin in 1810), nothing comparable to it existed in the relatively more politically democratic countries of England and the United States.

In Germany "academic freedom" was originally defined as *Lehrfreiheit und Lernfreiheit*, freedom to teach and freedom to learn. In the United States when academic freedom was first bruited about, no one paid any attention to *Lernfreiheit*—freedom to learn. Academic freedom was identified simply with *Lehrfreiheit*—freedom to teach.

The founding fathers of the American Association of University Professors—John Dewey, Arthur Lovejoy, and James Harvey Robinson—were concerned only with the freedom to teach, which hardly existed anywhere in the United States at the time. Until very recently when academic freedom was defended or criticized, normally all it meant was freedom to teach. Freedom to learn, which today is at the heart of most claims for student academic freedom, only came to public notice in this country a few years ago, adventitiously in the wake of other student demands that required an ex post facto rationale. Prior to that, the phrase "student academic freedom" would have been regarded as a neologism.

There are several important implications of the definition we have offered for academic freedom. First of all, it does not define academic freedom as the freedom *to teach* the truth but only as freedom *to seek* the truth. There is a crucial difference in the emphasis we put on the term "seek." For it runs counter to the position of all thinkers—from Augustine to the present—who have thought that they had *the* truth; that academic freedom was the freedom to find and teach that truth, and that, therefore, error had no rights. But academic freedom, if it exists, implies the right to be wrong. After all, no one can properly claim to be infallible, or to possess absolute truth. All we can ask of the teacher-scholar is that he should honestly seek the truth. This is not to equate truth and error; nor does it say that they have the same rights when they are known as such. If academic freedom is the right not to *teach* the truth but to *seek* the truth, then teachers must enjoy freedom from any ecclesiastical, religious, economic, or political dogmas that would bar the road to further inquiry.

Another significant implication of our definition is that the right of academic freedom is not a civil right or a human right despite widespread opinion to the contrary. For note that we have defined it as the right of *professionally qualified* persons. That makes it a special, not a general or universal right; it is a right that must be *earned*.

A human right, on the other hand, is a right that does not have to be earned. It is possessed by every human being because he is a human being, or a member of a civilized community. One doesn't have to earn the right to worship God according to his conscience, or the right to speak, publish, and assemble freely. It is his due as a member of a civilized community; intrinsic to his status as man and citizen. Anyone has a human right to talk nonsense about anything, anywhere, anytime. But returning to our definition of academic freedom, one must be professionally qualified to talk nonsense in a university!

To be sure, what one may think is sheer nonsense may turn out to be the newer or higher wisdom. It is risky to dismiss the apparently nonsensical mouthings of professionally qualified persons. What sounds like a paradox may, on further investigation, turn out to be a new or even commonplace truth.

It follows from our definition that the qualified teacher, whose qualifications may be inferred from his acquisition of tenure, has the right honestly to reach, and hold, and proclaim any conclusion in the field of his competence. In other words, academic freedom carries with it the *right to heresy* as well as the right to restate and defend the traditional views. This takes in considerable ground. If a teacher in honest pursuit of an inquiry or argument comes to a conclusion that appears fascist or communist or racist or what-not in the eyes of others, once he has been certified as professionally competent by his peers, then those who believe in academic freedom must defend his right to be wrong—if they consider him wrong—whatever their orthodoxy may be.

The viability of academic freedom rests not only on its support by the community of scholars but even more on the support of the general community, which ultimately is the source of the material means of its operation. Even the withdrawal of tax exemption may be fatal to its functioning. That is why understanding and support of the principles of academic freedom, when they are threatened, are often crucial to their survival. Such an understanding presupposes a considerable degree of sophistication by the public. Although difficult, this sophistication is possible to achieve. The general community, if it endorses academic freedom, must be prepared to support not a teacher's opinions but his right to be wrong, i.e., his right to hold and express them. Academic freedom, however, does not in the least imply immunity from criticism, even vigorous criticism from one's peers as well as others.

Polls of public opinion, and of representatives of the public, indicate that most laymen experience some discomfort with the notion that there is a right to heresy. But if they can be brought to reflect upon the fact that the heresy of today may become the accepted truth or orthodoxy of tomorrow, that no one can reasonably claim infallibility or absolute truth for any theory that would render it invulnerable to the possibility of its withdrawal or modification in the light of further evidence, they are likely to accept the right to heresy. On reflection they realize that the very nature of free academic activity implies an openness to all points of view, provided only that they express the conclusion of honest inquiry.

Does this mean that anything goes in a university or college, that a teacher who enjoys tenure is licensed to do or to say anything he pleases?—No. The right to heresy must not be confused with, or interpreted as, a right to conspiracy. By "conspiracy" in this connection, I mean a deliberate act in violation of the canons of professional ethics and integrity.

It will be recalled that we defined academic freedom as the right of *professionally qualified* persons to inquire, discover, publish, and teach the truth as they see it *in the field of their competence*. But sometimes, for a variety of reasons, teachers will disregard their obligation to teach their subject, and will consume class time in holding forth on matters utterly unrelated to the subject matter.

Suppose a professor of mathematics does not teach mathematics to his classes but, seized by one or another variety of religion, insists on denouncing sin or socialism or capitalism or birth control; or suppose a professor of English concerns himself mainly in class with a defense of Lysenkoism or other subjects completely unrelated to the field in which he has recognized competence. These suppositions are far from being as bizarre as some of the things that do happen.

Every experienced teacher can recount scores of cases—at other institutions, of course—in which the ethics of the profession have been violated. Not so long ago, a mathematics teacher at Wright State University in South Carolina gave "A" grades to all of his students in his algebra and calculus classes as a protest against the "established authority" of mathematics, a discipline he defined as "a Nazification of human reason."*

Were these professors to be challenged, criticized, and after due process and judgment by their professional peers, rebuked or transferred or even dismissed, they could not plead the right to heresy. For they would be violating the ethics of their profession.

Actually, although such behavior—and worse—is far more common than most laymen are aware, once tenure has been acquired, it is extremely difficult—even where the will is present—to convict successfully a tenured teacher of incompetence or dereliction of duty. There have even been cases of alcoholics who have managed to stay on for years protected by the tenure rules, or more accurately, by the unwillingness of colleagues and administrators to initiate the complex and protracted process required to retire them. The result has been that generations of students have suffered without remedy.

It is undoubtedly true that without firm rules of tenure the principles of academic freedom can easily be abused. But these very principles can and have been abused to protect the tenure of those who have been derelict in their responsibilities to their students and their studies. Despite grave drawbacks, the present system seem to be the least objectionable of those at all practicable. However, its operation could be substantially improved if there were periodic reviews of professional competence and a sterner desire to retire those who

* *Cleveland Plain Dealer*, February 6, 1969.

are unfit or misfit, even if it became necessary to pay them not to teach. The truth, which many in the academy are loath to admit publicly, is that those who suffer most from the abuses of the tenure system are the students.

A much more important violation of professional ethics is involved in another type of action. Suppose it were discovered that a professor was on the payroll of a corporation and instructed by its public-relations office to propagandize in his classrooms and other professional relationships in behalf of conclusions or positions dictated to him from time to time. Or, suppose it were revealed that a researcher had contracted to "cook" his experiments in advance in accordance with directives received from some outside agency. This would clearly be a case of "conspiracy," in the technical sense in which I am using the word, rather than heresy since the "findings" were not reached as a result of free inquiry but were dictated to him by the others. We would rightly say that such a person has surrendered his professional integrity; that he has given hostages to the enemies of free inquiry and therefore rendered himself—if the charges are confirmed—*ipso facto* professionally unfit.

The question of his fitness would be raised not on doctrinal grounds but on grounds of professional ethics. He would, of course, be entitled to a hearing and the protection of due process but the burden of proof would rest on him to show why he should not be dismissed if the facts were as stated. This would not be a heresy hunt. A colleague who honestly and independently reached the same conclusions as the hired mind of the conspirator, if he enjoyed tenure, would not be molested.

Similarly, suppose a teacher were a member of a political group or party, whatever its ideological affiliation or complexion, that explicitly gave him instructions to slant his position in the classroom, and "without exposing himself," to indoctrinate for the "party line" of the moment. If such instructions were given, whether it involved the line of the churches, political parties, or sects, we would on this analysis emphatically deny that such conduct fell under the right to heresy. This would be conspiracy, and render such a teacher presumptively unfit on grounds of professional ethics to continue teaching.

His actions would be comparable to that of a physician who agreed to recommend unnecessary operations to his patients in order to split fees with the surgeon, or to that of a lawyer who agreed to throw his client's case because of political bias. All would be guilty at least of unprofessional conduct. The difference between the behavior of the heretic—who because he reaches conclusions on his own is honest even if mistaken—and the conspirator—who acts on conclusions fed to him by others who have no educational qualifications or authority—even if the conclusion in any particular situation happens to be correct, is profound. It cannot be ignored without degrading the whole enterprise of scholarship and critical integrity. And although there may be difficulties in implementing the distinction, if the faculties themselves undertake the task of defending the ethics of the teaching-learning process from subornation, whenever evidence of its presence is manifest, the difficulties and dangers would be far less than if anything and everything were permitted. For in the latter case, the consequences sooner or later would invite efforts by those outside the educational community to enforce the distinction.

If there is no right to conspiracy, then no member of any group that prescribes, as a condition of affiliation, the express willingness to engage in unprofessional conduct in the classroom or on the campus is entitled to the protection of academic freedom. This is of importance because he is sure to invoke the principles of academic freedom when he is exposed as a member of such a group. Nor is it necessary to prove that he has actually carried out the official instructions of the group or to detect him in *flagrento delecti*. After all, it is not necessary to prove that a person who has voluntarily joined a ring to commit an immoral action must carry it out before we are justified—after a hearing in which he would have an opportunity to rebut the evidence—in barring him from the position that would enable him to act on his instructions.

This concept of academic freedom is notably and eloquently expressed in the Declaration of the Graduate School of the New School for Social Research, which was founded by exiles from Hitler's Germany:

> The New School knows that no man can teach well, nor should he be permitted to teach at all, unless he is prepared "to follow the truth of scholarship wherever it may lead." No inquiry is ever made as to whether a lecturer's private views are conservative, liberal, or radical; orthodox or agnostic; views of the aristocrat or commoner. Jealously safeguarding this precious principle, the New School strictly affirms that a member of any political party or group which asserts the right to dictate in matters of science or scientific opinion is not free to teach the truth and thereby is disqualified as a teacher.

The battle for academic freedom has not yet been completely won in the United States. But its principles are recognized by almost all accredited institutions of higher learning in the country, and challenged only in some small, usually denominational, institutions in the cultural backwash of the country.

Many of the provisions in the statements of the declarations of principles of academic freedom of professional associations have the status and force of law in some jurisdictions. We have certainly come a long way from the days when theological orthodoxy of some kind was a *sine qua non* of membership in a college faculty, or even from the days, which I can vividly recall, when professors were considered merely "hired hands" and could be arbitrarily dismissed. Although the corporate structure of the American university, for historical reasons, leaves nominal authority in the hands of a board of trustees or regents, they have even less actual power in terminating or renewing the appointment of university professors than boards of directors have with respect to employment in a closed shop, or even a union shop. Viewed in historical perspective, it is no exaggeration to say that never was *Lehrfreiheit*—the freedom to teach—in a healthier state than it is today.

The case of Professor Eugene Genovese of Rutgers University symbolizes the change in the attitude toward academic freedom not only within the university but without. A few years ago Professor Genovese declared at a public meeting on university premises: "As a Marxist and Socialist I welcome the victory of the Vietcong."

This was during a week when the Vietcong had been very active in the deliberate slaughter and mutilation of South Vietnamese civilians who had refused to pay tribute to it. Professor Genovese's declaration made the newspapers soon after casualty losses for American soldiers had been reported. A loud hue and cry arose.

Many organizations and prominent persons demanded that President Mason Gross dismiss Genovese. President Gross dissociated himself from Genovese's intemperate remarks but refused to breach the principles of academic freedom by taking any disciplinary action against him. In this view he was sustained not only by Genovese's colleagues and department, but by the Board of Governors of Rutgers University. The outcries became even louder, and an appeal was taken to Governor Hughes, then up for re-election. To the surprise of many, the Governor backed the position of the president and board of Rutgers University and claimed that the price for academic freedom was tolerance for unpopular and even dangerous views.

This gave his Republican-party opponent the issue he had until then been lacking. And he made the most of it. He focused his entire campaign on the issue of Genovese's right to teach. In November Governor Hughes was returned by an increased majority even though the polls of the time showed that New Jersey voters supported the American involvement in South Vietnam. This was the first time the issue of academic freedom was central to a state campaign. The almost unanimous judgment of observers and commentators was that the electorate had recognized and endorsed the right to heresy as integral to academic freedom.

It was a welcome sign of maturity. It was a pity, however, that none of Genovese's own colleagues challenged his juxtaposition of "Marxist" and Vietcong. There are Marxists who are firmly convinced that to be Marxist implies opposition to present-day totalitarian Communism in Moscow, Peking, Havana, and Hanoi. More regrettable was the failure of Genovese's colleagues, while defending his right to teach, to raise some fundamental questions.

Genovese should have been engaged in discussion and asked to square his eloquent invocation of academic freedom with support of totalitarian regimes that had destroyed academic freedom, root and branch, and exiled or executed multitudes of scholars and teachers and their families. His opposition to the American involvement in Vietnam was no problem. But support of a Vietcong victory by a staunch advocate of academic freedom seems inconsistent. At any rate the discussion would have been pedagogically instructive. Right or wrong, Genovese was a heretic, not a conspirator, and the defense of his right to heresy by citizens of a major state was heartening. It is a right that would be denied him by any totalitarian group he supported.

The situation in the United States, unfortunately, may change in the future, for reasons to be discussed in the next chapter. But at this writing the bulwarks established in the past forty years against the traditional enemies of academic freedom are holding firm. The novel element in the situation is that the greatest potential threats to *Lehrfreiheit*, to the academic freedom of teachers and scholars, emanate today not from reactionary business tycoons or superorthodox ecclesiastics, or chauvinistic politicians but from American students themselves! How is this possible?

This brings us to a consideration of the other aspect or phase of academic freedom that until recently has been comparatively neglected in the United States, to wit, the concept of *Lernfreiheit*, or freedom to learn.

# CHAPTER FOUR

# FREEDOM TO LEARN: "LERNFREIHEIT" AND STUDENT RIGHTS

We have already observed that one of the distinguishing fea-
tures of contemporary student restiveness is the demand for
academic freedom for students, for students' rights, for *Lernfreiheit*—freedom to learn. What does it mean?

Our task will be not so much to find or explicate a meaning already clearly in use as to propose one that will recommend itself after reflection. The phrase "freedom to learn"
cannot mean in the United States what it originally meant in
Germany. In Germany *Lernfreiheit* presupposed the successful completion of the all-prescribed curriculum of the *Gymnasium* that carried students through the equivalent of the first
two years of the American classical liberal-arts college, and
the passing of comprehensive final examinations (the *Matura*).

The assumption was that all university-bound students
would be free to organize their own program of studies; to
attend classes at any university, in their own time and discretion, in preparation for the state-wide final examinations
in their field of specialization. The American college system
was so completely different from the German educational
pattern, and so diverse in form, curriculum, and standards
that the German sense of "freedom to learn" could not be

adopted when the principles of academic freedom were first
formulated in the United States.

It is, therefore, necessary to explore the possible meanings
"freedom to learn" may have on the American scene. In passing, it should be mentioned that in Germany the sudden shift
from an almost completely regimented secondary-school and
junior-college curriculum to one in which students were cast
completely on their own with no curricular prescriptions or
order of studies whatsoever, and no faculty guidance or as-
sistance, with the sole control emanating from the necessity of
passing a final examination, has led to much hardship among
students and indifference to their pedagogical needs by the
professors. In recent years it has been the cause of much
protest.

Whatever meaning "freedom to learn" is given, some things
should be obvious. First, if there is no freedom to teach, then
the freedom to learn is itself therewith abridged. Students
have no freedom to learn if their teachers are not free to seek
and teach the truth as they see it. The converse, however, is
not true. It doesn't follow that there cannot be freedom to
teach where freedom to learn is abridged or absent. As we
shall see, there may be circumstances preventing freedom to
learn without freedom to teach being abridged.

Second, freedom to learn may be construed as freedom to
attend college or not to attend. There is no problem here provided one has the means to attend college. No one should be
compelled to attend college. Freedom to learn may mean—
again assuming the power to do so—freedom to select the
type and kind of college one finds congenial to his educational
needs and capacities. Today the range of choice, although not
unlimited, is enormous. There are colleges with all-prescribed
curricula like St. John's; there are others in which students
can dance or sing their way to a degree. The number and
variety of colleges are greater than ever before.

Third, if freedom to learn means freedom to select curricular options in the college of one's choice, then except for the
rare institutions in which the curriculum is prescribed, the

freedom of students to make such curricular choices is more widely recognized than at any time in the past.

These may be considered relatively trivial interpretations of freedom to learn. More important, we may mean by the phrase the student's freedom to challenge, to contest, to dissent, to doubt, to inquire. If this is what we mean, then American students are today freer than any other bodies of students in the world. They are certainly much freer than students were when I attended college, and freer today than they were yesterday. The freedom of American students today is so uninhibited that questions have arisen concerning the good taste, and even legality, of the language of dissent. The tone, the vocabulary, the manner of expression on the American campus of today are absolutely unprecedented. This freedom characterizes not only the form of expression but its substance.

In no other country of the world would a play like *McBird*, in which the Chief Executive of the nation is accused of having planned the assassination of his predecessor, be permitted to be produced on university campuses. Everything seems permissible. The fact that the problem today appears to be how far can students go in their uninhibited speech-behavior does not necessarily indicate that they are *intellectually* free. Students, like other human beings, can be enslaved by their passions. Later on we shall have something to say about the amenities of discourse in relation to freedom of inquiry. But even allowing for all the abuses of intellectual freedom today, the fact that the climate of opinion permits the possibility of this abuse marks the distance we have come since the early decades of the century.

I recall two incidents from my own educational career that may illustrate how great the span is. The first occurred in a Latin class. Caught unprepared one day, I was asked to translate from Cicero's oration against Cataline. As I stumbled along with progressively extended pauses, the teacher sardonically inquired about the reason for my apparent reluctance. Stalling for time, I explained that I found it hard to swallow Cicero's interpretation of Cataline's conspiracy and his motives.

The teacher's ears pricked up. "Why not?" he asked with unwonted and ominous gentleness.

"All we know about Cataline," I bulled along in a kind of glib despair, "is what his enemy, Cicero, tells us. Cataline seems to be defending the interests of the exploited farmers of his region against the predatory interests of the Roman ruling class for whom Cicero was an eloquent spokesman."

I forget the exact words I uttered, but the formula was the same that I had used as a soapboxer in Morris Hillquit's campaign as the Socialist candidate for mayor in 1917. I merely transferred the class struggle from the twentieth century to the first century B.C. When I stopped to catch my breath, the teacher was almost on top of me. He first paled and then turned a fiery red that seemed to suffuse not only his face but to mount to the top of his ivory bald head.

In a choking, rising voice in which anger struggled with incredulity he shouted, wagging a bony finger under my nose, "I have been teaching Cicero on and off for forty years and this is the first time anyone has dared to defend Cataline!" He pointed to the door. "Out, you——you Bolshevik!"

When I returned to class, I was never called on again even when I was prepared. What an opportunity that teacher had missed! Had he assigned the subject to me as a project on which to report, who knows but that I might have ended up as a classics scholar? What scandalized him was not so much my talking back but the outrageousness of my challenging something he had been taught to teach to others. What was true in that class was true in lesser measure in many others.

Even in history classes recitation was by rote memory. "Continue!" the instructor would say as he called upon a student after signaling the reciting student to stop. And the second student would continue reciting the text—almost word for word! Small wonder that in some subjects we got our education on our own from reading books.

The second incident occurred a few years later when I was a student in a government class at C.C.N.Y. The teacher conducted the class by letting the students give reports on the themes of the course. All he contributed was to say "Next" as each student concluded. But when in reporting on the Calhoun-Webster debates, I declared that it seemed to me that Calhoun had the better of the argument, that his logic was better than Webster's although his *cause* was worse, the instructor exploded and stopped me.

After emotionally recounting his father's services in the Civil War, he turned wrathfully on me and shouted: " Young man! When you're not preaching sedition, you are preaching secession!" Whereupon he drove me from the class. (The "sedition" was a reference to an earlier report on Beard's economic interpretation of the Constitution that he had heard with grim disapproval.) And this was at C.C.N.Y. in 1920! The incident wasn't typical, but that it could happen at all marks the profundity of the changes in attitudes toward students since then. John Dewey's influence has made itself felt even in the colleges today. But so have other influences that would have disheartened and dismayed him.

Granted that progress has been made in all the foregoing respects. There still remains an order of consideration that goes beyond curricular choices. Freedom to learn depends upon the material possibility of learning. There are thousands of potential college students in the United States who have been deprived of the freedom to learn because of poverty or prejudice or the absence of adequate educational facilities that may include deficiencies in transportation, housing, or professional opportunities. So long as such conditions exist, there is no freedom to learn for those individuals affected by them.

We have asserted that freedom to teach is not a human right. But freedom to learn is. One doesn't have to earn it. It is implied in the commitment to democracy as a way of life. The equality of concern for all its citizens to develop themselves requires that all individuals be provided with the education and schooling necessary to enable them to reach their maximum growth as persons. Therefore, as citizens of a democratic society we are under an obligation to support and to work for whatever measures of social reconstruction we deem necessary to remove the social obstacles to freedom of learning.

It is also perfectly legitimate for a university to study these problems, to locate the obstacles interfering with freedom of learning, and to pose solutions to them. In one department or another, all universities and colleges in the United States are already engaged in such a study. A considerable number of them have even integrated field work, apprentice programs, and clinical practice in various areas in conjunction with these studies.

This is one thing. And it speaks well for the educational adaptability of American institutions of higher learning that they are moving in the direction of integrating learning by controlled experiment and tying doing to theory. But quite another thing is the demand, sometimes made in good faith, sometimes not, that the university go far beyond this enlightened educational approach. It is held that the complex of social, political, and economic problems that affects the freedom to learn must become items not only on the agenda of *study* but on the agenda of *action* by the university; that the university itself as a corporate educational entity, in the very interests of the education it wishes to impart, must commit itself to a program of social reconstruction, that it must become an agent of social change.

There are some members of the university community who are puzzled as to why the university should be specially concerned with the problems of society that affect the freedom to learn of so many of our young men and women. The answer is or should be obvious. Aside from the fact that educational planning not only makes indifference to these problems unwise, their urgency and pervasiveness make their study in depth highly desirable if students are to acquire adequate understanding of the social world around them.

The alternative to indifference is not fanaticism. Concern,

interest, and study that include—where relevant and pedagogically desirable—field work and clinical experience are sufficient. There is no justifiable ground for demanding of the
university that, in order to live up to its dedication to the goals
of education and scholarship, it must become an action organization to reform or revolutionize society.

Earlier I said that such a demand is made not only in good
faith but in bad. I was referring to those whose explicit social
philosophy stresses the fact that neither education nor educators can ever reform or rebuild society, that educational
institutions merely "reflect" the social-economic order, and
that the latter is the area in which victory must be won to
effect any lasting or beneficial educational change. When those
committed to this variety of vulgar Marxism demand that the
university do what their own social philosophy declares
impossible, it is obvious that they really are functioning as
architects of social chaos. They hope that the resulting disorders and confrontations in the academy will somehow inspire, or ultimately contribute to, the national crisis of leadership and public confidence that may usher in the revolutionary
situation.

Here we are more concerned with those who make the demand in good faith. And there are a surprisingly large number
who out of naiveté or unfamiliarity with the complexity of the
issue support the demand. They overlook the fact that profound differences exist about the social means necessary to
achieve a society that provides the maximum freedom
to learn for all who are willing and able to learn. The agreement on the goal by itself has no more directive differential
force than agreement on the goals of good citizenship. The
rub always lies in the means and programs proposed. And
because of the profound differences concerning means and
programs, the university that espoused one particular solution would become as partisan and biased as other political
action groups that urge their special programs on the community.

In that case, the primary purpose of university education as conceived until quite recently would be altered. The university would become, in virtue of its programmatic commitments, an agency interested in political power. Class and group conflicts within it reflecting the diversities of the nonacademic world would rend its very fabric. Scholars would find themselves engaged not only as citizens but as scholars in a struggle for power not necessarily related to their quest for truth—a quest that differentiates the university from other institutions.

This new view of the university has begun to make headway in recent years even among scholars whose program of social change is far from revolutionary. I shall discuss it in detail in Chapter Seven. But to avoid confusions and misunderstanding of my argument at this point, I wish to point out that there are certain goals and objectives with respect to which the university as an institution *can* take an official position or make a public commitment without laying itself open to the charge of political partisanship or bias.

These goals and objectives are related to its educational mission, to problems concerning the defense of academic freedom, the budgetary needs of the university, and related matters. On all of these questions the assumption is warranted that the position represents a genuine consensus of the faculty. There are an indefinite number of issues relating to scholarship and research on which, because of the public urgency of problems related to them, the university or a specific school or department may be requested to offer its considered judgment on the basis of available evidence, provision always being made for the registration of dissenting or minority views. The individual professor is always free to do so in his own name. Such judgments, individual or group, are always legitimate. But in no case is the university justified in becoming a political or agitational instrumentality pressuring the community to act in a controversial context.

For example, let us assume that the medical faculty is convinced that the fluoridation of the public water supply is a desirable health measure. It may announce this. It may not throw itself into an electoral campaign where the community is divided over the conflicting values of safety and expense, on the one side, and medical health on the other, although as individual citizens its members are free to do so. Not only would the medical school be engaged on work foreign to its primary task, which on its educational side can be carried out by federal and state public health agencies, it would be preempting for itself a political role that does not necessarily follow from its commitment to the quest and publication of the truth. In a democratic community, it must be borne in mind that neither philosophers nor experts are kings. And it is wise, also, to remember that one does not have to be an expert to evaluate intelligently the contributions of experts.

This concept is fundamentally opposed to the elitist view of the university as a revolutionary action organization that is basic to the strategy and tactics of the so-called Students for a Democratic Society as it functions on campuses of higher education. The members of this society, proudly and avowedly of the New Left, eschew any official ideology except a vague socialism. This is more an attitude of anticapitalism whose only preponderant character seems to be an intense and bitter anti-Americanism. I refer to the SDS as "so-called" because their actions consistently show that they no more believe in democratic process than the leaders of the so-called Non-Violent Coordinating Committee are or were believers in nonviolence.

Among these actions we may list the disruption of meetings and classes of those with whom they disagree; the glorification of the leaders of dictatorial social movements—at Columbia, the signs erected in the buildings occupied by students read *Lenin won! Castro won! And we will win*; and the willingness to collaborate with totalitarian groups to further a particular goal. This last is particularly significant. No genuinely democratic group will make a united political front with those who wish to destroy democracy. The elitism of the SDS is further evidence of its undemocratic character.

To the extent that they are articulate about their strategy

of winning power, the leaders of the SDS are disillusioned both with the labor classes and masses. They regard them as corrupted by the affluent society. Although uncomfortable about the tendency of an elite to make a fetish of the elite of the elite or to succumb to what has been called since Stalin's demise "the cult of leadership," nonetheless the leaders of the SDS do not share power equally or readily with their members. They speak eloquently about participatory democracy but in action they practice manipulative democracy, skillfully imposing a predetermined position by the leaders of the moment on the large membership organization.

Wherever the SDS is active, it differentiates itself from other protesting students by repudiating or sabotaging efforts to restructure the university. The SDS is for confrontation; it aims for the administrative and faculty jugular in order to destroy, not reform, the university as it exists today. It recognizes that successful restructuring of the university will give students a voice and, in some areas, a vote in determining university policy. This would make the students, through their representatives, co-responsible for existing states of affairs, including what may appear to some as "grievances." It certainly would reveal for what it is the nonsense about students being "exploited" by the faculty.

The leaders of the SDS have warned their followers not to be trapped into the appearance of collaboration with the representative agencies of the academic community lest this prevent the radicalization of the university. This explains their ambiguous attitude toward representative official student organizations on campus. No matter how fairly elected, they are dismissed as tools of the administration and faculty.

If the SDS and its allies manage to infiltrate and capture the official student organization and student pressure is brought to bear on them "to play ball" with faculty—administrative committees, they will sometimes resign their posts of power in order to avoid the odium of compromise and to win freedom of action for "pure" opposition. After all, important concessions that increase the participatory role of students may undermine their own propaganda about the university. This is the strategy behind the promulgation of "nonnegotiable demands," and their escalation when they are sometimes granted.

There is no space nor necessity in view of the changing situation to list some of the strategems adopted by the SDS to radicalize the university. On every campus it is possible to discover some legitimate grievance, some requirement or procedure or mode of doing things that has persisted by sheer inertia because no one had experienced them as unendurably galling or unjust. Once attention is called to them, recognition may transform them into felt grievances, and objective grounds may be found for removing them. Instead of seeking peacefully to resolve these grievances through existing channels of consultation, the SDS will attempt to inflame them to a point where they can rally the student body for a confrontation.

Midterm examinations, for example, have been traditional in most colleges. Once the question of their pedagogical usefulness is raised, it is not sufficient to cite the fact that no one has previously questioned them. Their pedagogical validity becomes an open question that normally can be settled by faculty bodies in consultation with students. But before this is done, the SDS will strive to get the students to make their abolition a nonnegotiable demand. Sometimes in the absence of a plausible grievance, one may be synthetically created. In one typical piece of advice to SDS chapter members, they are urged to sign up for certain courses in large numbers and then denounce the university for its large classes.

One thing is or should be clear. Freedom of dissent, freedom of speech, freedom of protest are never the real issue. For these freedoms the SDS together with other students enjoy to the full. What the tactics of the SDS are designed to achieve is to give dissent the immediate form of violent action, euphemistically characterized as "confrontation." The measures that are finally adopted to counter this violent form of action, if the faculty and administration do not cravenly capitulate, may involve the use of the civil authorities, the

courts, and ultimately, the police. This is likely to be the upshot, wherever students engage in vandalism, arson, assault,
the pillaging and publication of university files.

The measures adopted to counter and restrain violent action are then seized upon for propaganda purposes by the
SDS spokesmen as a violation of academic freedom and morals,
and as a justification for the original act of confrontation
if this has not dropped out of sight completely. Sometimes
the original violence of the SDS is justified as a kind of "defensive action" in advance against the reaction it provokes.

It is disheartening to observe how often this cynical response
succeeds in obfuscating situations and shifting attention away
from the initial actions of violence to the measures taken to
counter them. It goes without saying that in the heat of the
crisis administrations or faculties may make a tactical error in
dealing with SDS provocations. (Actually their major errors
have been those of capitulation and amnesty for illegal action.) These errors are then equated by ritualistic liberal members of the faculty with the crimes of the students. They then
rise above the conflict and either pronounce a plague on both
sides or direct their main fire against the administration whose
previous actions of ommission and commission, even when
they were blameworthy, had never moved them to criticism.

Once these rifts appear among the faculty, the administration's position is eroded. The result is that the administration
becomes the scapegoat, the students are in effect amnestied,
and confirmed in their judgment that their strategy and tactics
were sound. With local variations Berkeley, Columbia, Harvard, Cornell—tell the story.

On occasions in an unguarded moment the leaders of student revolt will admit that the issue they exploited was a false
one, and used only as an enkindling slogan. After the Berkeley affair Mario Savo acknowledged that the issue of "Free
Speech" was a "pretext," (the word is his) in order to arouse
the students against the existing role of the university and
society. It was Mark Rudd who, after his victory at Columbia,
belittled the significance of Columbia's affiliation with the

Institute of Defense Analysis. In his words, "It was only a case of two or three professors." While the disorders were at their height, he is reported to have said to a circle of close supporters: "As much as we would like to, we are not strong enough to destroy the United States, but we are strong enough to destroy Columbia."

Nonetheless, the SDS leaders always speak of respect for "democratic rights" and there are innocents among the students and faculty who take them at their word. But their actions again and again show that they have absolutely no respect for the rights of others, whether it is the rights of their fellow students, their teachers, administrators, or visitors invited to present their point of view on campus.

The same students who seize and occupy a building shouting about their rights to this or that will brazenly defend depriving a majority of their fellow students of *their* rights to an education. When pressed about their inconsistency, they will feebly invoke Marcuse's notions about "repressive tolerance" —feebly because they seem aware of its absurdities. Part of their intellectual incoherence stems from the absence of any clear idea of the kind of society they wish to substitute for the current one. My experience here has been shared by others. Again and again in discussion with members of the SDS in answer to my question concerning their ultimate goals and programs, I have received variations of a reply that Tom Hayden, their aging leader, gave to Gore Vidal in their television debate.

Asked about the goals of the revolution he was preaching to students and others, Hayden said: "We haven't any! First we'll make the revolution, and then we will find out what for." This is truly the politics of absurdity.

Unfortunately this is not a local aberration. Aside from the vague and hackneyed talk about being alienated from their society, and the litany of grievances about the political state of the nation, the condition of our cities, poverty, housing—about which millions of citizens are rightfully and deeply concerned —nowhere is there a *program* of social action presented to cope with their problems. The talk about revolution is mostly rhetorical with no specific conception of the political instrumentalities by which it is to be achieved, its problems, costs, and consequences. Even the Freedom Budget proposed by the A. Philip Randolph Institute is denounced as a gimmick of corporate liberalism, not to mention proposals for a guaranteed federal annual wage or a negative income tax that would require a coalition of different social forces to implement.

Why do individuals who profess to be democratic hold this view? Among the reasons expressed in the responses usually made by present-day academic rebels to criticisms like those above is a blanket indictment of the university as it functions today that they believe absolves them of responsibility.

"After all," they assert, "despite your indignation with our disruptive behavior the university today is nothing but an institution which functions to preserve the *status quo*. Therefore the university is faithless to the ideals of the community of scholars. It has systematically betrayed its mission about which you speak so eloquently and misleadingly. The university has degenerated into serving as an instrument of the ruling class. Its so-called educational processes are really subtle processes of brainwashing that further the purposes and interests of that class." The language is sometimes less crude but the message is the same.

Even *if* such a charge were true, even *if* the university were nothing but a bulwark of the social and political *status quo*, this would at most justify criticism and protest. It would *not* justify violent and lawless action in behalf of a contrary goal, just as illegitimate, to convert the university from an agency of conservation and reaction to one of revolution.

But it is certainly not true! It is false to say that the universities of the country are nothing but bulwarks of the social and political *status quo*. Never was it so far from being the case as today. There is no institution in the country in which dissent and criticism of official views, of inherited traditions, of the conventional wisdom in all fields, is freer and more vigorous than in the American university. Examine the roster of visiting speakers in any season at a typical university. The critics and dissenters of the existing order in the particular field of the speaker's competence will be found to predominate. Examine the voting records of faculties; look into the social attitudes expressed in their publications—and they will be found to be among the most liberally oriented in the nation.

The American Association of Manufacturers and similar groups complain that business is downgraded in the American curriculum; that the economics of the welfare state is favored over the economics of free enterprise in most college and university departments of economics. Whether justified or not, that such charges are made and are given wide currency is itself a significant sign.

The sober truth is that the very freedom of dissent that students currently enjoy in our colleges and universities, and which the SDS abuses so grossly, is in large measure a consequence of the spirit of experiment found in most institutions, the absence of enforced conformity among them, and their readiness to undertake new educational initiatives. Those of us who remember the educational tyrannies of the past—when not only the ideas of members of the academy but their very lives were under the suspicious scrutiny of censors, busybodies, and vigilantes—and who succeeded in transforming the situation, and winning for students the right to be as free as they are today, find it ironical and bewildering to be told by irresponsible fanatics that the universities have to be destroyed because they have become the bulwarks of the *status quo*. What and where is the *status quo* in this world of tumultuous change?

Let us disregard for the time being those who talk about student rights primarily as a tactic of confrontation. Let us ask what are the specific rights students may legitimately expect, and in their continued absence, may legitimately demand, in conjunction with their enjoyment of academic freedom. These rights seem to me to fall within two generic classes—social and educational. Let us consider each in turn.

There is a growing recognition that students should be entrusted with the power to regulate their social life through their own organizations. As far as possible, students should be treated as adults and allowed to assume the responsibilities of governing themselves. But they must be held responsible for the abuse of those responsibilities. Moreover, they should not be deprived of rights they would enjoy as citizens where the exercises of such rights does not interfere with the educational mission of the university.

Although this should be a general rule, even in this area the faculty cannot abdicate all responsibility. With respect to student life and student organization, the faculty must retain the ultimate power of veto, when basic issues of educational policy or human rights are involved. If any action of the organized student body or of any student group threatens the educational mission or goal of the university, whether on campus or off campus, the faculty must be prepared to intervene.

For example, suppose students decide to establish fraternities or sororities. Normally a decision of this sort would fall within the jurisdiction of student authority and its representatives. But if these societies were organized along racial or religious or secular lines that interfered with the educational process or the right to learn, the faculty would be under an obligation to veto the proposed action.

In any situation in which the majority of students deprive a minority of its rights, after all appeals to the conscience and goodwill of the majority have been exhausted, the faculty must intervene to curb the dictatorship of the majority and to defend the right to learn or the academic freedom of the minority. Student bodies in the South a few years ago displayed racist prejudices and elsewhere they have been known in the past to be susceptible to the spirit of vigilantism.

In the present days of tension, as students take over control of their own social life on campus, often resorting to the tactics of confrontation to implement demands they make against administration and faculty, it is advisable for the faculty to stipulate in advance certain guidelines to permissible limits of dissent. In the nature of the case, these must consist mainly in indicating what conduct cannot be tolerated if any individual or group wishes to remain a member of the academic community. After several recent shocking incidents, some students blandly insisted that there were no explicit provisions condemning disruptive sit-ins, and that any punishment for their action was *post hoc* and unfair.

One curious aspect of current debate about disciplinary measures for the disruption of the educational process has been the contention of some civil libertarians, sympathetic to student activism, that university punishment of students' actions that also fall under the sphere of competence of the civil authorities is a form of double jeopardy, and hence a violation of the student's constitutional rights.

Students have also taken up this cry and denounced as paternalist tyranny or worse any effort of the university to enforce its own penalties over and above those laid down in the criminal code for *all* citizens. This claim has not prevented them on occasion from demanding that the university intervene on behalf of students who have run afoul of the law in order to get criminal trespass and even more serious charges dismissed.

The contention that any university punishment, whether sanctioned by student organization or faculty and administration, for an offense punishable under the law places the individual in double jeopardy is odd on its face. For the punishments by the university, which run from censure to expulsion, are never of the same order as civil punishments.

A student who breaks into a print shop off campus to steal university examination papers for a sale to his fellow students, when apprehended and convicted, is punished for breaking and entering. If the university punishes him—as it always has in such cases without a murmur of protest ever having been heard—by suspension or expulsion, is this double jeopardy?

A student arrested on the campus for pushing drugs to fellow students is punished under the law. Should he, therefore, be exempt from university punishment? There is such a thing as conduct unbecoming a student or member of the academic community. Such conduct may or may not be subject to the sanctions of the criminal code. But that has nothing to do with the legitimacy of university discipline enforced in a nonarbitrary fashion through academic due process.

The fact that a practice has been long established does not testify to its wisdom or its justice. When challenged, its rationale must be explored in the light of current needs and conditions. It should be obvious, however, that if nothing punishable by law can be punished by the academic community by relevant educational measures, and if everything legally permissible were educationally permissible, the university could not function as a genuine educational organization. Plagiarism either by students or faculty members of something in the public domain is not a legal offense. In fact, it may have constitutional protection under the First Amendment. Would it, therefore, be unjustified to impose some academic sanctions for gross and deliberate intellectual dishonesty?

Another curious feature of contemporary agitation over student rights is that although the movement for the abolition of course requirements is growing, students seem oblivious to the compulsion, often outrageously abused, involved in the imposition of student activity fees that run into hundreds of dollars in the course of their academic career. These fees are collected by the university and turned over to official student organizations that disburse them as they see fit.

In some Eastern colleges, student organizations elected by a handful of students have donated thousands of dollars to the Black Panthers and SDS, whose views are strongly opposed by the majority of students. They have also underwritten the traveling expenses and speakers' fees of crusading propagandists for causes quite foreign to the interests of those whose money has been conscripted. Although such situations can be remedied, the possibility of abuse would be greatly reduced, if not eliminated, if all such fees were made voluntary. Extracurricular activities would then reflect the genuine interests of the mass of students rather than the interests of special groups whose members have managed to slip into the strategic positions of influence and power.

Academic freedom for students in determining their social life is subject to a great many complications flowing from the fears of parents about the morals of their daughters, restrictions of towns concerning the consumption of alcohol, and the controls of state legislatures on the budgets of colleges and universities.

In one college, a suit by the irate parents of a pregnant sixteen-year-old coed, on the ground that the college had failed to exercise the proper supervisory care of its dormitories, was narrowly averted because of the fear of publicity.

The uneasy relations between town and gown can easily be exacerbated by public and conspicuous consumption of drugs and liquor. Budgetary reprisals by legislatures may cripple the educational future of the university. Usually the legitimate demands of students to determine their social life can be granted without fuss and feathers if provocative actions are avoided. Most students are sufficiently sensible to proceed with discretion in situations where the state of public opinion is such that public reaction may damage the quality of their educational experience. However, the responsibility of faculty and administration is primarily to make the alternatives clear to students so that they are aware of the consequences of their decisions. In the end, it is the students who must make the choice about their personal lives.

What does academic freedom for students mean with respect to strictly educational matters? On this question, confusion abounds. The divisions of opinion run in all directions.

My own view is that students are justified in presenting three kinds of demands wherever a situation exists that makes these demands relevant. First, students should have the right of educational participation in the form of *consultation*. They should have the right to be heard, to receive explanations, to present their own views concerning *any* educational measures that affect them. This should apply to proposals to increase tuition, to requirements for graduation, to the use and modification of grading systems—even to the content of their courses.

Actually, although it has become customary to use the language of "rights" concerning participation of this kind, it is an imperative of effective teaching. Any scholar or administrator worth his salt would welcome such interest and discussion, and greet with enthusiasm this active participation and consultation by students. For in this way they can be more readily motivated and inspired to begin the processes of self-education and independent judgment.

Unfortunately, in the past students have been profoundly indifferent to educational matters. There is reason to believe that their present interest is belated and transitory, and that few students have as yet developed a sustained sense of the importance of pedagogical questions. Concerns that have moved students into confrontations have, with the exception of some aspects of the black-studies program, never been strictly educational questions.

To those fearful members of faculty and adminstrative staff who are dubious about discussing these matters with students and inviting them to present alternative solutions to problems, one may address a single question: "If you have a good reason for making or refusing to make some administrative or curricular change, if you are not acting arbitrarily but reasonably, on what possible ground can you refuse to justify the position taken?" Students have sometimes been known to make valuable suggestions or counterproposals. The exercise of their right to consultation can itself become a vital educational experience introducing them to a complex of interesting social problems, and motivating them in an authentic and hopefully lasting way.

Consultation, discussion, dialogue, even debate with students on educational questions are one matter. The power of *decision* on educational questions is something else again altogether. One of the sorriest aspects of the contemporary chaos is the confusion between the two. Even some normally levelheaded persons in the academy have become infected with strange notions about what democracy in education means. The SDS, of course, on ideological revolutionary grounds makes the vehement routine demand that students should have the power "on an equal footing with the faculty" to make decisions on all educational matters. Sometimes its members speak as if students should have the preponderant power. This means that the students, or their representatives, would have the power to outvote or at the very least veto the faculty on any proposed curricular change, and nullify the decisions of any professor who seeks to organize his course in a manner they disapprove of.

Well, why not?— For many reasons. First, this is to draw an equation between the authority of ignorance and that of knowledge, of inexperience and experience, of immaturity and maturity. To be sure, there are some students who in all these respects are precocious and some teachers who have slipped through the professional safeguards against incompetence and are inglorious mediocrities. But it would be absurd to base a general policy on rare and exceptional instances. There are ways of containing the incompetence of teachers, and a perceptive teacher can grant to specially qualified students the opportunity to determine their own educational projects. But the decision to do so must lie in *his* discretion, and his discretion alone.

Is it arbitrary to assume that there is a presumptive authority that attaches to the teacher's function?—No more so than it is arbitrary to assume that the master craftsman in any field should exercise the authority of his superior skills. In what field does the apprentice enjoy the same authority as his teacher to determine the order of studies and the nature of the disciplines required to become a master journeyman? This is obvious if one considers the student as potentially an apprentice teacher, or assumes that every student may someday qualify for a professorship so that he is a potential colleague —a very large assumption, indeed. How much more obvious with respect to those who, so to speak, are just passing through the subject or field, oblivious to the depth, riches, and lasting values of the subject matter of the teacher's speciality?

A second reason for leaving the *decision* as to what factors constitute the necessary and sufficient conditions for the achievement of a liberal-arts education or any other kind of university education, general or professional, to faculty bodies is that by law and custom *responsibility* is vested in them for granting the degrees and certification of competence.

Everyone in the community has a stake in maintaining the best standards of education and in safeguarding against their erosion. One need not overdramatize the possibilities, but even an incompetent medical or laboratory technician may imperil a person's health or life. The student who receives a degree carries with him the judgment and reputation of the faculty "to whom it may concern," and it concerns a great many.

It is not for nothing that degrees from different colleges are rated differently by those in the know. The differences reflect the different standards of the faculties. Were students to share as coequals in the planning, execution, and evaluation of their curriculum, their degrees would be debased. Invidious distinctions—much worse than those current today—would develop, reflecting the degree of involvement of students in the evaluation and certification of their education. The best students will not attend universities in which their fellows are the peers of their teachers.

A third and even more weighty reason for leaving the decisions on curricular matters to the faculty is that concern with its basic problems normally is a life-long commitment. Students come and go every four years. And if they are well educated, they have more intellectual humility, are more aware of what they don't know, when they leave college than when they enter.

Most teachers grow old in their profession. The range of evidence open to members of the faculty is of an altogether different dimension from what is available to any one student generation. The judgment of the relative importance of different social factors, the assessment of future developments, the immunity to fads and pressures of public opinion and popular culture—whether mediated by alumni or government or the mass media—as these bear on the construction and necessary revision of curricula of study require a historical perspective that only the faculty can acquire. Having fought, over a half century, for curricular reforms inspired by John Dewey's philosophy of education, I can testify that on occasions faculties have lacked historical perspective, and oscillated between the extremes of holding on to fixed curricula inherited from the past (whose excellence was proved in their eyes by the fact that they had been nurtured by them) and a willingness to add anything to the curriculum that would draw enrollment and subsidies. But unfortunately no group exists—neither trustees, nor administrators, nor alumni, nor students—that can supply historical perspective if the faculty lacks it. The only improvement possible to an educational institution suffering from the weaknesses of a poor faculty is to develop a better faculty, not to elevate the students to positions where they preempt the role of the faculty.

Finally, because the class concept has recently been introduced into the discussion of higher education, and the relation between student and teacher assimilated into the class struggles of industrial society, it cannot be stressed too strongly that the educational interests of teachers and students in the colleges are common. Every piece of new knowledge won, every problem clarified, every intellectual power sharpened and developed, every original insight or vision that lights up the darkness, is a gain for all. One excellence does not exclude another. All intellectual values are shared. That is why when students have won the right to consultation, they can with good conscience and good sense leave the ultimate or final decisions on educational matters to the faculties. There is no spiritual inequality among those who constitute the academic community of teachers, learners, and administrators in virtue of the differentiation of status and functional roles anymore than there is in a family where mother, father, older and younger children accept different tasks and responsibilities. If the right to consultation is granted students, beneficent changes are sure to result—if we do not confuse ourselves and others by smuggling into the concepts of consultation and communication the notion of decision, too. Unfortunately this confusion is very much in evidence in recent measures adopted by some faculties who feel themselves threatened by student unrest, and, in order to head off confrontations on campus, have rushed to put students as *voting members* in key curriculum committees, or have made them an integral part of the faculty senate with the same privileges with respect to decisions on curricular affairs as the senior members of the faculty. This has the consequence—in the event of a divided faculty vote—of giving unqualified students the strategic balance of power in deciding issues of the gravest educational importance.

These decisions have been reached in haste, and are justified by the invocation of the weasel expression, "Giving students the right to help determine educational policy." The operating word here turns out to be "policy"—whose ambiguity is the key that opens the door to educational absurdity. If the students have the right to consultation and participation, this certainly gives them the right to help determine educational policy to the full extent of their rationality, ingenuity, and persuasiveness. More than this is not required. But if, as is only too often the case, the right to help determine educational policy is construed as the right to help make the decisions, to cast votes just as members of faculties do, the upshot is likely to be continued and intensified educational disruptions.

One can write the scenario in advance. Once faculties have yielded on the principle of student decision on educational matters, the students will demand a more equitable representation on faculty committees and faculty senates. It will not be long before the SDS or the Peace and Freedom party or some other would-be revolutionary student group captures the student seats as they so often have done with respect to student-editorial and student-government posts, whenever they set out to do so. An issue will arise, or one can easily be created, on which the students will be defeated. They will then take their case to the general student body agitating for greater if not equal representation.

Faculties, in order to buy peace, will first declare that the principle of increased representation is negotiable ("Why risk having the place burned down on our heads over such a procedural issue?"), and then declare, as threats of coercion mount, that it is not necessarily undesirable, and finally conclude that it is desirable at least on "an experimental basis." In this fashion the university will become more and more politicized, reinforcing other tendencies in the academic community discussed in subsequent chapters.

Even without the potentialities of political embroilment, there are dangers flowing from the presence of students on committees dealing with matters in which, in the interests of *other* students, strict privacy is desirable. At Oberlin College, notable for its liberalism and high academic standards, in the spring of 1969 student members of the Oberlin Committee on Admissions, unable to convince faculty members of the wisdom of one of their proposals, published confidential material from student-admission folders; and shrugged off the charge that they were guilty of a grave breach of ethics and a disgraceful violation of the rights of privacy.

There are certain inescapable risks involved even in student participation but they are worth taking because of the immense possible educational advantages. But there are no compensating advantages in the risks incurred when students are given the powers of *educational decision.*

That is why with respect to the first legitimate demand for student rights, we must say: "Consultation, yes—decision, no."

The second legitimate educational request students have a right to make is one rarely heard although it is far-reaching in its implications. This is the right to the individualization of the curriculum as far as possible within the resources available—and where not available, the right to request the reordering of educational priorities to make it feasible.

It is a commonplace that each student differs from every other in his needs, his background, his interests. He responds differently to different kinds of instructions, to different stimuli. Those teachers who set out to teach a class of students equally, that is to say, with an eye on what they presumably have in common, rediscover Aristotle's insight that such equal treatment does an injustice to every student who has more or less than what is assumed to be common.

Teachers cannot do justice to those who are very bright and those who are very slow, to the student of quick perception because of a highly prepared apperceptive mass, and the student who is taking the first groping steps in the subject. After all, we make special provision for students who suffer from physical disabilities—who cannot see or hear or walk properly. But the range of psychological, intellectual, and cultural differences among students is usually far greater than the range of their physical differences, and educationally far more significant. The procedures cannot always be the same.

The ideal curriculum for each student would be a tailor-made curriculum fashioned to fit his individual needs, his past history, his ambitions, his capacities in order to maximize his desirable growth. If the community possessed adequate resources, every student would become the center of a special course of studies taking its point of departure from his individual potentialities and achievements, even when designed to prepare him to meet the challenges of his society. This is the way kings and queens receive their education, and even then it is not always successful. A democratic society that reorganizes the right to an education as a human right should not aim less high for its citizens than the elite societies of the past for their nobilities.

Although unrealizable as an ideal today, every college should move in this direction, and strive to individualize the curriculum. As each student meets the general requirements, he should meet it in specific and special curricular ways, devised by a sensitive guidance system and other forms of consultation.

William James once said that there wasn't very much difference between any two human beings, but that whatever differences exist make all the difference in the world. It is that personal individual difference that is lost sight of when one curriculum or course of study is mechanically imposed on all students.

A better understanding of what is involved in individualizing the course of study for students would obviate some of the stupidities and excesses of forcing colleges and universities, under threat of disruption, of accepting unprepared or illprepared students into courses already established for students with much higher levels of intellectual achievement. The educational system of a democracy has a responsibility to each student to provide him with the schooling that will enable him to reach the maximum of *his* potential. Each one's needs are morally as significant as anyone else's—whether he is bright, dull, or mediocre. We have had occasion to say and we will have occasion to repeat again and again: *Because all persons in a democracy have a moral or human right to the best possible education, it does not follow that they all must have the same education any more than it follows from the right of every human being to medical services that this requires the same medical regimen for everybody.*

Finally, perhaps the most important of the rights that students may legitimately claim is one that is least heard in the raucous tones of those who shout loudest about academic freedom for students. This is the right to expect of those responsible for their education a central and continuing concern with the character of teaching on the college level, and the corollary right to evaluate their teachers on the basis of their classroom performance. No matter what else students learn or achieve while at college, if the teaching is inferior their stay has largely been a waste.

It is no secret that the worst teaching in any of the institutions that constitute the educational ladder of the country takes place on the college level (I am dissociating the college from the graduate school here because until recently the graduate school was primarily a research institution in which students were junior colleagues, and because the arts of teaching are generally irrelevant to the art of research.) If anything, the situation with respect to teaching in liberal-arts colleges is worse than in other colleges because in the latter a certain amount of apprentice and on-the-job training is likely to expose students to some excellent models. But the art of teaching is neglected or slighted in almost all colleges because of the dubious assumption, implicit in their hiring practices, that anyone who knows anything can teach it effectively. This certainly is not true.

The greatest educational crime on the college level is boredom. Unfortunately, too many students are the victims of it. The subject matters of a liberal-arts education are so intrinsically interesting, they bear so directly on the great ideas, the great personalities, the great social and historical movements that affect present alternatives and enter into the students' own quest for identity, that there is no excuse for boredom. What always needs to be explained is the *absence* of an atmosphere of intellectual excitement in a liberal-arts college— something that is not necessarily the same sort of thing as the spirit of activism or "creative vandalism." The absence of a bracing atmosphere of intellectual excitement in a liberal-arts college is prima facie evidence of educational failure, an indictment of its curriculum or faculty or both.

It is not the difficulty of subject matter or the rigor of teaching that generates boredom. Actually students are the first to acknowledge this. Even when they find the teacher rather harsh in his methods and exacting in his standards, they rarely complain about his teaching if they learn something from him, if he opens up a new subject or a new vista for them. Nor is the presence or absence of "relevance" the clue to effective teaching. "Relevance" is a relational term. One must ask, "Relevant to what?" Anything worth teaching must be relevant to the learner, and anything that strengthens the student's intellectual powers, instills him with a passion for excellence, motivates him to embark on educational adventures and excursions of his own, renders him more sensitive to form, color, sound, and stretches his imagination is relevant to his growth as a human being.

The relevant is not synonymous with the contemporary. Those who attribute poor teaching to the absence of connection between what is being taught and the immediacies of current events have much too narrow a concept of modernity. There are certain experiences that are common to all human beings, and nothing that enriches the understanding of those human experiences is irrelevant to any human being.

Even casual observers note that there is nothing that brings teachers and students more closely together than a common interest or enthusiasm in the subject matter and problems of a course. Let a teacher succeed in this, and other virtues will be added to him. And unless the range of student capacities is so great that they are not even within hailing distance of each other, discipline takes care of itself. In such situations teaching becomes not a task but a joy.

When students *praise* a teacher for good teaching, this is not always sufficient evidence that he actually is a good teacher. For sometimes students are taken in by a teacher who woos them, who courts popularity, caters to their radical or reactionary prejudices, and, so to speak, sells himself rather than his subject matter. But when students complain that they are learning little or nothing, when they are critical of the methods of teaching, they are almost always right. (The only exceptions have been obviously politically motivated attacks on teachers by a few students repudiated by a majority of their classmates.)

An inescapable responsibility lies with the college to provide them with instruction from which they can learn something significant, to recruit teachers who can make their subjects come alive. Students are extremely loath to complain about poor teaching. They will be surprised to learn how readily their complaints about poor teaching will be received by departmental chairmen and administrative personnel who often must rely on hearsay, since in most institutions to observe the teaching of one's colleagues is an unforgivable breach of decorum. But whatever the reasons for the timidity of students in failing to protest and so being deprived of their educational birthright, they ought to be encouraged to make known what the character of their experience has been.

How can this be done with the least embarrassment to all parties concerned?—Most simply by requesting students to fill out detailed evaluations of their teachers' classroom performance upon the conclusion of a course and making them available to each teacher so that he can determine how he is affecting his students. Even if every sentence a teacher utters is the quintessence of wisdom, if he has failed to communicate, his teaching is a vain beating of the air. Anything worth doing is worth doing well, and despite occasional remarks to the contrary, most teachers are wounded to the quick at the evidence of their bumbling ineptitudes. Student evaluations should be a normal part of the educational experience of the college and be officially administered.

In some institutions where teacher evaluations are undertaken by student groups and published as the "low-down" on courses, many abuses have developed. The evaluations are often not representative of the judgment of the class but are based on the assessment of cronies. Sometimes the evaluations reflect sectarian political bias; sometimes personal grudges are paid off. Worst of all, some junior faculty members, fearful of advisory evaluations that may prejudice their professional career, court student favor by excessive permissiveness.

Good teachers, except in introductory courses in language and other disciplines with relatively fixed subject matters, are good scholars—not necessarily creative scholars—but *au courant* with developments in their fields and capable of critical response to such developments. That is why the explanation offered for poor teaching in terms of the necessity of publishing will not wash. It is sheer myth. Scholarship and research have never hampered effective teaching. Most good teachers publish more, much more, than most poor teachers. Nor is it true that good teachers are not honored for their teaching in the absence of research publications. The greatest honors, of course, go to the pathfinders and discoverers. But there are honors enough to go around even aside from the unique experience of quickening minds into maturity and helping students burgeon from the state of pupils, dependent upon teachers' stimuli, to that of potential colleagues with their own critical self-consciousness.

As I have already intimated, the chief reason for failure to develop a central and continuous concern with teaching is the tenure system. There is irony in the fact that militant activist students are unaware of this. They seize upon every opportunity to disrupt academic life when tenure is denied probationary teachers after their initial period of appointment runs out. Nonetheless, the simple reason why colleges cannot rid themselves of poor teachers is that once they receive a tenured appointment, they are in effect tenured for life.

Theoretically a teacher can be dismissed for incompetence even after he has procured tenure. But I have never heard of any teacher who has been tried and dismissed by his peers on the ground that his teaching and/or scholarship have fallen below the minimum acceptable level of performance. On the face of it this is truly astonishing. There are hardly any other professions or ways of earning a livelihood that practically guarantee life tenure after six years (and sometimes less) of service.

There are excellent reasons, of course, why this massive protection of the tenure of incompetent teachers has developed. They have to do with the protection of the academic freedom of *teachers*. But if it is true that academic freedom *for students* requires that they be assured of competent instruction, especially in the field of their specialization, then intellectual honesty requires that we recognize that the tenure system as presently constituted almost guarantees that many students will not enjoy academic freedom of the kind that really matters, despite their revolutionary agitation for reform of school and society.

The first few years of a teacher's appointment to a college or university are crucial. Normally he must make good by the time the second renewal of his three-year period of service comes around. The judgment of his peers, including department chairmen and deans, is weighted most heavily on the score of research and publication. This is not a matter of public relations but rather of intellectual prestige and pride. If the appointed teacher shows signs of being a productive scholar, any deficiences in teaching are likely to be overlooked in the wishful expectation that he will improve with time and experience.

In most institutions, there is no method by which this is confirmed. If the appointed teacher shows no sign of creative or critical scholarship but is a person of reasonably adequate intelligence and goodwill, his excellence as a teacher will almost always win for him tenure. This is especially true in liberal-arts colleges but not the case in the few universities preeminently oriented toward publication and research, where the undergraduate college is overshadowed by the graduate school.

And now a sad thing is observable. Roughly half the young men who have been given tenure in the expectation that they will make substantial contributions to the field of scholarship gradually lose their intellectual drive and peter out. They work episodically, not systematically. As they acquire families and added obligations, they look for outside sources of income. They teach in evening and summer sessons and, where it is permitted, even do moonlighting at other institutions. They grow tired and discouraged and rely more and more in their teaching upon the notes built up in the early years of their romantic enthusiasm. The greater the original ambition, the more poignant the contrast between promise and performance. They lose zest in teaching their subject and become indifferent about awakening the interests of their students.

It is at this point that they become boring. They meet their classes, go through the same routines, seek to avoid controversy and challenges. Their job has become a well-paid sinecure in which they can finish their days, provided they do not run afoul of the criminal law. Far from having developed themselves, they are now in a state in which they would not qualify for the posts they originally filled, for the light and the promise is out of them.

How can the rights of students to the best possible education be furthered at the same time as tenure is preserved?— No one knows the answer. Were colleges rich enough, they could buy up the contracts of teachers who have outlived their usefulness. There is no magic in small classes. Students are better off with excellent teachers in large classes than with poor teachers in small ones. The use of television in teaching opens up interesting possibilities that should be explored, but there is no substitute for the dialectual interplay of minds between teacher and student by which the intellectual powers are developed and new and exciting ideas are born.

It is true and will always remain true, however, that regardless of how we define academic freedom for students, students cannot enjoy it unless there is academic freedom for their teachers. There is no *Lernfreiheit* without *Lehrfreiheit*.

Today that academic freedom is under attack by those who should be in the forefront of its defense.

# CHAPTER FIVE

# THE ATTACK ON ACADEMIC FREEDOM

"Our reason for closing down Fayerweather Hall," explained one SDS leader with a bullhorn during the disturbances at Columbia University in the spring of 1968, "is to call attention to the unconscionable violence in Vietnam, the police state in Harlem, and the intolerable oppression by the United States in Latin America."

Not only at Columbia but in other institutions students have stormed buildings, manhandled administrators, ransacked confidential files, and deprived faculties and fellow students of *their* educational rights in order to call attention to some evil in society or government that they have regarded as unendurable, refusing to rely on the remedies open through the democratic political process. The statement quoted could be matched by similar ones in almost all situations in which students have disrupted academic life.

It is quite clear even to the violent demonstrators themselves that their actions are not necessary to call the "attention" of the country to the major problems of our time, and that they are not likely to persuade American citizens by their arrogant and contemptuous words that Harlem is "a police state" (actually there is more community control and tolerance of divergent life styles in Harlem than in most other American communities) or that American acts of omission and commission constitute "intolerable oppression" of Latin America. To be sure, other issues are also raised, more university-centered than large questions of foreign and domestic policy, like the investment portfolio of the university, the place of R.O.T.C. in the curriculum. But these issues are always related to the larger ones.

Since, with sufficient ingenuity, almost any grievance on a campus can be tied to the problems and attitudes of the larger society (e.g., the presence of a relatively small number of black students on campus even when the admission policy is patently nondiscriminatory becomes "symbolic" of racism), the question arises why these social problems and issues have *now* been moved into the center of focal academic concern. After all, almost every one of these problems, especially those connected with racism and poverty, were much graver in the past than in the present.

This is the fatal weakness in the reports of various commissions that discount and sometimes explicitly deny the significance and causal impact of ideas and attitudes in explaining student disruption. In attributing the causes of academic unrest to unsolved objective problems in the larger society without, they fail to account for the striking fact that when these problems—of poverty, racism, hunger, and unemployment—were much worse than they are today, the phenomenon of student disruptions was absent. The systematic underplaying of the subjective factor of student revolt in these reports testifies to the residual strength of the outmoded nineteenth-century deterministic beliefs that "social forces," not men, make history. It suggests that the general character of the conclusions had been reached before the investigation on which the reports were allegedly based began.

Among other reasons (enumerated in Chapter Two) for this shift in emphasis has been the emergence on American campuses of small groups of revolutionary students with highly developed organizational skills who view the university as a bastion of "the capitalist system." Some are convinced that the effect of the university on the nation's youth can be neutralized by exposing its true function of intellectual brainwashing. Some, relatively few, harbor the hope that the university can be transformed, first by converting the students and then most of the faculty to the nobler ideals of a new society, and eventually, forging them into an instrument of revolutionary change. Now that the working class, corrupted by bourgeois affluence, is no longer the carrier of the revolutionary principle, the students and intellectuals must play that role.

Finally, there are those groups, numerically the largest, that still accept the Marxist view, in its simplistic version—that no significant educational change is possible without fundamental social and economic revolution in the larger public arena. The aim of student rebellion is not to restructure the university to make it a more viable and effective educational institution, but to create situations that will polarize the academic community and radicalize the student body. In this way the engineers of the social revolution would be recruited.

From this revolutionary point of view, distinctions between liberal and conservative institutions, humanist and authoritarian teaching traditions, are superficial and irrelevant. In different ways all are engaged in indoctrinating, subtly or overtly, for the middle-class values that gloss over the realities of exploitation on which the class system rests.

If anything, it is the liberal and humanistic institutions, with their pose of tolerance and sweet reasonableness, that are the most dangerous. For they nourish the illusion that social change can be achieved by the appeal to reason and imagination. Worse, by institutionalizing the processes of dissent, they tame the Promethean spirit prepared to storm the very gates of Heaven.

These views represent a departure from more intelligent versions of Marxism, which—recognizing the influence of social and economic forces on all aspects of culture, including education—nonetheless acknowledge the presence of causal reciprocities among these factors and the relative autonomy of the modern university, especially in democratic societies.

These concepts of the university by the student rebels, together with the belief that they possess the truth about the nature of the present unideal society, the nature of the future ideal society, and the methods by which the existing community must develop from the former to the latter, are the chief source of one kind of growing threat to academic freedom. Students who hold these views sometimes deny that academic freedom exists in the United States on the a priori ground that the dominant economic class sets fixed limits beyond which it will not permit free inquiry to go. Or, where it is admitted that academic freedom exists, the bold contention will be made that there is nothing sacred about such freedom, and that whenever its exercise results in the discovery of methods or conclusions that are harmful to the prospects of liberation of the exploited classes at home, the Third World abroad, or colonial liberation anywhere, it must be curbed. Sometimes, convinced that they know the truth about men and society, and that error has no rights, these students will disrupt the classes of teachers who, they believe, are disseminating error. On occasion they will insist upon confrontation between their teachers and speakers brought in from the outside if they feel themselves unable to do justice to the logic of the revolutionary cause.

The things that have occurred on the campuses of American colleges, in the classrooms, laboratories, and private offices of respected and distinguished scholars, have been altogether unprecedented in the history of American education. This is not the place to document in detail the record of harassment, intimidation, disruption, and even outright physical violence on campuses and in classrooms from one coast to another.

To begin with Berkeley—where, ironically enough, the student rebellion exploded in 1964 under the banner of the Free Speech Movement—bombings, arson, and extensive vandalism have marked the activities of students demanding control of special curriculums. Classrooms have been invaded for purposes of political harangue, and research projects attacked in fields disapproved of by those who consider themselves the saviors and/or the conscience of society. Sometimes, to avoid threatened disruption, classes are shifted to secret meeting places.

Convinced that they have "the truth," some students have organized systematic campaigns of harassment against the persons and classes of professors whose inquiries seem to challenge that truth. For example, they have demanded the dismissal of Dr. Arthur Jensen as a "fascist" and "racist" for publishing an article in the *Harvard Educational Review* in which he suggested that hereditary as well as environmental factors accounted for the differential achievements of matched Negro and white, disadvantaged and nondisadvantaged, children. The student charges are irrelevant and their epithets absurdly false. Presumably, however, in the eyes of these fanatical young totalitarians, "fascists" and "racists" must be driven from the American campus, whereas the right to teach of avowed Communists, even when they are members of the Communist party, must be defended if need be by closing down the university.

At San Francisco State College not only have the classes of faculty members been disrupted, and the campus transformed into a battle area between rioting students and police, the offices and homes of some professors have been attacked and their lives threatened. The chief, but not the only, target of the student attack by the BSU and the SDS has been the distinguished scholar, Dr. John A. Bunzel, also noted for his consistent and courageous political liberalism.

At U.C.L.A. a course in race offered by the Department of Anthropology was withdrawn because the students objected to the professor, a person designated by his peers as well qualified. In a not untypical reaction that marks the extent of the erosion of principles of academic freedom on some campuses, the instructor concurred in order to avoid open conflict. His decision was probably influenced by the bombing and other acts of terror against Professor W.R. Allen and the Economics Department.

These events, together with the policy of recruiting some

unqualified black militant students with longstanding criminal records and the murder of two students on campus, led to
the resignation of the outstanding economist, Dr. James B.
Buchanan, on the ground that he could not properly teach "in
an atmospere of violence, intimidation and fear."

At San Fernando State College and California State College
at Hayward, as well as several community colleges on the
West Coast, administrators and faculty members have not only
been threatened but physically assaulted. The case of Professor Marilyn-June Blaure of Hayward was a particularly
crass illustration of terrorism.

At Columbia during the academic year of 1968-9,
unmollified by the amnesty won for its violence during the previous spring, the SDS broke up judicial hearings, called under rules drawn up with student participation
and concurrence, brutally clubbed a professor unsympathetic to their cause, and violently disrupted more than forty
classes conducted by members of the faculty whose views
they considered untenable.

At Cornell the armed take-over of Willard Straight Hall
produced a shock that startled the entire country, frightened
the faculty into reversing the findings of its own faculty-
student discipline committee, and generated secondary tremors
among the already alarmed citizenry.

These events at Cornell were the denouement of a pattern of retreat before onslaughts against academic freedom,
clearly recognizable even before the assassination of Dr.
Martin Luther King. A visiting Professor of Economics, the
Reverend Michael McPhelin, was taxed by three students
with racism for allegedly asserting that human resources
could be considered a natural resource and that such human
resources varied; that economics was one of the sciences
developed by Western man; and that those brought up in a
poverty-stricken environment, in the jungle of the city, must
develop cunning and other traits appropriate to that environment to survive. The three students insisted on taking over

the class. To prevent this maneuver Professor McPhelin dismissed his class. Within the hour, several score students invaded the office of the Chairman of the Economics Department, and held him a prisoner until he consented to sign a statement to bring to Cornell at university expense someone selected by the students to impart the truth.

At Harvard University, a few days after the student seizure of University Hall, their removal by the police, and the call for a student strike, members of the SDS disrupted the class of Professor Samuel Huntington by insisting that he abandon his analysis of Venezuelan military coups and discuss the strike issues.

What happened at Harvard has occurred episodically on other campuses around Cambridge. These class disruptions are sometimes not reported either because the instructor is openly or covertly in sympathy with the aims of the disrupting students, or out of fear of further disruption or involvement in the disciplinary action that might follow the lodging of a complaint.

These direct threats to academic freedom from students are not always inspired by the same ideological considerations that move the SDS and other activist political groups. But when justifications are offered for them they are couched either in the vulgar Marxist idioms of the SDS or drawn up in the form of a blanket indictment of racism against the university on the a priori ground that, as a major institution of society, it *must* reflect the worst racist practices of that society.

People who charge racism exempt themselves by definition from being guilty of it despite the fact that the specific demands by Black Nationalists for a separate curriculum and separate living quarters for blacks exhibit the same patterns of segregation, save in reverse, that have prevailed in the Southern States before the desegregation decision of the Supreme Court.

There is a third kind of justification offered by those individuals among students and faculty who may be regarded as being on the periphery of the radical student movement and who loyally support the SDS and its leaders in a showdown with the college or civil authorities. It is alleged that these disruptive tactics—the violence, the arson, and the vandalism—were the only methods available by which to achieve the much needed reforms in university structure. Although this is easily said, I am not familiar with a single case in which such a claim is even plausible. Many of the demands that intransigent students make are not even within the power of administrations and faculties to grant. When they are, and students have presented a reasonable case for them, they have been granted like the decision not to report class standing to draft boards or petitions for revisions of curriculum.

Despite allegations to the contrary, the history of American education is a history of radical changes undertaken without benefit of student violence or threat of violence. Any *sustained* campaign of peaceful protest and dissent is very likely to achieve the desired results if a prima facie case can be made out for the change. Finally, no matter what the alleged remediable campus evil has been, the costs of eliminating it by escalating student violence have been far greater, far more harmful in its effects on comity and moral life of the academic community than the original alleged evil. This is true not only of strict campus issues but even of those that affect the local urban area. The people of Harlem have been deprived in consequence of student violence of the use of a gymnasium that their representatives gladly approved when it was first projected by Columbia University. Nobody gains by restoring the site to a barren outcropping of rock. Everybody loses. Whatever potential disadvantages, even of a symbolic character, were involved could easily have been rectified as a consequence of sustained orderly protest.

The attack upon academic freedom by the use of physical

violence against the person of professors and students de-
grades not only the victims and assailants but the entire
educational process. For nothing is so foreign to the life of
mind as the brutalities of force. The resort to force to answer
an argument or to prevent an argument from being made is
more often than not an expression of frustration because of
one's inability to meet the argument. A violent person may
love the object of his violence. He can never by violent
means understand it.

Apologists for student rowdyism and disorder tell us that
students are trying to communicate with us through their
violence. But a blow never communicates properly when we
reach out for understanding. Mao Tse-tung's stale dictum,
"Power comes out of the barrel of a gun," is not always true
even when the issues are political. It is never true when the
issues are intellectual. Insight and truth have other sources.
Students of another generation were well aware of this.

Most condemnations of fascism would begin with a cita-
tion from Goering: "When I hear the word 'culture,' I reach
for my revolver." Today there are activist students who applaud Fanon's line: "When I hear the word 'culture,' I reach
for my knife."

Violence on the campus may be indirect as well as direct
and be just as prejudicial to the exercise of academic freedom.
When students prevent their fellows from attending class by
blocking doorways, or prevent faculty members from gaining
access to their offices and laboratories, or vandalize libraries
by throwing books into heaps and scattering them in different
alcoves, they are crippling the life of mind in the university
just as much as episodic violence does.

There is another threat to academic freedom that has
mounted in intensity until it now constitutes a serious challenge to the possibility of reasoned discourse about genuine
differences of policy on American campuses. This is the
growth of obscenity, the deliberate use of the violent language of the gutter, to disconcert and degrade those who

cannot be refuted by logic and evidence. Its use disorganizes by its insulting irrelevance any meeting of minds in institutions dedicated to the life of mind.

I am not now referring to the employment of earthy language in a suitable context to drive home a point. I refer to the systematic employment of the foulest kind of obscene epithets, which the law recognizes as provocative of violence, and sometimes as legally punishable, in the literature, propaganda, and discussion of some student activist groups on American campuses. There has been nothing like it in the history of American education or, for that matter, the education of any country.

This vulgar and filthy speech is directed not only at men but at women as an explicit avowal of contempt and disrespect. Once introduced, it destroys the possibility of intelligent dialogue, for those who resort to it can only be put out of countenance by being subjected to a stronger stream of abuse, beyond the capacity or willingness of the academic targets of the attack. Nor is silence in the face of these insults an effective retort. For everyone is diminished in the noisome atmosphere created by cloacal invective. The normal response to calculated offense in face-to-face relationship must be inhibited in order to prevent a riot. Those who introduce obscenity are aware both of its effects and the immunity to punishment they enjoy because of the inhibitions of their victims.

There are some individuals who feel that student obscenity is rather "cute," an adolescent *jeu d'esprit* at which only middle-aged squares or gray-headed stuffed shirts can take umbrage. When a student dresses down the dean of Columbia College before the assembled student body as "a motherfucker"—he doesn't intend anything personal, of course. It is only a way of emphasizing a grievance. But this attempt to explain the obscenity away simply ignores its social effect. So successful was its use by the SDS at Columbia in demoralizing meetings with faculty members and administrators that it became one of the chief means of physically disrupting the sessions of the disciplinary tribunal set up to consider the case of a law student charged with (a) assault and battery against university personnel, and (b) physically hindering access to a university faculty member by other students.

In the letter of transmittal to Dean Warren of the School of Law of Columbia University dated December 26, 1968, the chairman of the committee writes that the sessions were conducted "under circumstances often violative of the principles of decorum observed in a hearing room, and with insults and lies hurled at the tribunal by members of the audience . . . [The first meeting] was adjourned when members of the audience mounted the podium, kicked the papers to the floor, and directed a demonstration of such magnitude as to render further proceedings inaudible."

The transcript reveals that the interrogation of the panel was punctuated by obscene jeers from the audience. Among the least offensive were outcries like "Are you going to set Gus [the defendant] free? None of this bullshit about procedure! Murderers up against the wall!" the transcript concludes (page 55) with the following paragraph:

> Chanting calls of "Bullshit! Bullshit!" Call of "Shit or get off the pot!" Whereupon a man from the audience seized the gavel from the tribunal's desk and walked along the desk, kicking aside the papers thereupon. The tribunal left their places briefly and conferred.

The committee adjourned the meeting and fled. A second closed meeting was invaded by several hundred SDS students headed by Mark Rudd who called the law professors "Pigs!" and incited the students to additional obscenities.

Finding the law student guilty as charged on one of the two counts, the panel punished him not by expulsion or even suspension (the punishments called for by the Interim Rules for his offense) but by disciplinary probation. This meant that the student got off scot-free and that he was permitted to complete his law course without any interruption. He was merely warned not to repeat the offense.

He repaid them by publishing a scathing and abusive letter in the *Columbia Spectator* whose concluding sentence reads:

> To these petty little men, and the more guilty ones that control them, I conclude with the message of the valiant math-commune: "Up against the wall, mother-fucker. This is a stick-up!"

Because it lowers the whole moral and educational tone and level of discourse in a university, this forced draft of obscenity threatens academic freedom. What A. M. Rosenthal, an editor of the *New York Times*, says so persuasively about the effect of violence on the body politic applies all the more to the educational scene!

> Not much of discourse takes place when one participant smashes another in the face. And the techniques of present-day militancy often simply are verbal blows in the face.
> Obscene epithets are blows in the face, and in political struggle they have a deliberate, thought-out function. To look at a man and speak to him vilely is to throw filth in his face.
> Fascists of the right and of the left know that when a man is so addressed he is humiliated and brought down and they know that when filth is thrown the recipient, however decent, suddenly stands amidst the reek.
> Obscenity is simply one more weapon in political street warfare, and so is racism, but much more powerful, much more destructive of discourse. Conceivably there is a difference between calling a man a Jew pig and calling him a nigger, but it is rather difficult to see.
> *(New York Times,* January 6, 1969)

One of the curious consequences of the threats to academic freedom by rampaging militant activists of the SDS and Black Nationalists has been the efforts of administrators to purchase peace at any price by sacrificing essential principles of academic freedom. This effort at appeasement rarely succeeds because the demands of these and other political groups of the same kidney flow not from sound basic educational principles—on which agreement can be won among members of the academic community without violence or threats of violence—but from strategic considerations on how to radicalize the student body, polarize the campus, and extend privileged enclaves of student power. These strategic considerations dictate the escalation of demands until society is transformed.

The likelihood that peace can be won by appeasement and capitulation is remote, even when sound educational principles and the safeguards of academic freedom are sacrificed. The recent events at Cornell University, San Francisco State College, and the College of the City of New York are graphic illustrations.

Some administrators appear not to be aware of this, especially those who see their role as somewhat like that of labor mediators who hope by getting concessions from both sides to restore peace and amity. They naturally are impatient with those who raise difficulties about first principles in what appears to them to be an essentially bargaining situation. The analogy between the industrial conflict and the educational situation is fundamentally unsound for many reasons, some of which I shall detail. Suffice it to say here that the college administrator who conceives of his role as that of a labor mediator overlooks the obvious facts that he is a party to the dispute, especially where he represents, as he should, the reflective will of the faculty; and that where *political* issues are raised in strikes the labor mediator has a very limited role.

The life of an administrator in our times is an unhappy one. At best patronized by the faculty, who know that a career of scholarship is impossible in the embattled posts of administration, he is the first and most conspicuous target for attack by students and public. Called upon to make important decisions in many fields in which he can only guess, unable to count on the gratitude and loyalty, and in the pinch of crisis, even the confidence of a faculty whom he has served often sacrificially—it is a matter of wonderment that any first-rate mind can be found to serve as a university administrator. And yet, great faculties do not get built by themselves. Administrative leadership is essential.

One must, therefore, judge with forbearance the actions of university administrators, particularly in the light of the tendency of faculties to make them scapegoats for the faculties' own ineptitude and neglect. In the martyrology of college administrators, the names of Clark Kerr and David Truman rank high as men of liberal principles, imagination, and compassion, repudiated by faculties they had served with great distinction.

Nonetheless, there are other administrators whose outlook and attitudes have positively contributed to the erosion of academic freedom, who have self-righteously pursued policies independently of their faculties, with disastrous consequences not only to their own institutions but to the entire cause of education in a free society. If we single out some administrators by name, it is not on personal grounds but only as illustrations of *types*, for unfortunately there are others of the same kind.

Perhaps the most conspicuous of the deliberate violations of the principles of academic freedom are those for which Dr. James Perkins, the former President of Cornell University, has taken responsibility. In his mind the toleration of attacks on academic freedom appeared to be necessitated by vague principles of "social justice." I say "vague" because none of the issues on which he yielded seemed required by any principles of social justice in which equality of concern is central.

There may theoretically be a conflict between principles of academic freedom and other freedoms—as when some mad scientist demands the right to experiment on a human being against his will to make an allegedly important discovery. But the quest for social justice cannot conflict with principles of academic freedom, especially in an age when we are seeking to formulate and apply principles of social justice in new situations. The openness to discovery, to new possibilities and alternatives, is what needs to be stressed rather than dogmatic pronouncements, and this is impossible where academic freedom is curtailed.

What President Perkins meant by "social justice" was revealed in his interview with Evans and Novak (*Newsday*, May 2, 1969) in which he reported that "he had told faculty members 'they could not use the cloak of academic freedom' to cover up statements which might anger black students." The principles of academic freedom, as we have seen, give qualified teachers the right to utter statements that might anger anyone. Any administrator who is unaware of this— and is unprepared or unwilling to defend a faculty member against those inside or outside the university who are angered by his statements, and seek to refute him not by argument or evidence but by force and violence or threat of force and violence—is manifestly unfit to be an administrator. Even if in his misguided notions of what constitutes social justice, he is willing to permit himself to be manhandled by students and publicly humiliated when he capitulates to their lawlessness, as was true of Dr. Perkins, he has been guilty of intellectual treason. Worse than the student lout, white or black, who roughs up those to whom he can make no rational response, is the teacher or administrator who kisses the hand that strikes him down.

Another type of administrator, avowedly liberal in his educational philosophy, will sometimes high-handedly appoint an individual to a strategic educational post without consulting the relevant departments or knowledgeable scholars in the discipline. Pleading the necessity for emergency action, he will shortcut the faculty procedures by which competence and professional standing are established. The result sometimes is the recruitment of a controversial figure who, unsure of the conditions of his tenure, tends to espouse extremist attitudes as a kind of insurance against dismissal.

The chief architect of the planned chaos, so to speak, on the campus of San Francisco State College was none other than its President John Summerskill, who on February 9, 1968—without even consulting his faculty, or the Council of Academic Deans, or the Vice-President for Faculty Affairs —appointed Dr. Nathan Hare to be Special Curriculum Supervisor (at the rank of lecturer but with pay based on the academic rank of Associate Professor) to help design a curriculum of black studies.

Dr. Nathan Hare, as President Summerskill was aware, had been dismissed from Howard University, the well-known Negro university in Washington, D.C., on charges that he had incited the students to riot and violence. Hare's incredible version is that he had been fired simply because he was black. Hare characterizes himself as a "black revolutionist." In several speeches he has declared that seizing the symbols of power (such as seizing buildings) is not enough. It is the implements of power, he argues, that must be acquired— "money and guns." In this, his views are similar to those Maulana Ron Karenga expressed at the Yale Symposium on the Black Experience and Black Studies in the spring of 1968, in which Dr. Hare also participated.

More relevant are Dr. Hare's views of black studies presented at the Yale Symposium and elsewhere. Among other things he believes that no white person is capable of teaching black experience; that black studies should be restricted to black students (although he is not opposed to white students studying the black experience in their own classes!); that a separate department of black studies be established granting a bachelor's degree in black studies, and that this department have complete autonomy (which no other departments have) in hiring and firing staff; that among the legitimate courses in black experience are courses not only in black history and economics but black mathematics, black statistics, and black science.

Being "black" is a necessary but not sufficient condition of competence to teach in the black-studies program. "Black Anglo-Saxons" need not apply. Only those committed to the cultural values of what has sometimes been called "Negri-

tude" and to the ideals of revolutionary black nationalism are
eligible. It is just as if someone were to contend that Jewish
studies in any field could only be taught by those who sub-
scribed to the extremist variety of political Zionism!

With views of this character, it was not long before the
presence of Dr. Hare made itself felt on the campus of San
Francisco State College. An already difficult situation
was made worse. Surrounded by the massed membership of
the Black Students' Union breathing down their necks, faculty committees adopted a program of black studies. Subsequently the faculty and the trustees approved a black-
studies degree. The Council of Academic Deans authorized
the establishment of 11.3 positions and a Black Studies Department "with full faculty power commensurate with that
accorded all other departments at the college."

However, Dr. Hare and his cohorts among students and
faculty were not satisfied with all this. Nothing but complete autonomy and twenty positions would do! They called
a strike in order to close down the college. By this time
President Summerskill had long since resigned and fled the
campus, leaving others with the educational mess he had
created.

There is something odd about the way in which faculty
members, dropped for incompetence—or, more rarely, for
conduct unbecoming a teacher—reappear on other campuses.
There should not, and cannot, of course, be an automatic
bar to the employment of teachers elsewhere if they have
failed to make the grade in the institution of original
appointment. But in justice to everyone concerned, a full
exploration of the circumstances under which an individual is
released or dismissed is always in order.

Administrators have been known to hire teachers without
even inquiring from their erstwhile departmental colleagues
about their qualifications as classroom teachers and scholars,
relying only on the letters or assurances of individuals who
are friendly to the candidate but who are not in the field of
the candidate's discipline. The Summerskills of the academy

who act this way leave the resulting embarrassments and disasters to their successors—both administrators and faculty —aware that although it is easy to make a mistake in education, to undo it is one of the most difficult things in the world.[1]

There is a third type of administrator who weakens the defense of academic freedom against its enemies and detractors. This is the headline-hunting administrator who, on the assumption that man-bites-dog is always good for a story, will say something perfectly outrageous to call attention to himself or to some pet curricular plan that, judged on its merits, would be left to wither on the vine. Like those who in time of plague peddle some cure-all nostrum, or who in periods of national confusion urge conversion to some recondite propositions in theology as the only path to salvation, they seek in the situation of educational chaos to further educational projects that could not command attention on their intrinsic merits.

We may cite as typical of this breed Mr. William Birenbaum, president of the Staten Island Community College, who charges that the responsibility for campus violence of every variety rests not on the SDS or the Black Nationalists or their allies, but on the authoritarian structure of the colleges and universities themselves and the attitudes of the oligarchy of professors who run them. "Student lawlessness and disorder on the campus are a direct function of the authoritarian and oligarchical order imposed by those who possess the law-making power in the university."[2] Either Mr. Birenbaum does not know what a "direct function" is or he is willfully disregarding the evidence. For the evidence shows that his statement is incorrect. The worst excesses have occurred not on truly authoritarian campuses but on the most liberal ones.

[1] Additional material on the situation in San Francisco State College will be found in John Bunzel's chapter "Black Studies at San Francisco State" in *Confrontation*, edited by Bell and Kristol, New York, Basic Books, 1969.
[2] I am quoting from an account of a speech delivered before the 49th annual meeting of the American Association of Junior Colleges, reported in *The Chronicle of Higher Education*, March 10, 1969.

By any measure, the University of California at Berkeley, San Francisco State College, Roosevelt College, Oberlin, Swarthmore, and N.Y.U. are more liberal than the University of Utah, Fordham, Virginia Polytechnic, and scores of others—but the former have been more affected than the latter. This is not an argument for an authoritarian university, we hasten to point out, but merely an indication that the causation of student rebellion is far more complex than the simplistic hypothesis advanced.

The worst classroom disorders at Columbia University took place *after* the disciplinary structure was liberalized with substantial student participation. On many campuses, faculties and administrations have left to student determination what recruitment policy should be or whether students should be free to elect the R.O.T.C. curriculum. Despite majority student support for a policy of open recruitment and free election of R.O.T.C. on many campuses, violent disruptions have occurred. Mr. Birenbaum is obviously unfamiliar with the literature of some revolutionary student groups who reject the principles of academic freedom for students or freedom of curricular choice if students choose what—in the judgment of these groups—is not good for them.[3]

Not satisfied with picturing the victims of student violence as if they were aggressors, Mr. Birenbaum warns that the chief dangers to "education for freedom" come not from the rioting students and their allies but from those who would enforce the law against them. He creates an amalgalm between conservative governors and legislators who counterpose educational vigilantism to academic anarchy and "liberal university professors" critical of the SDS. But the liberal university professors he attacks have been educational reformers all their lives. They oppose not reform, but reform by violence, as self-defeating and counterproductive. If there is a choice, it is between reform—where neces-

[3] See the important article, "Letter from Columbia," by Arnold Beichman in *Encounter*, May 1969.

sary—by the pooled intelligence of all elements of the academic community, and reform by coercion or the imposition of antecedently held, fixed "nonnegotiable" educational solutions.

The educational panacea proposed by Mr. Birenbaum to bring peace and order on the campus, to save it from the oligarchy of the professorial elite, is a mixture of the obvious, irrelevant, and absurd:

> Because we must live in the cities, we must restructure our institutions to honor and understand the mentality required for successful city life. To do this we must methodically break down our own walls, and launch vast new programs aimed at the disruption of our own un-American academic monopolies.

What necessary connection the centering of the curriculum on urban affairs will have with the behavior of student disrupters, whose battle cries focus on national issues more often than on local ones, is not indicated. Much of any good curriculum in social studies *already* relates to the culture of cities. Actually some of Mr. Birenbaum's specific curricular suggestions were already implemented at San Francisco State without moderating in the least the student extremism and violence.

And what a narrow and constricting curricular frame he proposes! Men live not only in cities but in states and in nations and in a world whose problems require a vision beyond particular cities, if any city is to survive. Men live also in a world of ideas, in societies of the spirit—religious, artistic, scientific. An education worthy of man must not deny him access to the great legacies of the past. We need not break down the walls between the college and society, provided there are open doors for easy entrance and exit.

Even for the curriculum of a junior college, exclusive orientation to urban problems is too confining. To make it the model for all colleges and for all talents is to ignore relevant differences in need, aspiration, and capacity. To look to the college as the instrument of social reform, to convert it into a center for social work and social relief, is to usurp the function of other institutions in the democratic community.

It is one thing, as I have argued in the last chapter, to bring into college students whose right to an education from which they can profit is frustrated by low incomes and socially disadvantageous environments. It is quite another to make the study and removal of the social obstacles to educational opportunity—an essentially political task—the central subject matter even of junior colleges—and all the more so if such schooling is to be terminal.

Some such conception of the college, or at least of one of its chief functions, explains the introduction of racist practices by the administrations of Northwestern University and Antioch College. Yielding to threats from the dominant Black Nationalist factions among their Negro students, segregated black dormitories and black-studies institutes were established just a few months after Congress adopted the Civil Rights Act of 1968 providing open occupancy in housing.

The rationalization offered for this lapse into racism on liberal premises is almost as deplorable as the action itself. The facilities have not been segregated, say the administrators, because in principle whites have not been excluded. They simply lack eligibility or have not expressed a strong desire to live in black dormitories or attend classes in the black institute. This is rather reminiscent of the claim of Southern registrars who denied Negroes their right to vote not because of their color but only because of their alleged illiteracy. In justification of the practice at Antioch, which led to the resignation of Dr. Kenneth Clark, its Negro trustee, President James P. Dixon, is quoted as saying: "Here [at Antioch] we tend to accept what people say is good for them as being good."

This is a preposterous attitude for educators in quest of what is sound, who periodically evaluate what they are doing in the light of new needs and developments. What if the things people say are good for them are educationally bad for them? What if they are also bad for others?

Administrators and faculties must always *listen* to what students say is good for them. But saying something is good doesn't make it so!

Would President Dixon accept with similar complaisance the demand of white students for segregated housing or studies irrespective of the rationalizations offered, especially their contention that such segregation was good for them?

The real reason why the demands of the black students were granted at Antioch, Northwestern, and elsewhere is that they threatened to tear the place apart if they were denied. The administration and faculty yielded out of fear. When this happens, academic freedom is a shell. Its spirit has fled the campus.

Administrators cannot betray the principles of academic freedom without the connivance of the faculty. The saddest chapter in American higher education has been the actions of university faculties themselves in undermining the principles and practices that were established with such difficulty during the last fifty years. The story is particularly painful for individuals like the author who have advocated an increasingly larger role for the faculty in the determination of university policy.

It is a story that can be told here only in the form of episodes. The first episode begins with Berkeley, the birthplace of the American student rebellion. At Berkeley an administrative blunder was the occasion for the first act of student lawlessness. After the blunder was retrieved, however, students seized Sproul Hall and the faculty refused to condemn the action. Instead they adopted a rule that the content of speech be completely unrestricted on campus. This opened the door to the filthy-speech movement and the tides of obscenity, insult, and slander that have lowered the level of

THE ATTACK ON ACADEMIC FREEDOM 99

intellectual discourse and made the dialogue of reason all but impossible.

The second episode was the formal acceptance by the faculty of Harvard University of the principle that students in the black-studies program have the right to determine the content and personnel of instruction, which in effect gives them the power of veto. By itself it has little significance and was adopted to buy peace at Cambridge. But its repercussions have been far-reaching. If Harvard can do it, what objection can there be for less prestigious institutions to follow? It has facilitated the take-over of black-studies programs by Black Nationalist students, thus insuring that black studies become a political instrument of the separatist anti-integration factions among the Negro community. More important, it plays into the hands of the SDS and similiar groups that have made the same demands as black students to control the content and personnel of *their* studies. Indeed, if the principle is valid for black students, why is it invalid for white?

Those who approve of the principle for black studies but disapprove of it for nonblack studies do not dare to say what is in their hearts—that it makes little difference who teaches black studies and what the content is since, in the rude language of the students, they are mostly "crap courses," and that what can be tolerated for such courses cannot be tolerated for courses that have real intellectual content. To say this would be a crass expression of racism and justifiably resented by black students genuinely concerned in getting as good an education as their white fellow students. In any event, if the principle is sound with respect to the education of black students, it is also sound with respect to the education of whites. It seems to me, however, demonstrable that it is unsound with respect to the education of both.

Whatever may be worked out at Harvard, it is safe to predict that before long the SDS and other political groups will agitate for the revision of courses that are, in their judgment, "class-biased," "imperialistic," "irrelevant," "capitalistic," and "fascistic." These epithets have actually been used by members of the SDS to characterize existing courses. They have even demanded that research projects be dropped in areas related to defense. They are not content to be heard, to have their criticism evaluated as suggestions. They frankly want power. If it is not granted to them, they are prepared, whereever they believe they can do so with impunity, to impose their will by disruption and take-over.

The stormy history of Stanford University in recent years is evidence of how far they are prepared to go. Like all revolutionaries, convinced that they are fighting for values of transcendent importance, they are prepared to sacrifice the principles of academic freedom, which they tend to regard merely as a redoubt of professional privilege.

If the episode at Harvard may be called the "Munich" of American higher education, someday the episode at Cornell may be described as its "Pearl Harbor." The spectacle of armed students with rifles at the ready leaving Willard Straight Hall—which they had illegally occupied by driving the visiting parents of other students out of their rooms into the chill dawn—shocked the entire country. But the incident was the culmination of a series of disastrous actions by the administration and faculty in which every principle of academic due process was jettisoned, the academic freedom both of teachers and students betrayed, and the hysteria of blue funk concealed by empty rhetoric about building a new form of "racial harmony on campus."

The enormity of the action taken by the Cornell faculty becomes apparent when it is recalled that it had set up a faculty-student commission on discipline, under whose code six black students were cited for participating in serious disorderly actions. These students refused to acknowledge the authority of the commission. After considering the evidence and deliberating on the charges, the commission voted "censure" of three of the six students found guilty, the mildest possible punishment.

THE ATTACK ON ACADEMIC FREEDOM

Instead of appealing the judgment to the faculty, militant black students of the Afro-American Society seized Willard Straight Hall, the student center, armed themselves, and demanded complete nullification of the sentence. The administration agreed. But since it had no authority to override the faculty, it summoned the faculty to an emergency meeting on Monday, April 21. The faculty refused to endorse the capitulation of the administration to the threats of force. Leaning over backward to show it was not punitive minded, the faculty invited the black students to attend a meeting convoked for Wednesday, April 23, and state their case.

The black students did no such thing. Instead they denounced faculty members who had taken principled positions against surrender as "racists" who "will be dealt with." A spokesman for the Afro-American Society declared that Cornell had "three hours to live." The slogans "Death to racists!" and "Death to pigs!" were proclaimed. On the advice of security officers, members of the faculty who had been denounced and threatened as "racists" abandoned their homes and went into hiding.[4]

Meanwhile, the SDS organized sympathetic students and seized Barton Hall. Together with their faculty allies, they threatened to tear Cornell apart if the faculty did not repudiate the decision of the joint faculty-student committee it had set up the previous year both to democratize and generalize the disciplinary procedures. The seizure of Barton Hall was as illegal as that of Willard Straight Hall, but it received the ex post facto blessings of Dr. Perkins "as one of the most constructive forces which have been set in motion in the history of Cornell."

Cowed by the threats of violence from the Afro-American Society and the SDS, the faculty, without even considering the evidence on which the decision of the Commission on

[4] Word of these threats was telephoned to me by some members of the Cornell faculty who had joined the University Centers for Rational Alternatives. I attempted to get in touch with Professor Walter E. Berns to discover the true state of affairs but he was then beyond the reach of any available communication.

Discipline was based, repudiated its findings. The censure of the three students was lifted.

Since that time, rationalizations galore have poured from the mouths of those who voted "in fear and trembling" for the new era in race relations. It was not cowardice, argued some, because it requires courage to abase oneself publicly in order to atone for the crimes of white society. It was wisdom, argued others, because the danger was great that "someone might have been killed." There was no capitulation because of danger, affirmed others, because "the rifles of the black students were not loaded." The very men who denounced with fiery scorn those who surrender a prisoner to a lynch mob threatening to burn down the court of justice, explained: "We are not fanatics of justice and due process. We do not live by the Kantian maxim, *Fiat justitia pereat mundus.*[5] We have saved the temple of reason from being burned down by irrationalists."

There may be salvation by surrender—but reason and truth can never be saved this way.

Actually an unhysterical assessment of the situation shows that whatever physical damage might have been inflicted on Cornell would have been less costly morally than the loss of self-respect involved in the capitulation. Not all the Negro students at Cornell lined up in support of the Black Nationalists. The strategy of the latter was simply provocation. The contention that they had not participated in setting up the judicial process under which three students were censured is altogether without merit except on the assumption that they were a sovereign group independent of the rest of the students.

The rules set up were general guides to all student behavior. The fact that the Black Nationalists blew up to such extravagant proportions the significance of the mildest possible penalty, "censure," which could have no real bearing on the behavior of those censured, is evidence that the issue was

[5] "Let justice prevail though the world is destroyed."

not one of life and death. They were testing the administration and faculty to see how far they could go.

After their victory, they carried this testing further. They proposed that none other than John F. Hatchett be appointed Assistant Director of the Projected Center for Afro-American Studies. Hatchett had been dismissed by the New York City Board of Education for insubordination and subsequently relieved of his post as Director of Black Studies at New York University because of his virulent anti-Semitism. Although the plan for the Center of Afro-American Studies, accepted by the administration, provided that the center was to be completely autonomous, that the university faculty was to have neither voice nor power of veto in selecting staff, the Cornell administration rejected Hatchett. The tidal wave of national outrage and protest had mounted so high already that the administration feared it would be completely swamped if it accepted Hatchett.

Although they had a better case for fighting in the Hatchett issue, since they had been promised autonomy, than in the refusal to accept the rules of judicial process, the black students yielded. Would the black students have yielded if the Cornell faculty had remained firm on the more fundamental issue? And if not, what would they have done? No one can answer with confidence. Some reports from the black students themselves indicate that half of those who seized Willard Straight would have "quit Cornell to punish it." Other reports say vandalism would have occurred. There is no good reason to believe that they would have shot it out with the sheriff's deputies, for the reason they gave for arming themselves is that they feared retaliation by other, white students.

The Harvard faculty, although it gave its black militants educational autonomy, voted to uphold punishment of students who had invaded University Hall. The Cornell faculty made no effort to punish students for seizing either Willard Straight Hall or Barton Hall, for sporting guns on campus after they had been specifically banned, for threatening the persons of members of the faculty. These actions remained punishable even after the judgment of censure had been rescinded. But no one dared propose to the Cornell faculty to enforce the rules that covered such grave—it is not too strong to say heinous—misconduct. The writ of law ran not for those who successfully violated it.

The upshot of events at Cornell may best be described in an unprecedented letter written by two visiting professors at Cornell on May 6 and published May 10, 1969, in the *New York Times*.

> To the Editor:
> The authors of this letter are visiting scholars at Cornell University, one in the Society for Humanities, the other in the English Department. Eleven days ago we took the step, perhaps unprecedented among visitors to a great American university, of announcing that we were suspending our teaching for the rest of the semester, although we would remain available to our respective students for private consultation.
> Implicit in our invitations to Cornell were the conditions of free speech and personal safety that have normally obtained in the academic communities of the civilized world. In our judgment these conditions no longer obtained. We see no reason to change our decision; for although the situation at Cornell is today superficially calmer, academic freedom remains in jeopardy.
> We advise our colleagues in other universities that the revolutionary "restructuring" now going on in several departments and in the government of this university, with the approval of the administration and many among the faculty and student body, threatens to destroy the intellectual standing of Cornell.

> Harold Bloom,
> Professor of English,
> Yale University.

Matthew Hodgart,
Professor of English,
University of Sussex, England.

Ithaca, N.Y.

The thinking that makes it possible to resign oneself to the
events at Cornell, if not to condone them, is exhibited in the
text of a letter to President Nixon adopted by a substantial
majority of the faculty, administrators, and student body of
Amherst College. This letter, released May 21, 1969, received
wide distribution and comment. It repays careful study because of what it says and fails to say.

It says that campus turmoil and disruption of the kind we
have been discussing—

> will continue until you and the other political leaders of
> our country address more effectively, massively, and
> persistently the major social and foreign problems of our
> society. Part of this turmoil in universities derives from
> the distance separating the American dream from the
> American reality.

There will always be a difference between the American
dream and the American reality, and we need not be fearful
of the discontent that impels us to reduce the gap. The statement overlooks the fact that the meaning and content of the
American dream have changed with our growth in power
and productivity. Because we have raised our sights higher
than ever before, we are more aware of the disparity between ideal and performance. But surely this is no ground for
ignoring or denying the distance we have come in the last
fifty years with respect to the recognition of the rights of
labor, of racial and religious minorities, and in standards of
living and acknowledging how much *more* still must be
done.

But if there is a connection between student disruption
and concern with major social and foreign problems of our

society, the Amherst statement fails to explain why our campuses were quiescent during the long periods of the past when there was no effective, massive, or persistent attempt to meet these problems. When trade unionism was a subversive doctrine (the twenties), when sixteen million were unemployed (the thirties), when elementary civil rights were being denied to Negroes (the forties), when an undeclared war was raging in Korea (the early fifties), our campuses were relatively quiescent. The Amherst academic community issued no statements.

Today during a decade when more social legislation, more civil-rights legislation, more progress in mitigating poverty have been achieved than in any decade since the Civil War, why are our campuses—in many places, literally —aflame? If unsatisfactory social conditions are responsible for student turmoil, how explain that the more social conditions have improved, the more massive and the more persistent—as compared to the past—the effort to better these conditions, the more flagrantly and violently have student disorders flared?

The Amherst statement then quotes a report that five cabinet officers "seemed to agree that the disorder was caused by a small minority of students."

To which it replies in a shocking and arbitrary substitution of meanings:

> Our conviction is that such a view is seriously in error if it is taken to mean that no legitimate and important reasons exist for the anger and sense of impotence felt by many students and faculty.

But, of course, the statement that the disorders are caused by a small minority of students means no such thing. It means what it says—that a small minority of students have seized buildings, vandalized them, rifled files, disrupted classrooms, assaulted fellow students, faculty, and administrators, committed arson, bombed the homes and threatened the lives of those who have criticized them. This is what disorder means. The report rejected by the Amherst community asserts that the disorder was instigated by a small minority. This is verifiable truth. No one denies that there are legitimate and important reasons for anger and the sense of impotence not only among students and faculty but among the citizens of the country. The only relevant question is whether these reasons are a sufficient ground for condoning the student disorders?

And here what the Amherst letter does *not* say is extremely significant. It does *not* say a word in criticism or rejection of these disorders. This omission, advices from Amherst indicate, was deliberate. Under the circumstances, would it be unfair to infer that the Amherst academic community believes that until the American dream becomes reality, student disorders will and should continue, and that it is wrong to condemn them?

If this is, indeed, what Amherst College believes, the citizens of the general community would have "legitimate and important reasons" for a sense of anger against it. But surely this would not be a sufficient ground for burning it down or acting in the way the small minority of students acted at Cornell, Harvard, and Columbia.

The irresponsibility of the Amherst letter is all the more striking because it was adopted after the unhappy events at Cornell, Harvard, and elsewhere had been blazoned in the headlines of the nation's press. If we test the statements made in that letter against the specific happenings on the campuses, and ask what action taken by the students was caused by the failure of the federal government "to make a decisive response" to our crisis, the utter irrelevance of one to the other will be apparent.

Test the Amherst declaration against, say, the six famous demands that the Columbia SDS made when it seized Hamilton Hall and then the president's office in the Low Library:

(1) The lifting of disciplinary probation against students who had violated the rule banning indoor demonstrations.
(2) The revocation of the rule itself.
(3) Judicial decisions should be made in public open to all.
(4) All relations with the Institute for Defense Analysis (IDA) should be severed (already under reconsideration by a faculty committee).
(5) Construction of the Columbia gym must be stopped.
(6) Amnesty must be granted all students for violations of law.

The only issue remotely concerned with national policy was Columbia's relations with IDA, which were minimal. The key issue was the students' demand for amnesty, to which they clung even after their other demands were, in effect, conceded. On all of these issues, to put it mildly, intelligent persons of goodwill could hold contrary views. The resolution of not one of them required the violence initiated by the SDS.

As the students opposed to the behavior of the SDS put it: "The question is not one of liberalism vs. moderation. It is a question of whether democracy can survive on a campus dominated by one faction victorious only through physical coercion."

One might ask, Could democracy survive at *Amherst* under such conditions?

The Amherst statement admits as an afterthought that "not all the problems faced by the colleges are a reflection of the malaise of the larger society." Believing this, the Amherst academic community was under the intellectual obligation to spell out which problems were which and to relate them to the disorders that have occurred.

Many of the problems involved in the race riots that broke out on the campus of the College of the City of New York raised questions about educational theory and practice, the function of a university in modern society, and the definition and responsibilities of academic freedom. At Cornell the basic issue was the nature of academic due process. On these matters the Amherst statement that summarized two entire days of deliberation remained silent. Yet these considerations are really central.

To anyone aware of Amherst's impressive intellectual past, the spectacle of its current failure to distinguish relevant issues, of its unwillingness to condemn the violence of the means used in behalf of ideals not less stoutly believed by the victims of that violence, is disheartening. It is a measure of the retreat of liberalism from intelligence to ritual, from grappling with specific problems to pious rhetoric. It makes one fateful presupposition that must be challenged, even if it were established—as it has not been—that student turmoil is chiefly caused by failure to solve our major domestic and foreign problems. This presupposition is that in a democratic society the failure to solve these problems—and there will always be problems—at a rate and in a direction satisfactory to any particular group, students or not, justifies that group to resort in the name of democracy to violence and other forms of confrontation. This belief is widely shared, particularly among those who want to be revolutionists and democrats, too, in a democratic society.

To this view, we now turn.

CHAPTER SIX

# THE WAR AGAINST THE DEMOCRATIC PROCESS

We are living in a time of great fear and confusion in our country. The fear and confusion are so profound that our very language has become infected with mischievous ambiguity. The disorders rampant in our cities and schools have brought the slogan of "Law and Order" to everyone's lips. But there is no agreement about what it means.

One looks behind the words to the motives of the persons using, them. This remains true even when the slogan "Just Law and Civilized Order" is counterposed to it. "Justice for whom?" ask militant students with a sneer at liberal illusions.

"The only difference between civilized and uncivilized order," I have heard it said, "is the difference between the veteran cop and the raw recruit. Both wield clubs."

The relations between law and liberty and their place in a free society are complex questions, themes for perennial dialogue or discussion. Until recently we had thought that certain elementary truths could be accepted about law and freedom and democracy as a basis for understanding and improving our society. Among these truths are the propositions that if freedom is defined as the absence of restraint on our powers of action, then no freedom can be absolute; that one freedom limits another; that law creates and protects certain freedoms only by restricting certain other freedoms; that where freedoms conflict, the best hopes of rational and peaceful resolution are through the democratic process; and that, finally, the only alternatives to the democratic process are—as Lincoln put it when the nation faced the torment of civil war—anarchism, on the one hand, and despotism, the normal reaction to prolonged anarchy, on the other.

Today these truths have been put in dispute not only by the behavior of many of our citizens but by the justifications offered for this behavior. In the past we used to believe that we could turn for intellectual guidance to our colleges and universities as relatively disinterested centers of inquiry in these matters. Unfortunately, colleges and universities have themselves become embattled storm centers of controversy, not only about the presuppositions of the democratic process but about the nature and goals of the university.

A few years ago there was a movement in educational circles that advocated that the study of communism, fascism, and other forms of totalitarianism be incorporated into the curricula of our colleges, that we teach in a scholarly and objective fashion about the fighting faiths and subversive stratagems of the enemies of a free society. Judging by the nationwide behavior of student bodies, during the last election, in refusing to give a hearing to points of view they did not share, we have failed, for the most part, to teach our students properly even about the meaning of democracy.

Instead of the colleges and universities functioning as centers of enlightenment to a bewildered and distraught population, because of what has occurred on their campuses, they have become objects of revulsion and disgust to large numbers, and have strengthened the furies of backlash and reaction. There is little room for doubt that events at Berkeley as well as Watts contributed to changing the climate of political opinion in California. The riotous happenings at Columbia and other campuses definitely cast their shadows on the elections in 1968. The defeat of school-bond issues in many areas of the country, and more particularly in California, has been attributed by informed observers to the almost daily televised spectacles of campus confrontations and disorders.

That many of our students have not been properly taught the meaning of democracy is apparent in the reasons they sometimes offer for their disillusionment with the democratic process when they have failed to convince others of the validity of what they firmly believe to be true or right.

In extenuation of conduct that breaks out of the frame of academic civility or political due process, militant student leaders have been heard to say: "You advise us to rely on democratic processes when we have legitimate demands. But what's the use of resorting to such processes when it results only in frustration? We make demands that are good for the country, we talk, we even get a hearing but our proposals on the war or draft or military spending are not adopted. We are only invited to talk some more! We have learned that rocks and riots can make people listen to reason when arguments fail. When we put our bodies on the line, we get results."

This is, indeed, a very odd conception of the democratic process. The failure to convince others may indicate that the evidence or argument is not strong enough, or that even when it is valid one must learn how to be more persuasive, to wait a little longer and work a little harder. In some respects the democratic process is like the scientific process. Its validity does not depend upon any one specific outcome but on a whole series of decisions. It can't guarantee that any particular policy we passionately regard as valid will be adopted any more than the particular findings of a scientific inquiry will be true.

A guess may sometimes turn out to be right and the conclusion of a careful investigation wrong; an old wives' remedy may, on a rare occasion, work when scientific medicine fails. But no sensible person, therefore, discards scientific method. A democrat knows that a majority may sometimes be wrong. But he believes that in an open society where the processes of freely given consent operate, conflicts of interest can be more satisfactorily resolved by majority rule than by minority rule, and that he must therefore appeal from the decision of an unenlightened majority to the decision of an enlightened majority.

The assumption made in certain students quarters today that what *they* want or believe desirable is what the majority of the electorate wants or believes desirable is very questionable in the light of reliable polls in the past on our policy in Vietnam, the draft, defense spending, and many other issues. On these matters the thinking of students has differed from that of the general population, as the election returns show.

Let us grant, for the moment, that the students are right and the others wrong. What follows? Surely not—if they are democrats—that they have a right to disrupt society. And surely not that they have a right to make the university the scapegoat for the mistakes of the majority. For even ir- responsible fanatics must grant that the university is not responsible for American involvement in Vietnam, for the draft, for failure to enact proper legislation to solve prob- lems of race and poverty. There is something contemptible in compensating for one's political weakness by taking it out on the university—that soft underbelly of society vulnerable to any violent thrust by minuscule groups.

Even if the university faculties supported the policies stu- dents opposed (in fact, they have been the chief critics of these policies), and even if society, so to speak, could be held up to ransom by demoralizing universities, this would not justify the strategy of student extremists, were they truly commited to democratic principles. Although they oc- casionally invoke these democratic principles, they are con- fused and ambiguous about them, except for members of one or another Communist faction for whom "the dictatorship of the party" is an expression of "socialist democracy."

No matter how convinced we are as democrats that we are right, this does not give us a mandate to impose what is right on the general population. Deny this and we surrender to the logic of totalitarianism. This elementary truth has been persistently ignored, and sometimes contested, by student rebels. They seem to be unaware of the elitism behind their imperious political attitudes.

They will agree it is wrong for any group convinced that smoking causes lung cancer to march on tobacco warehouses and fire them because the democratic majority refuses to outlaw the sale of cigarettes. They will scoff at those convinced of the harmful effect of alcohol on the nervous system who, outraged by the preferences of the majority for the joys of drink over the sobrieties of abstinence, act like disciples of Carry Nation. But they seem to expect the country to come to heel if its "intellectuals," among whom they include themselves, disapprove of some political policy. They have not the slightest compunction in disrupting voluntary R.O.T.C. courses or other curricular or extracurricular activities approved by a majority of their fellow students.

The elitism of student militants makes them knights of the double standard. They will cry out that the police or the military have no place on any educational campus. But they heartily approve of the use of bayonets to guarantee the enforcement of the court order to make it possible for black students to attend Central High School in Little Rock, Arkansas, and to enable James Meredith to enroll at the University of Mississippi. It is "democratic" for a minority, no matter how small, to defy the decisions of the majority if it disapproves of them. It is "undemocratic" for a segregationist minority, no matter how large, to do the same. It has to be the right minority. And who determines that?—The right minority, of course.

There are some additional misconceptions both of the democratic process and of the educational process that have contributed to current confusions and bid fair to confound them. Indeed, there is a real danger that unless they are exposed, they may inflame disorders both in school and society. The disconcerting thing is that these misconceptions are being circulated not by demagogues and rabble-rousers, appealing to the vigilante spirit, but by members of the intellectual establishment—individuals in a position of influence and power both in the academy and judiciary.

It was said of Florence Nightingale that she began her great reforms of the hospitals of her day with the maxim that whatever hospitals accomplish, they should at least not become centers for the spread of disease. Similarly, it is not too much to expect that one who professes to live by the word of reason should not encourage propaganda by the deed, that educators not apologize for or extenuate violence on the campus, and that members of the judiciary not incite even indirectly to lawlessness.

The first misconception I wish to consider is the role of violence in a democratic society.

One of the standard responses made to the condemnation of violence by those who are more fearful of excessive law enforcement than of widespread violation of law is the equation of violence with force, and the contention that since force and the threat of force are natural, even essential, to any ordered society, violence is not a phenomenon that per se should provoke moral outrage. This overlooks the difference between violence and force. As long as law exists, force is potentially present. Otherwise, there can be no law enforcement. This is a truism.

Violence, however, is the *illegal* use of force. Those who resort to it in a democratic society while continuing to regard themselves as democrats call into question the processes of freely given consent on which laws ultimately rest. A democracy provides the mechanism by which grievances may be remedied, but the manner and form of remedying grievances cannot be determined only by those who suffer from them but by the community. Otherwise, the grievances of one group may be remedied by imposing greater grievances on another group.

We sometimes hear it said that those in position of governmental authority cannot consistently condemn violence because the government itself is engaged in violence. This is the sheerest nonsense ever when it is mouthed by eminent scholars. The government uses force, to be sure, but unless that use can be shown to be illegal—and in a democracy the existence of an independent judiciary makes it possible to do so—such force may be wise or unwise but it cannot properly be called violence. Furthermore, the government cannot be counterposed to the people in a democratic society unless it can be established that it has usurped or forfeited its authority.

The use of force by a democratic government may be immoral even when legal but as long as one remains a democrat he eschews violence against a democratic government to get it to reverse its course, and works through the political process that permits nonviolent civil disobedience as well as other forms of peaceful dissent.

We are accustomed to hear the Rapp Browns and Stokely Carmichaels say that "violence is as American as cherry pie," but one gets quite a turn when he hears Dr. Harvey Wheeler of the Center for the Study of Democratic Institutions characterize rioting as "an American way of life" and speak of its "creative uses." As the coauthor of *Fail-Safe*, a book that frightened large numbers of citizens unaware of the fact that it was based on a complete misunderstanding of the simplest facts of the American defense system, he now reveals a corresponding lack of understanding of the American political system.

"Direct action," he says, "the sort that now issues in violence too often [apparently there is no objection to its often issuing in violence], must be given fuller constitutional protection."[1] I am not concerned for the moment with the absurdity of a law that would make the violation of a law legal. This is comparable to speaking of a legal right, as distinct from the moral right, of revolution. What is irresponsible to the highest degree is the view that because something is allegedly American, whether "rioting" or "cherry pie," it is therefore good or acceptable.

[1] *Saturday Review*, May 11, 1968.

"Violence is as American as cherry pie," but so is a lynching bee. Does this make it good? There are many things that are American that as democrats we should deplore from our earliest history to the present. What makes an action good or bad is not whether it is American or un-American, but its consequences for justice and human welfare. Lynch law on the American frontier sometimes resulted in justice but most times it did not.

And what does this talk about "direct action," for which constitutional protection is demanded, actually mean? Dr. Wheeler is saying that if students—impatient with the refusal of the faculty and/or administration to grant their demands— seize a building and bar access to classes by other students and teachers, thus bringing the university to a halt, they should have *legal* protection for their action. Presumably violence occurs only when attempts are made to prevent lawless students from preventing other students from carrying on their legitimate educational business—acquiring an education.

According to this view, if the faculty or students invite a speaker of whom some other students disapprove and these latter bar his access to the campus or shout him down, the disrupters should have legal protection against any disciplinary measures taken against them. I shall have more to say about "direct action" in a moment, but surely such student conduct goes far beyond the expression of orderly dissent and protest. It would be too much to demand that dissent and protest be reasoned or reasonable. But is it too much to ask that it be orderly and peaceful? Otherwise, it is as obvious as anything can be that this call for the constitutional protection of "direct action" is an invitation to chaos.

Suppose one group of students resorted to "direct action" against the "direct action" of another group of students. Since the law must be equitably enforced, it could not prevent any group from preventing those who would prevent others from carrying on. What we would have is a kind of academic Hobbesian war of all against all, with the police standing idly by as those in pursuit of the good, the true, and the beautiful pursue and decimate each other.

When anyone says that in a democratic society, in which the legal process has not broken down, persons should resort to "direct action" to get their way, he is using a calculatedly ambiguous expression to conceal the fact that he is advocating the use of violence. When anyone urges "direct action" on students in a university, in which due process cannot be strictly legal but must be interpreted as the use of rational procedures, he is urging the substitution of mob rule for the rule of reason.

After all, what is "direct action" as distinct from "indirect action"? It is action that shortcuts deliberation and consultation in order to produce confrontation. Even when passive, its consequences may be harmful to person and property. Union picketing is a right under the First Amendment only when it is *peaceful*. But direct action is not necessarily peaceful any more than resistance is. That is why it is a clear evasion, and further evidence of confusion, when Mr. Wheeler equates his new constitutional right to direct action with the demand that "We must have a new constitutional right to civil disobedience."

A constitutional right, like any legal right, is a claim made by an individual or group that the state must be ready to enforce. Presumably, then, Mr. Wheeler would have the state protect Southern racists standing in the doorway of integrated school buildings to prevent, by their show of direct action, Negro children from entering. How then could the law enforce the constitutional rights of these children? The law itself would suffer a breakdown from a new disease—legal schizophrenia.

It is a striking phenomenon that more has been written about civil disobedience in the last few years than in the entire period of American history that preceded it. But the nature of civil disobedience in the political democratic process has been radically misunderstood by many, and when these misunderstandings are applied to the academic world, the results border on the grotesque.

There are two fundamental misapprehensions about civil disobedience in general that have seriously misled many. The first is the assumption that each law in a democratic community posits as a legitimate question to every citizen whether to obey that law or to disobey it. What is overlooked is the fact that, except on rare occasions, the prior allegiance of the *democrat* is to the legitimacy of the process by which the law is adopted. There is always, to be sure, a moral right to reject the whole democratic process on revolutionary or counterrevolutionary grounds, but we are speaking of civil disobedience by *democrats* in a *democracy*.

The democrat cannot make an issue of obeying or not obeying *every* law without repudiating the principle of majority rule and the democratic process to which that rule is integral. It is only on a matter of the gravest moral importance that he will be civilly disobedient, and the limits of his civil disobedience, *if he wishes to remain a democrat and operate within the democratic system*, will be drawn at that point in which the consequences of civil disobedience threaten to destroy the democratic system. That is why there is presumption that a good citizen will obey the law that passes by majority vote of his fellow citizens or their representatives, even if he happens to be on the losing side. Else why have a vote?

The implicit obligation to the law, once the decision has been freely made after open discussion, is prima facie binding. It is also clear that despite this prima facie obligation, any democrat may find *some* decision so unjust that he publicly refuses to obey it and, confident he is not destroying the democratic system, accepts the legal consequences of his refusal. But he cannot make *every* law of which he disapproves, *every* vote that that has gone against him, a matter of conscientious brooding, of potential commitment to civil disobedience or defiance.

An analogy may make this clear. In the ethical universe of discourse and behavior, we assume that the truth must be told. But only a fanatic will assume that we must tell the truth all the time; and we can all conceive of circumstances in which, despite Kant, a moral man will tell a lie. Yet, if anyone therefore inferred that as a moral man he must *always* grapple with the option to speak the truth or not to speak the truth whenever a question is put to him, he would either be the victim of doubting mania or would be disclosing the fact that he was not so much a moral man as a confidence man. There is a prima facie obligation to speak the truth, even if in order to save a human life or a woman's honor (to use an old-fashioned phrase) one must lie.

The trouble with much of the literature on civil disobedience is that in recognizing that it is *sometimes* justifiable, it does not recognize the presumptive validity (not necessarily wisdom) to a democrat of laws passed by means of the democratic process. Whoever, like Thoreau, says that as an individual he will obey society's laws when he can benefit by it, but will not accept its laws when they limit his freedom of action or offend his conscience is a free loader. The failure to recognize this point is evidenced in the remarks of a newly minted college president who says that to a democrat, every law should be seen not as a law of pre-. sumptive validity, but *"as a question."*

Because there are some laws—for example, those restricting a man's right to worship God according to his conscience or enforcing racial segregation—that are so unjust as to justify morally our civil disobedience, the inference is drawn "then that option should be open to every citizen with every law." By the same logic, we could say: "Because we may sometimes lie with a good conscience, let us always recognize the option about any question asked us—to lie or not to lie." I submit that this attitude would destroy the possibility of ordered democratic society as it would that of a moral community.

The second misconception of civil disobedience has far more dangerous fruits. The civilly disobedient democrat violates the law and accepts punishment in order to bear witness, to reeducate the majority by provoking them to second thoughts. Having failed to persuade his fellow citizens about the wisdom or justice of some measure by using all the methods open to him through the democratic process, he cannot honestly use civil disobedience as a strategy to prevent the majority of his fellow citizens from achieving their political ends.

A citizen may refuse to pay a tax he regards as morally objectionable and go to jail to bring about the repeal of the tax. But he has no right to prevent his neighbors from paying the tax. A student may refuse to take a course required of him and suffer the consequences. But he has no right to prevent other students who wish to take it from doing so. He may even go on strike and urge other students to join him but he has no right to prevent his fellow students from attending class if they so desire.

What I particularly wish to challenge is the application of the principles of civil disobedience to the university as fundamentally confused. The university is not a political community. Its business is not government but primarily the discovery, publication, and teaching of the truth. Its authority is based *not* on numbers or the rule of the majority, but on knowledge. Although it can function in a spirit of democracy, it cannot be organized on the principle of one man, one vote—or if it takes its educational mission seriously —of equal vote for student and faculty in the affairs of the mind or even with respect to organizational and curricular continuity.

The fact that a society is politically organized as a democracy does not entail that all its other institutions be so organized—its families, its orchestras, museums, theatres, churches, and professional guilds. I think that we may expect that all the institutions in a political democracy function in a *democratic spirit*, and by that I mean that all participants of any institution should be regarded as persons, should be heard, listened to, consulted with. But as we have already argued, the responsibility for decision cannot be shared equally without equating inexperience with experience, ignorance with expertise, childishness with maturity. The assumption of a political democracy is that each citizen's vote is as good as any other's. If we make the same assumption about universities, and define a citizen of that community as anyone who functions in any capacity on the campus, we may as well close up educational shop.

All this is denied, directly or indirectly, by the newly appointed President of Bryn Mawr College Harris Woffard, Jr., who in an address in the summer of 1968 to the American Bar Association in Philadelphia maintained that our chief danger in college and country has not been civil disobedience, but "undue obedience to law."

I leave to the victims of our riot-torn cities the proper rejoinder to this observation as it concerns them. I limit myself to the university. Why does Mr. Wofford believe that our students suffer from undue obedience and that they should be encouraged to accept "the theory and practice of civil disobedience"? He admits that "speech, lawful assembly, or peaceful petition for the redress of grievances are permitted in most of our colleges and universities." He asserts that "the right of students or faculties or visitors to advocate anything on our campuses—Nazism, Communism, sexual freedom, the legalization of marijuana, black supremacy, the war in Vietnam, the victory of the Vietcong—is generally accepted by academic administrators."

Surely this takes in a lot of ground. *Why isn't this enough?* Why, if students have the right to speech, which in effect means they can talk to faculty and administration about anything, and can make a reasonable case, do they need to be encouraged to resort to direct action? Speech means the possibility of communication. Reasonable speech means the likelihood that procedures can be established in which grievances can be heard and settled. What academic rules exist comparable to the Nazi laws against Jews and Alabama laws against Negroes, which, as Mr. Wofford claims, an "increasing number of our students feel a basic need to destroy"? Certainly not at Berkeley or Columbia!

Mr. Wofford fails to cite any. But with respect to both the community and the academy, he does say, "We need to develop a different and stronger dialectic than mere words and periodic elections." What can this mean when a thorny issue arises, but a resort to direct action that truly corrupts words by making them "mere," and defeating the popular will? What can this mean except a discreet invitation to resort to violence in order to get one's way after "mere" words have proved unavailing?

Mr. Wofford wants "to encourage civil disobedience and discourage violence." But having justified civil disobedience as a method of resisting or *preventing* the occurrence of what is regarded as evil, rather than as a self-sacrificial educational act of *teaching* what is evil, he is in effect countenancing student violence, although he sincerely believes he is not.

With respect to violence, he is the epitome of confusions. On the one hand, he says that "we should prosecute and punish violence and lesser crimes." On the other, he scorns using force to counter force, as if the arrest and prosecution of violence never required force. His confusion hides an actual ambivalence about violence. He would rather that the Columbia students had not forcibly held a college dean captive and burned a professor's research papers—the trespass and denial of other students' rights do not concern him. But more important than these actions, he tells us, is the fact that through them the students were communicating what they wanted. Here, indeed, lies the central issue. *The truth is that they communicated nothing that could not be, and had not previously been communicated by words.*

To a liberal mind, nothing that was communicated by the words and actions of the students was of greater moment than their violation of the canons of academic decency and integrity. This point should be crystal clear. No matter what grievances the small group of Columbia students had, curricular or extracurricular, strictly educational or political, there was no warrant whatsoever for the violence, physical harassment, or obstruction to which they resorted. This is the issue that transcends everything else of significance. It is amazing how many relatively well-informed persons, including some faculty members, talk around it.

It is not startling, therefore, to discover that Mr. Wofford misstates or ignores the facts. For him, the issue at the center of the student uprising at Columbia was "student participation in the government of the university." Actually this was not one of their six demands. The most intransigent of their demands, even after the administration yielded on the construction of the gymnasium, was complete and total amnesty for all their depredations and violations of law. These students, Mr. Wofford to the contrary notwithstanding, were not being civilly disobedient. Not a single law they violated affected them. They were insurrectionists who had vowed either to transform the university into an instrument of their political interests or to destroy it. Their refusal to accept voluntarily the punishment a genuine conscientious objector would have proudly insisted upon is sufficient evidence that we are not dealing with disciples of Gandhi or Martin Luther King.

In this connection, another important confusion gets in the way of understanding. There are some ritualistic liberals—Mr. Wofford among them—who make a sharp distinction between human rights and property rights, and profess relative unconcern about illegal interference with property rights, especially the lawless occupation of public premises. In some context this distinction between human rights and property rights may be illuminating, particularly in legislative decisions where the public interest sometimes conflicts with large vested interests in corporate property. But in the educational context it is misleading and specious.

Is the right to learn a human right or a property right? When a handful of students seize buildings at Berkeley or Columbia and prevent the great mass of other students from learning, is a property right or a human right being violated? If the right to learn is a human right, how can it be exercised if classrooms or libraries are blocked or burned?

When a teacher's or administrator's office is being occupied and vandalized, is this not a grave violation of his human right to exercise his profession, an arrogant abridgment of his freedom of movement? When his files are rifled and his letters destroyed or published, is not this the gravest violation of the personal right of privacy? Even if we do not agree with the Supreme Court justice who held that the most basic of all human rights is the right of privacy, surely it ranks high among personal rights. Are a professor's research notes, burned by the Columbia students, even when they represent ten years labor, merely a property right?

When the Nazi Storm Troopers burned the books of Socialist and Jewish professors, were they merely destroying some property rights? Actually, in basic political terms, the exercise of most human rights, especially civil rights, depends upon the possession of some property rights in things, particularly in the means and instruments of communication. Madison made much of this. It is an essential political truth recognized by Marx but not by many "vulgar Marxists."

The first thing totalitarian regimes do in depriving their subjects of civil freedom is to deprive them of those forms of private or personal property on which such freedom depends. A man's home is his property. When the law says his home is also his castle, it recognizes the extent to which his other freedoms or human rights depend upon this property right. Have I a *human* right to freedom of the press if I am *forcibly* deprived of my *property* rights to typewriter, mimeograph machine, printing plant, paper, and ink?

Actually the justification for some student sit-ins on the ground that only property rights, not human rights, are being violated is often hypocritical. For sometimes sit-ins have been justified to protect property even at the cost of human rights.

For example, at C.C.N.Y. in 1967, students, by lying

down in front of bulldozers, prevented the removal of some trees that were on the only ground available for the construction of necessary dormitories for new Negro students. Here was a conflict of values—ultimately, of human rights. After the petitions and arguments have been heard on both sides, by what right does any self-constituted group set itself up as the arbiter of the common good?

The decisions in matters of educational policy cannot always be taken by simple majority vote—even on matters exclusively affecting students—because sometimes a minority and the educational needs of that minority must be protected against a majority. In such cases, the instance of final decision should be the faculty, whose primary concern is the educational health and excellence of the institution. Of course, the faculty is not infallible, but because no one is infallible, it does not mean that all are equally qualified to decide.

It is this presumption—that whenever there is a conflict of values or judgment, only those who are prepared to defy the outcome of reasoned inquiry, if they disagree with it, have right on their side—that makes the apologies for student disorders sound so overridingly arrogant.

Mr. Wofford, for example, asserts that student sit-ins and strikes last year, whatever their excesses, were justified whenever colleges and universities refused to suspend classes on a particular day to give collective testimony against the Vietnam War. By what right does he assume that all have the same point of view either about the war or about how to discuss it? By what right does he or protesting students presume to dictate to teachers, some of whom have already given effective testimony one way or another as citizens against the war, that they should *not* hold classes, if in the judgment of these teachers such instruction is necessary?

There are plenty of occasions to discuss the war, but there is rarely enough time to cover the materials in the course. The almost unconscious assumption that Mr. Wofford and others make that the *outcome* they favor is much more important than the *due process of reaching it* is another crass illustration of their fetishism of antecedently held conclusions over the process of inquiry.

By now I hope I have made abundantly clear that the democratic spirit in institutions of higher education has its locus not in any specific mechanisms of voicing ideas, opinions, judgments, requests on any relevant matter of educational concern, but in the realities of participation. I know of few educational institutions in which participation of students in the discussion of issues is not welcomed—and where it is not, it seems to me to be elementary educational wisdom, as well as discretion on the part of the faculty, to see that the situation is remedied as soon as possible. But once it is present, there is no place for the violence and lawlessness that paralyzed Columbia University in the spring of 1968 and that is currently being prepared for other universities on the visitation list of the Students for Democratic Society and similar groups. And here let it be said that they do not represent most students, and in criticizing them we are not criticizing all students and all youth.

We have noted an understandable uneasiness about the presence of violence on university campuses on the part of Messrs. Wheeler and Wofford, betrayed by their ambiguous and inconsistent remarks about direct action. We must, however, consider finally a more forthright defense of violence in the academy, recently presented by, of all people, a leading figure in the Federal Judiciary, Judge Charles Wyzanski, Jr., apropos of his discussion of the Columbia imbroglio. Judge Wyzanski begins his discussion by expressing agreement with Harold Howe, II, former U.S. Commissioner of Education, that "the colleges were to blame, not the students, for what has been going on at Ohio State, Columbia, Boston University, Paris, and Italy."[2]

This is not an auspicious beginning. For to couple such disparate events and to imply that colleges at home and abroad are equally to blame, or are blameworthy in the

[2] *Saturday Review*, July 20, 1968.

same way, is to overlook the fact that European students re-volted against conditions of squalor and material scarcities not found anywhere except, perhaps, in small denominational colleges in the South. On no important American college campus that has spawned violence have students suffered the material deprivations and the rigid authoritarian rules of the French and Italian university systems.

Furthermore, the statement that periodically comes from government bureaucrats, trying to act as mediators between embattled administrators and *enragé* students, that universities have brought their troubles on themselves by their ineptitude, can only be explained by the simplistic belief that where no one is free of guilt, all are equally guilty. The faults of administrators are many and real, but to equate them with the physical outrages, the bombings, and beatings that have oc-curred on American campuses as a preface to a pious dis-avowal of both sides is a sentimentalism that can thrive only as a result of carefully cultivated ignorance.

Judge Wyzanski goes on to speak of the specific situation at Columbia University. He says that "one can see how justified students were in resenting a proposed gymnasium that would have a separate entrance for Harlem residents." The word "separate" here, suggesting segregated facilities, is ex-tremely misleading. First of all, the entrances were not sep-arate, but *different*, one for Columbia students, white *and* black, and one for Harlem residents, blacks and a few whites. This was not a Jim Crow gym.

Secondly, the entrances were different because the build-ing, which occupied less than two acres of stone outcropping not serviceable for anything else, had to be built on two lev-els. No one has been able to uncover a scintilla of discrimi-nation in the business. Thirdly, whatever the wisdom of spending money on a gymnasium rather than on books, flowers, and music, the project was approved at one time or another by forty-four Harlem organizations and officials.

Let us grant that the students were justified in feeling resentment, although no poll was taken at the time to determine whether they wanted a new gymnasium; nor was a poll of Harlem residents taken to determine whether they preferred the existence of the stone outcropping in its barren uselessness to the presence of the gymnasium with its impressive, even if limited, facilities.

The pertinent question is not whether the students were justified in feeling resentment, but whether they were justified in expressing their resentment as they did. To mention just a few things, were they justified in (1) invading and seizing five university buildings, (2) holding an assistant dean captive and threatening him with violence, (3) pillaging the personal files of the president, (4) committing acts of arson, including the destruction of the research notes of a professor they disapproved of, the fruit of years of labor, (5) carrying out widespread vandalism costing in the neighborhood of $350,000, (6) destroying records, (7) publicly denouncing the dean of Columbia College before the assembled students, and other members of the administration and faculty, with some of the choicest gutter obscenities, and (8) to cite only one action symbolic of the practices of the gutter as well as its languages, spitting in the face of University Vice-President David Truman, who, as Dean of Columbia College the previous year, had received a standing ovation from both students and faculty for opening up new lines of communication between the administration and student body?

Suppose for a moment that Judge Wyzanski were to make an important legal decision that some citizens of the community resented. This is not an unusual occurrence. What would we normally say if they expressed their resentment at Judge Wyzanski's decision in a manner comparable to the behavior of the resentful students toward the Columbia administrators? Would we content ourselves with saying that these citizens were justified in feeling resentment—as well they may!—and remain silent, as Judge Wyzanski has, about the horrendous method of expressing it? Would we say, as so many have, that these outraged citizens were trying "to communicate" something by making a shambles of the court-room and disrupting its procedure? Grant that the dignity of the academic process cannot be compared to the awful majesty of the judicial process. But in either case, is not the basic or paramount issue, not the fact of the resentment, however justified, but the violent disruption of the educational or legal process? That this is no fanciful comparison is evidenced by the increasing number of incidents in which deliberations in our courts of justice have been hampered by organized groups massed to intimidate judge and jury.

There is something much worse—something that is a grave sign of hysteria of our times. Not only does Judge Wyzanski defend "black power," which he mistakenly identifies as merely one pressure group among others, thus overlooking its racist character, he also asserts that the Columbia students are not wrong in their concept of the legitimate scope of violence.

"I ask you to reflect carefully," he says, "about the Boston Tea Party, or John Brown and the raid on Harper's Ferry, or the sit-down strikers in the plants of General Motors. Every one of them is a violent, unlawful act, plainly unlawful. In the light of history, was it plainly futile? There are occasions on which an honest man, when he looks at history, must say that through violence, regrettable as it is, justice of a social kind has worked itself out."

Let us follow Judge Wyzanski's injunction and reflect carefully—wondering, as we do, whether he himself has reflected as carefully as he should have about the meaning and implication of his words in their present historical context. Is the appropriate question to ask about violence whether or not it was futile or successful? One would have thought the important question is, Was the violence morally justified and historically necessary?

If the question is—as Judge Wyzanski seems to think—whether violence is historically effective or futile, *then any violence that results in victory for those who use it would be justified;* and the more ruthlessly effective it would be, the more justified it would be. Mere might would determine right.

Surely this should give us pause! The only pause it gives Judge Wyzanski is the doubt whether we can always know in advance that violence will be as effective and as justified as "the three instances I have cited, the Boston Tea Party, John Brown's raid, and the General Motor sit-ins, and many others I might have mentioned [which] have shown that violence worked."

This bastardized pragmatism is prepared to bestow the crown of moral legitimacy on any violence that works—independently of the cost, the bloodshed, and the agony. Every lost cause may not necessarily be a wrong cause in this view, but every winning cause is a right one. And like the Boston Tea Party, which was also illegal, the violent actions of the Columbia rebels, according to Judge Wyzanski, were successful and therefore right. Coming from a judge on the Federal Bench, this pronouncement is both morally scandalous and juridically bizarre.

That violence sometimes works, no one disputes. That sometimes through violence justice of a sort has been done is also true. But the relevant question, in the context of student outbreaks, is whether violence was *necessary* to do justice, whether it did not result in greater injustices. Could not a Southern segregationist urging forcible resistance to federal directives he deems unjust also invoke the violence of the past as justification? After all, reference to the Boston Tea Party was not uncommon in the speeches of fire-eating secessionist hotheads on the eve of the Civil War.

Let us look at the comparison between the actions of the Columbia rebellion and the Boston Tea Party more closely. It is a comparison made often by the student apologists—by Mr. Wofford, of course. It was made by the students themselves, in appealing for a federal injunction against Columbia University's feeble efforts to hold disciplinary hearings on the lawless conduct of some of its students. Why was the Boston Tea Party justified?—Because at the time democratic process was not available to the colonists, because there were no means by which the colonists' grievances could be peacefully remedied. But what was justified in the *absence* of the forms of due process is not justified once they have been introduced.

The Columbia students had not been deprived of previously existing rights, had not been denied a hearing; all the remedies available to them had not been exhausted— despite the claim to the contrary on the ground that they had failed in a few efforts to get their way. One does not need to exonerate the Columbia administration from blunder and ineptitude and even with the easy after-the-event judgment of authoritarian tendencies, to deny that it functioned like the tyrannical English Crown. The administration was guilty more of a laissez-faire decentralization than of despotic centralism, guilty more of indifference and lack of sensitivity to student concerns than of oppression and cruelty. And what it was guilty of did not begin to compare in magnitude and gravity of offense to the violence to which it was subjected.

When the Columbia students played their card about being the descendants of the Boston Tea Party patriots, they proclaimed: "Had the Americans agreed that the rule of law, however despotic, must prevail; had the Americans not focused on fundamental principles, this country might still be a colony today."

Fortunately, it was not to Judge Wyzanski that this appeal was made but to a sober-minded brother-judge of the Southern District of the U.S. District Court, Judge Marvin Frankel, who replied—in an opinion I recommend to Justice Wyzanski's careful consideration—that arguments of this sort that invoke the Boston Tea Party are:

> ... at best useless [and at worst deeply pernicious] nonsense in courts of law. It is surely nonsense of the most literal kind to argue that a court of law should substitute "the rule of law" in favor of more "fundamental principles" of revolutionary action designed forcibly to oust

governments, courts, and all. But this self-contradictory sort of theory—all decked out in forms of law with thick papers, strings of precedents, and the rest—is ultimately at the heart of the plaintiff's case.

But it is not only from a legalistic or constitutional point of view that this reference to the Boston Tea Party as a justification for violence is altogether misconceived. Its invocation from a political and common-sense point of view is pernicious and irresponsible because it, in effect, asserts that the political systems under which the colonists lived and under which present-day American students and minority groups live are substantially the same, which is demonstrably false.

Thus, in their foreword to *The Politics of Protest*, a report of the National Commission of the Causes and Prevention of Violence, which takes more than four hundred pages to say the same thing as Rapp Brown, that "violence is as American as cherry pie," and with the same misleading associations, i.e., that therefore it is as unobjectionable as cherry pie, Grier and Cobb write:

> If the Boston Tea Party is viewed historically as a legitimate method of producing social change, then present-day militancy, whether by blacks or students, can claim a similar legitimacy.[3]

And why was John Brown's lunatic raid against innocent people justified?—Because the North won the Civil War? Who knows that but for John Brown and direct-action fanatics, there may never have been a civil war of such magnitude and intensity and bitter consequences. It was John Brown and those with a mind set like his on both sides who sent glimmering Lincoln's project or hope that the slaves could be liberated by purchase at a price considerably less than the cost of the Civil War.

[3] *The Politics of Protest*, edited by J.H. Skolnick, (New York, Ballantine Publishers, 1969).

Judge Wyzanski's reference to the General Motor sit-ins warrants somewhat more extended consideration because it has become quite fashionable to compare present-day university sit-ins and their accompanying violence with the labor sit-ins at Flint, Detroit, and elsewhere during the 1930s. The comparison is usually a preface to a justification of the student action. Occasionally the reference is made in order to reassure the public. Student violence and lawlessness, it is said, are merely evidence of the growing pains of the American educational system as it matures into the twentieth century, just as the labor sit-ins were evidence of industry's coming of age.

This comparison overlooks several crucial differences that make the comparison extremely misleading.

First, the workers who sat in at General Motors and other factories made no demands unrelated to their industry and to its framework of possibility. They did not protest the stand or the absence of a stand by General Motors, or the U.S., on foreign policy, the Spanish Civil War, investments abroad, expansion in the city, the feeding of the hungry, or other issues that fall within the provenance of the federal, state, and local governments.

Second, they did not demand the abolition or restructuring of the entire industrial system in the way that SDS and its allies demand the revolutionary transformation or, more moderately, the restructuring of the university.

Third, the only issue the workers raised was recognition of their right to collective bargaining, which was already the law of the land. Students everywhere have won the right to student organization, and much more besides. A student organization is not and cannot be a trade union, but it enjoys many comparable privileges. For example, a student activity fee is automatically collected from all students and turned over to the student organization.

Fourth, there is an objective "antagonism" between the interests of the workers and of the General Motors Corporation in that no matter how much is produced, the more one party receives in wages, the less remains for profits or dividends, and vice versa. In the academic community there is a shared interest, a cooperative rather than antagonistic interest, on the part of both the faculty and the student body in the product of the educational process—the new knowledge, insights, and vision won. The more one produces, the more there is for all to enjoy. Educational values that are shared become not less by being divided but more; they grow more significant.

Fifth, the attitude of American industry toward union recognition—until the principle of collective bargaining was made the law of the land—was, on the whole, inflexible, hostile to change. Change in the institutions of American education, on the other hand, has been the law of its life. None of these changes, especially profound curricular revolutions, was brought about by violence or the threat of violence. *Valid* educational grievances invariably have been remedied by prolonged expressions of lawful dissent without violent confrontations. Whenever a sit-in has occurred on an American campus in recent years, the right to vigorous dissent and peaceful demonstration *had already been won.*

Sixth, the demands made by the workers were made by representatives of the great majority of the workers, and for the benefit of all of them. University sit-ins are undertaken by minuscule student groups. Some of their demands, such as equal power with the faculty to determine what the curriculum should be and who is to teach it, threaten the rights of their fellow students to get the best possible education. The sit-in that prevents other students from attending classes or denies them access to laboratories or libraries deprives them of their rights to *any* college education.

Seventh, the workers did not engage in acts of destruction and kept the machinery of the plants in apple-pie order. Student rebels have often engaged in costly acts of vandalism, including arson.

One could go on detailing other relevant differences, but enough has been said to indicate how far-fetched the comparison is. As in the use of metaphors, such historical comparisons are no substitute for a sober analysis of the situation created *today* by student lawlessness, administrative compliance, and faculty passivity and fearfulness manifested in failure to lay down in advance fair guidelines of permissible student activism and *to enforce them.*

The industrial sit-ins of the thirties may be adjudged right or wrong. They have little bearing on the question of academic confrontation today. The criteria by which we assess the justice of the one or the other are incommensurable.

What is objectionable in all of these comparisons is the assumption that the position of the Columbia students is assimilable to those of the oppressed American colonists, the enslaved Negroes, and exploited workers. The notion that students are the victims of academic imperialism, that they are a subject-class ground down by the lettered minions of the capitalist establishment for purposes of profit and power, is part of the juvenile literature of vulgar Marxism distributed by the Students for a Democratic Society.

It is difficult to believe that any seasoned mind shares these absurdities. At any rate, the SDS, as distinct from its academic and juridical advocates, is faithful at least to the logic of its absurdity. It declares that its purpose is to revolutionize society, to exploit the university as recruiting grounds for the revolutionary vanguard, and, failing that, to destroy the university. What makes altogether odd Judge Wyzanski's plea in extenuation for the Columbia student rebels is their own frank proclamation through the mouth of one of the SDS leaders (Paul Rockwell): "The issue of due process is secondary to the issue of [student] power."

How far we have come in the short period of time since the colleges sensibly, if belatedly, abandoned the notion that they stood *in loco parentis* to their students. How far we have departed from the notion that the university is a community of scholars, teachers, and students not in quest for power, but in quest for the truth wherever it can be found.

Actually, those who speak of student power do not speak for *all* the students but are comparatively a mere handful, whose actions rarely command the support of the majority. But modern political history should teach us not to underestimate the capacity of a small minority, whose chief virtues are courage, organizational skill, and daring, to manipulate thousands. Its position is fortified by the shrewd appraisal of the failure of nerve on the part of administrators, faculty, and moderate students to act intelligently and vigorously at the first outbreak of lawlessness.

Discussion, dialogue, orderly protest, eloquent dissent are always appropriate within the university. They should be encouraged and protected. But once the university yields to threats of force or intimidation, it recognizes a vested right to what has been illegitimately gained; the subsequent cancellation or negation of this right can be skillfully exploited by dissenting students to win the sympathy of the uninformed and uninvolved. Not everything can be negotiated. Student demands that weaken academic freedom and the self-respect of faculties cannot be taken as points to bargain over.

A faculty that respects itself must respect its students as persons. We treat individuals as persons when we hold them responsible for their conduct, when we avoid—in the absence of empirical evidence to the contrary—the assumption that they are creatures without intention, pushed out of their passivity by external forces completely beyond their control.

There are those who dismiss the entire concept of responsibility as meaningless on the ground that all causation is ultimately reducible to the influence of objective conditions on human behavior. But I know of no one who in considering human affairs can consistently exclude reference to responsibility from his talk and thought.

At the time of Little Rock, Arkansas, if someone had blamed the riotous behavior of the white racists against Negro woman and children altogether on the objective conditions in which they were nurtured, we would dismiss such an explanation as evasive apologetics. Not all people brought up under the same conditions rioted. Sometimes conditions do reduce men to the state of things. In that case moral judgment on human behavior becomes irrelevant. But whoever would explain away the assaults against academic due process as the result not of deliberate action, but primarily of the state of the world or nation, of the Vietnam War or the draft, has barred his own way to understanding the problems we face in attempting to extend human freedom under law both in schools and in society. Whatever the conditions are, as long as we are recognizably human, we are still responsible for our actions if the conditions permit alternative courses of conduct. Sometimes we are responsible for the conditions under which we act, too, but, of course, not in the same way and not to the same degree.

One sign of responsibility is the making of an intelligent response not only to events that have occurred, but to the possibilities of what might occur. The faculties and student bodies of this country can only measure up to their responsibilities by addressing themselves now, separately and cooperatively, to the problems of achieving the best liberal education possible under the imperfect conditions of American society. That is still their main function. Those who take it seriously are committed to a proposition that is justified by a variety of independent considerations, viz., that in a democratic culture there is *no* justification for the use of physical coercion or the threat of such coercion as a method of resolving differences in a university. Force—not violence—may sometimes have to be used to enforce the right against those who violate it. It never determines the right!

There remains to consider two observations about violence or the illegal use of force in a democratic society that have been very influential in recent thinking about the subject. It is sometimes said that peaceful reforms, even in democracies, are the result of fear of violence or the accommodating reaction to actual violence. Therefore it is wrong to condemn violence, whether riots, mutinies, seizure of buildings, arson, looting, even assassinations, if we wish to progress.

According to this view, a legitimate, if not the best, way to improve the conditions of the ghetto is to burn it down periodically, or the neighborhoods it adjoins; a legitimate, if not the best, way to reform and improve the universities is to seize them and build barricades. This is an opinion widely held today among militant Black Nationalists, extremist student radicals, and an assorted group of junior faculty members, newspaper columnists, and revolutionists of the pen who extenuate and sometimes openly encourage the strategy of violence. It is a dangerous view. But dangerous or not, is it true?

As a matter of fact, it is worse than false. It is thoroughly confused. First of all, it does not distinguish between the effect of *fear* that violence will break out if evils are not properly remedied, and the effect of the *actual* violence when it *has* broken out.

Fear of violence does have an influence upon willingness to reform conditions; and up to a point, it is altogether reasonable that it should have. To survive, a democracy must rest upon some shared values. Basic in any hierarchy of such values is a shared interest in survival. Where conditions are so oppressive that those who live under them are tempted to a revolt that may encompass our common doom, self-interest reinforces the weight of ideals and human sympathy in motivating the necessary reforms. If deficiency of imagination and moral feeling make me indifferent to the plague, the poverty, the crime that flourish beyond my narrow horizon, the realization that the diseases they carry may infect my own children will sting me into proper action. Under certain circumstances, therefore, a common fear may further co-operative effort.

It is a profound mistake, however, to assume that reforms, both past and present, necessarily depend upon the fear of violence. Vast social-welfare legislation for children, women, the aged, the sick and handicapped, the unemployed, tremendous advances in penal practices and in the defense and extension of civil rights, have been adopted in the absence of any credible threats of violence. Not a single landmark decision of the Supreme Court, including its outlawing of school segregation in 1954, was made under the threat of the gun, the mob, or fire. Numerous progressive measures in controversial fields such as marriage, divorce, and sexual relations owe their enactment to the growth of enlightenment, not to violence or the threat of violence.

Although the *fear* of violence is often a persuasive factor in expediting reforms, the same cannot be said of the *threat* of violence. Least persuasive of all is the brute outbreak or fact of violence that threatens the security of life and personal property. For the consequence of such violence is the generation of hysteria and panic among the victims, particularly when children and women are in the path of the violence.

Hysteria and panic are blind. They breed unreasoning, not intelligent, fear and hate. If enough people among the majority group are swept away by these emotions, a reaction sets in that makes reforms more difficult to achieve, not less. It can stop the movement toward reform and sometimes reverse it.

Whoever then calculates on the educational value of violence on the community, who anticipates that violence will strengthen the influence of moderates and facilitate reform, is taking a considerable risk. For it may provoke a backlash hardening opposition toward further reforms and support a counterviolence that, as it escalates, moves the conflict toward civil war, the cruelest of all forms of war.

There is not much point in discussing possibilities in the abstract. Each historic situation must be assessed in its own specific context. Since the Civil War, the greatest gains in the condition of the Negroes in the United States were made not in consequence of violence or the threat of violence but by the use of administrative and legal processes. The ghetto riots that periodically swept cities during the first four decades of this century brought no substantial reforms despite great losses of life.

Truman's Presidential decree outlawing segregation in the armed forces, the influential report of his Commission on Human Rights, the series of Court decisions opening up Southern universities to Negro students and outlawing discriminatory zoning laws and practices in public carriers and places, *Brown v. Board of Education of Topeka*, which reversed *Plessy v. Ferguson*, the great victories of the civil-rights movement headed by Dr. Martin Luther King—all these were accomplished without violence.

On the other hand, urban Negro riots delayed the adoption of an open-housing law for years. Although the contrary has been claimed, there is no convincing reason to believe that riots in the black ghettoes brought positive gains to the black communities that could not have been achieved in other ways, and without the cost and suffering involved.

What is true for the relationship between violence and reform with respect to the black citizens of the United States is also true for the relationship between student violence and university reform. The important differences between these phenomena result from the interesting fact that student grievances were, in the main, unrelated to the structure of the university. It is true that reforms have been adopted on some campuses where violence was feared or actually erupted. But was this student violence necessary to achieve these reforms, assuming their desirability?

After all, the causes of student violence from Berkeley to the present were not sparked by failure to meet student demands for university reform. Such demands in most instances were not even formulated. The universities rushed to reform themselves in the expectation that they would head off further violence. There is no guarantee it will succeed. Had students demanded the restructuring of the university by persistent and peaceful demonstrations, there is good reason to believe that the reasonable proposals among their demands would have been accepted.

That student violence has often been counterproductive is evident in California. Here, because of popular reaction to campus rioting, the electorate has refused to approve measures for the extension of higher education. This means that because of their violence, radical student militants are largely responsible for depriving tens of thousands of qualified young men and women of the opportunity of a higher education or, at the least, of the possibility of such education under adequate facilities.

The punitive measures proposed both in Congress and in many state legislatures to meet the frightening manifestations of student disorders are another indication of the pervasiveness of the backlash against students as well as of its intensity. This confirms what public-opinion polls so strikingly showed, for legislators do not bestir themselves on these matters to the degree they have, without feeling the touch of the whip of outrage from home.

Actually no legislation is needed to preserve order on any university campus. The faculties have all the power necessary to cope with the lawlessness and violence of students. Where necessary, they can impose penalties, for good and sufficient reasons, ranging from a warning to expulsion. Every court of the country before which the power of faculties to distribute these punishments has been challenged has upheld their right to defend the integrity of the educational process from disruption. The great difficulty has been that until now, with some notable exceptions, faculties have been reluctant to exercise these powers. Most violations of codes of student conduct, even when very grave, have gone unpunished.

Student disruption and violence have already done enormous harm to American universities. But potentially they threaten to do even greater harm by provoking anti-intellectualist tendencies among the general citizenry, curtailing educational budgets, and worst of all, giving a pretext and color of reason for government intervention and control of matters that hitherto have developed in relative autonomy of the state. Where student groups in effect declare war against school, society, and government, the great likelihood is that others besides themselves will suffer in the ensuing battles.

Student radical activists and Black Nationalist militants have their defenders who exonerate them of responsibility for the reaction to their violence. The most eloquent of those who speak in their behalf is perhaps Tom Wicker, an editor and columnist of the *New York Times.*

Mr. Wicker denies that violence produces any significant backlash. Any controversial action, he tells us, is sure to produce some opposition. But he also argues that if there is a backlash to student and black militant violence, the fault is not theirs: it merely reveals the bigots and reactionaries for what they really are. If they really were liberal or even decent people, they wouldn't react as they do.

Wicker concludes with the charge that those who reproach black militants and student extremists for their tactics of violence are giving them a choice merely between accepting the status quo or passively suffering the backlash.

The consequences of holding this position are momentous. For if one adheres to it, it justifies disregarding the probable reaction of the public to any tactic employed in behalf of a good cause. If anyone turns against the cause because of the character of the means used to fight for it, why, in Mr. Wicker's eyes that proves he didn't really believe in the good cause in the first place; he exposes himself as a hypocrite or reactionary.

To those, however, who judge a cause, among other things, by the means and tactics employed to realize it, Mr. Wicker's *apologia* will appear as the height of political irresponsibility. For indifference to or disregard of public reaction to the tactics used not only coarsens and blunts the moral sensibilities of those who fight in a good cause, so that they are prepared to use any means at hand to get their end, it guarantees the defeat of any good cause that needs allies and sympathizers for victory.

To do justice to Mr. Wicker's position, we must quote his own words:

> It is remarkable . . . that the suggestion is being seriously put forward that blacks and students somehow are responsible morally and tactically for the reaction they have provoked—ultimately, even, for Yorty—and therefore shouldn't have done what they have done, and certainly shouldn't do it again for fear of even worse consequences.
>
> This is sophistry; it is as if to say that prejudice and bigotry and hysteria are understandable and maybe even justified when the tactics of protesting or disadvantaged parties become questionable, when they inconvenience or frighten people . . .
>
> It is as if to say to black militants, who are militant mainly because nonmilitant political action has availed them so little, particularly in cities like Los Angeles and Berkeley, that direct protest will avail them even less; they can choose either the status quo or white backlash.
>
> The black kids who sat in, years ago, at Southern lunch counters heard the same argument . . . Martin King heard the same argument at Selma . . .
>
> The truth of the matter is that the people of Los Angeles are responsible for Sam Yorty's re-election . . . And those who reproach "militant" tactics have still to show that, for students and blacks, any other kind of action gets them even a hearing, much less action.[4]

Before analyzing this amazing passage, I wish to express my agreement with the only observation in it that is valid: "The truth is that the people of Los Angeles are responsible for Yorty's re-election"—not the social conditions under which they live. Excellent! Would that Mr. Wicker recognized that blacks and students are responsible for *their* actions, for their rioting and violence, not the objective con-

[4] *The New York Times,* June 3, 1969.

ditions he always cites when he explains their actions away, sometimes minimizing, sometimes justifying them. But to return to the passage. To begin with, Mr. Wicker is wrong about the historical facts. The peaceful sit-ins at Southern lunch counters produced no backlash. On the contrary, it was Southern violence in repressing these peaceful sit-ins that produced an upsurge of support for the Negro cause throughout the nation. It made all but the most vicious racists ashamed and angry at the tactics that were used against the demonstrators.

Dr. King achieved his great triumphs precisely because his protests were nonviolent. His tactics may have alienated a few, but they won over millions more. Any leader of a reform movement who scorns to reckon the public reaction to his tactics in considering their advisability is intellectually and morally bankrupt. For he is refusing to consider the very real possibility that his efforts and those of thousands he influences may be self-defeating. Mr. Wicker misstates the facts. The arson, the bombings, and the beatings at Berkeley, San Francisco State, and other campuses were *not* the tactics followed by those who sat in at Southern lunch counters. Nor were they the tactics followed or advocated by Dr. King. It is worse than sophistry to assimilate one to the other.

Mr. Wicker is wrong about the elementary facts of human psychology. When people are frightened by the spectacle of violence and arson, and in consequence vote to preserve the political status quo, rather than for a change they are sincerely convinced threatens them with greater evils, they are not therewith bigots and racists. They are only behaving as human beings, as Mr. Wicker himself would behave in any situation in which *he* was truly persuaded that these were the only choices. That many of those who voted for Mr. Yorty (like those who voted against the Police Review Board in New York City a few years ago) sincerely believed that this was their choice is incontestable. Reporters on the scene confirmed it.

If this belief was mistaken, as Mr. Wicker contends, is it not incumbent upon him to ask what caused this belief? By all accounts, it was the spectacle of violence by militant students and blacks that caused it, and the demagogic exploitation of that violence. Otherwise, we could not explain the numbers who voted in the Los Angeles local campaign (or, in New York, the defeat of the Police Review Board measure in normally liberal districts). Unless one can show that violent tactics are necessary, the normally intelligent leader condemns them because he is aware of their effects in mobilizing public opinion against his cause.

That is why student and Negro leaders who are *not* committed to revolution strongly condemn violence as inimical to reform. Those opposed to reform secretly hope that the tactics of violence will alienate the great majority. If there is no such thing as a backlash or it is of little effect, how does Mr. Wicker account for the fact that *agents-provocateurs* are sometimes hired to use tactics of violence to defeat reforms? Those student and black leaders who incite to violence are acting just as *agents-provocateurs* would act if they were seeking to discredit a cause or movement. If they were to succeed, Mr. Wicker presumably would condemn the majority repelled by this violence as reactionaries whose true colors have been revealed.

Mr. Wicker is all at sea about the educational scene. He implies that the Black Nationalist and white student extremists on campuses in California and elsewhere are being doomed by liberal critics of violence to a choice between the status quo and the backlash. Actually, there is no status quo. Changes are taking place all the time. But if there were a status quo and the backlash threatened to be worse than the status quo, and these were the only alternatives, common sense would impel one to defend the status quo. Even the Communists learned—too late—that the status quo of Weimar and the backlash threat of Hitler's rule, which they equally condemned with fine disdain, represented a choice between life with hope and death.

However, it is emphatically not true that the choice in education is between the status quo and the backlash of reaction. Mr. Wicker is obviously unfamiliar with the situation at the University of California at Berkeley, at Los Angeles, at San Fernando State, at Heywood State, and especially at San Francisco State, which loomed so large in the consciousness of so many voters. Many and important educational changes have been introduced in those institutions without violence. Educational agencies, academic mechanisms, and curriculum committees exist at every one of these institutions before which students can always get a hearing. Mr. Wicker's denial of this is a measure of his ignorance.

When he says that "those who reproach 'militant' [read "violent"] tactics have still to show that, for students and blacks, any other kind of action gets them even a hearing. . . ." he convicts himself of irresponsibility unless he can cite cases in which hearings have been denied them. The simple truth is that there has not been a single demand made by students and blacks for which they did not have a hearing or could not have had one if they had requested it.

Perhaps Mr. Wicker believes that the test of whether a student has been given a hearing is whether he gets what he demands, no matter what—even the right to hire and fire teachers, to determine the content of instruction, and to destroy academic freedom. If he believes this, it is evidence of an even greater irresponsibility.

Sober Negro leaders who have given a lifetime to the cause of racial justice, like Roy Wilkins, Bayard Rustin, A. Philip Randolph, and others, are profoundly concerned about the consequences the use of certain tactics may have on the struggle. They believe, with justification, that the view that progress depends upon urban and student riots, or that tactics should be chosen with no thought to a possible backlash, is practically an invitation to take the road of violence to the solution of the racial problem. But the road to violence will not solve racial problems unless it leads to the extermination of one or both races.

The Civil War in the United States saved the Union. It did not solve the racial problem. If there is no hope in the nonviolent methods of reform then there is no hope in any other available method. But the history of the last twenty-five years shows that there is hope in such nonviolent methods of reform, and that if gains commensurate with those made in the past are continued, by the end of the present century, a rough equality and justice between races will probably have been established.

The war against democratic process (and much more needs to be said) is also a war against academic freedom. But another war has been declared that more directly threatens academic freedom. This is the war against the university or against that concept of the university that grows out of the committment to academic freedom.

# CHAPTER SEVEN

# THE BARBARISM OF VIRTUE: THE WAR AGAINST THE UNIVERSITY

During the last five years American universities have more often made news as fields of battle than as centers of learning and intellectual discovery. They have been disrupted by student disorders unprecedented in scope and intensity by anything previously experienced in our history. The shock waves of violence, reverberating from coast to coast, have not merely shattered the placidities of the physical scene and the routines of campus life; they have had a profoundly disturbing effect on traditional assumptions about the character of American education, and therewith unsettled the intellectual climate.

One of the most significant signs of this change in climate has been the emergence and growing influence of a novel-sounding set of doctrines about the nature of the university and its vocation in a time of troubles. If acted upon, these doctrines contain the promise or threat of educational changes so vast that they can only be called revolutionary—or counterrevolutionary.

It is doubtful whether these doctrines about knowledge, scholarship, and the university have actually inspired student disorders, whose causes have been many and complex. Up to the present time, formulations of the new outlook have appeared in some situations mainly as rationalizations for student actions after the event. Potentially, however, they have enormous social and educational significance. If these doctrines are accepted as valid, they can plausibly serve as ideological premises for attempts at the transformation of the university so far-reaching as to bring up short all but their most tough-minded partisans.

The relationship between the phenomenon of student revolt—when it is self-consciously revolutionary, as in the case of the so-called Students for a Democratic Society—and the novel-sounding doctrines of scholarly and university engagement may be characterized as follows.

The chief student advocates of revolutionary change declare that they are not interested in educational change ("We do not want a 'free' university in this society"—Mark Rudd, *New York Times Magazine*, August 4, 1968) but in political change, since no genuine educational reconstruction is possible in a society where "totality of exploitation" exists.

On the other hand, the chief protagonists of the philosophy of engagement assert that learning and scholarship are themselves not value-free, that there is a ubiquitous, even if implicit, commitment to a moral, and therefore basically political, standpoint in the vocation of the scholar and in the mission of the university. Consequently, to the extent that the scholar and the university, and some imply even professional associations like the Modern Language Association (MLA), are faithful to their educational and cultural calling, they must espouse the cause of the party of humanity—which in the crunch of specific issues about war and peace, slavery and freedom, poverty and welfare, is inescapably a political, and virtuously partisan, cause.

Those who hold this latter position do not necessarily approve of or condone students' violence or their commitment to total social revolution. If they believe in revolution, for most, it is in piecemeal social revolution; and, even then, they would deplore the word "revolution," preferring adjectival terms like "progressive," "advanced," "forward-looking," "human," to characterize desired change. But what both groups have in common is the view that scholars as scholars and their institutions have a primary commitment not only to the pursuit of truth by the arts of reason but to virtue where virtue means not simply the values of intellectual integrity but "allegiance to humanity" and other synonymous expressions equally edifying.

I propose to examine some of the facets of this novel-sounding philosophy of education independently of its bearing on student activism and movements for restructuring the university.

The first thing to note about this philosophy is its high-mindedness, its exalted concept of the role of the scholar and scholarship, and of the university as a community of scholars. One representative of this view believes that "the republic of learning" has a moral responsibility to contribute to "the civic republic" and to civic virtue, and urges recognition of this responsiblity upon all professional associations.[1]

Another speaks of "the moral obligation" not only of the citizen but of the scholar and "of the University as a corporate body."[2] And no wonder, for the university even more so than the church is the temple of the human spirit: "The University is meant to house and celebrate the spiritual existence of man."

The responsibility to the human spirit is not only integral to the life of scholarship, it is universal. The scholar must serve by his scholarship not only his family, his class, his society, nation, and race but all of mankind. As a citizen he is inescapably limited by duties to the nation that bestows citizenship upon him, but as a scholar he is a citizen of the world.

Discounting the rhetorical exaggeration, almost any scholar could subscribe to this. In a sense, in serving truth one *is* serving all mankind. In a religious age when it was assumed

---

[1] Carl E. Schorske, "Professional Ethos and Public Crisis: A Historian's Reflections," *PMLA*, Sept., 1968.
[2] Richard Lichtman, "The University: Mask for Privilege?" *The Center Magazine*, Jan., 1968.

that the end of knowledge was to glorify God, the scholar might have piously proclaimed to the men of action and other citizens of the city of man, "Yes, all of us serve God: you in your way and I in His."

The quest for the truth has often been called divine service. But we would badly mistake the intent of the philosophy we are discussing if we interpreted it in this innocent way, as if it meant that the scholar and the citizen each serve mankind equally, and, if need be, independently, but tolerant of each other.

No, it is meant to deny the view that the life of scholarship, even in its own specialized or professional function, can ever be sufficient to itself. It means to assert that to conceive it as such is irresponsible and immoral.

The requirement that knowledge serve man or at least not harm him remains quietly in the background as a watchdog on intellectual activity but like a good watchdog emerges when the occasion arises, takes in a lot of ground, and has a sharp bite. The amount of ground varies with different protagonists, with perhaps the extremist claim coming from a philosopher.

Have we, for example, imagined ourselves in the last few days to have been engaged as a "free and human community of scholars" in the uncoerced pursuit of truth through the exchange and clash of opinions? If so, we have been mistaken, for in this view "a free and human community of scholars can only flourish when the multitudinous communities of the exploited, the wretched, and the brutalized peoples of the earth have broken the bonds of their subservience and established themselves as men of full stature."[3] One measure of the sincerity of our vocation as scholars is the extent to which our scholarship helps liberate humanity and prevents its exploitation.

And now for the bite! This is illustrated in another influential defense of the view that expressly declares that scholarship must serve the ends of a "liberating tolerance."

[3] Lichtman. See note 2.

If this be its function, once we encounter doctrines that are "regressive" and "repressive," we know *ipso facto* they are false, and cannot enjoy the same right of propagation as those that liberate.[4]

These exalted notions of the vocation of the scholar, the university, and the professional association testify to the presence of goodwill and virtue on the part of those who entertain them. But there are certain obvious difficulties that arise just as soon as scholarship is placed in leading strings to anything beyond its professional ethos.

If the commitment of the scholar and the university is moral and not only intellectual, to virtue and not only to truth, to the liberation of man in the truly liberal society, how can this supply guidance or a principle of decision when the scholar encounters conflicts among moral values?

The moral experience grows out of a conflict among values, a conflict not between the good and bad, which is a mark that we already know how the conflict is to be resolved, but between good and good, right and right, and the good and the right. Scholarship in the service of man seeks to further happiness, enhance justice, realize freedom, achieve peace. But what if these and other values conflict with each other as they always do, and sometimes with the truth? Who is to judge what values are to be given priority, what is to be compromised, and when? These are the inescapable moral and political decisions with which the citizen concerns himself and the scholar as a citizen. Must the scholar *as* a scholar, must his profession *as* an association of scholars, must the university *as* a community of scholars also make these decisions? How can they do so without becoming arenas of political struggle in the ordinary sense of politics, from which the high-minded devotees of commitment to virtue inconsistently shrink—explaining as they do that there are higher and lower, central and peripheral, important and unimportant spheres of politics?

[4] Herbert Marcuse, "Repressive Tolerance," in Wolff, *A Critique of Pure Tolerance* (Boston, Beacon Press, 1965).

If the scholar can only be faithful to his vocation if he concerns himself with the "multitudinous communities of the exploited, wretched and brutalized," with the threats to human freedom and world peace, who is to draw the line and say—here the politics begins, and here it ends, this is central and this is peripheral, this is important and this is not?

Not only are these difficulties obvious, they are familiar, and warrant greater attention than they have received by those who would commit scholars to the redemption of man. And they cannot be glozed over by quotations from Matthew Arnold who, as interpreted by those who cite him in this connection, epitomizes the confusion between the virtues of scholarship and the virtues of morality, between the true and the edifying, between science and salvation.

One writer quotes Arnold to the effect that culture is the desire "to make reason and the will of God prevail." (It is not altogether coincidental that these are actually the words of Bishop Wilson, which Arnold counterposes to Montesquieu's ground for the pursuit of knowledge: "to render an intelligent being yet more intelligent.") The writer then adds: "I doubt that there can be a justification of culture, scholarship, or the MLA that does not in part rely on this fundamentally social aim"[5]—to make reason and the will of God prevail.

There is a teasing ambiguity in the phrase "in part"—does it mean that one must be partly committed to reason and to God to justify the MLA, or that total commitment to reason and God is only part of the justification? Either way, it is high-sounding nonsense. Suppose one does not believe in God, in whole or in part, and like David Hume and his twentieth-century offspring, Bertrand Russell, holds that "Reason is, and ought only to be, the slave of the passions."[6]

[5] Richard Ohmann, "The MLA and the Politics of Inadvertence," *PMLA*, Sept., 1968.
[6] "This sentence . . . expresses a view to which I, like every man who attempts to be reasonable, fully subscribe . . . There is no such thing as an irrational aim except in the sense of one that is impossible of realization," Bertrand Russell, *Human Society in Ethics and Politics* (New York, Simon and Schuster Inc., 1955).

Shall we drive him out of the MLA or proclaim him an enemy of culture and scholarship? If we don't treat him that way in behalf of God and Reason why should we act otherwise in behalf of Man and Welfare, particularly if his lyre or verse is sweet, his argument cogent, and his learning impeccable?

Before examining in further detail the claims made about the responsibility of scholarship in a world in crisis—or simply the responsibility of scholarship, for in our epoch we have never lived in a world that was not in crisis—let us look more closely at the philosophy of learning under attack as inadequate or craven or hypocritical by those who believe that there should be an indissoluble union between the basic goals of the scholar, the community of scholars, and basic public policy.

Summarily put, the philosophy under criticism holds that the primary goal of the university—or "mission" if one prefers a grander word—and of the scholar and professional association of scholars is not the quest for virtue or power but the quest for significant truths, their transmission and critical evaluation by teaching and/or publication, and the promotion of programs of study, research, and teaching to further the goal.

Although it has roots in the past, this concept was never widely accepted in ancient or medieval times. It is comparatively modern, no older than the principles of academic freedom in which it is implicit. It has made its way against great obstacles, especially attempts to harness the allegiance of the scholars to the city-state, the church, nation, and the party, including the party of humanity. In speaking of this goal as an ideal I am saying that it *should* function as a guide in questions of scholarship and scholarly behavior, not that it always has. Although comparatively modern, the strength of this ideal of the university should not be underestimated. There were always some lonely voices in past ages that, in muted tones, spoke for this ideal; today most scholars in the basic sciences and humanities accept it as the rationale of their calling. Its growth explains the indisputable, and welcome, development of tolerance and hospitality to dissenting views in the university, especially in the United States.

Anyone informed of the history of academic freedom in the United States cannot but be impressed by the contrast between the present and past. Those who cry loudest that the university is only a tool of capitalistic interests cannot explain their own presence in it.[7]

The adherents of this ideal of the university must expect to find themselves embattled against those who fear that its pursuit may undermine the social and political status quo, as well as against those who are impatient with its irrelevance to the struggle to bring a new world into birth. Despite the fact that this ideal is dismissed as a familiar and tired cliché, judging by some recent discussions, it is radically misunderstood by some of its most vehement critics.

First, it does not make a separation or divorce between the scholar and the citizen. It makes a distinction between them. It leaves the individual free to map or pursue any course to Heaven or hell as a citizen without losing his professional standing as a scholar. But it denies him or any group of individuals the right to impose on the community of scholars in their professional associations or on the university as a corporate entity any particular goal or path to Heaven or hell. It is historically pertinent to observe that those of us in the academy who, as citizens, have spent the better part of our lives passionately engaged in good causes, whether won or lost, would never have presumed to demand that the university as such be committed to them—with one "exception" that turns out to be no exception. For our experience has

---

[7] In some institutions, latterly, a kind of fetishism of dissent is observable. Fear of even the *appearance* of intolerance of dissent has been abused by incompetents. Unable to win tenure because their scholarship or tenure has been adjudged unsatisfactory by their colleagues, they threaten to arouse students to protest the alleged violation of their academic freedom. Administrators and chairmen sometimes put pressure on departments to grant tenure to avoid disruption and disorder.

been an unremitting and hotly contested struggle for scholars to exercise their rights as citizens to engage in political action without jeopardizing or prejudicing their membership or standing in the professional community.

The irony of the situation, as we shall see, is that the academic freedom, so largely but not completely won, is under attack by some who enjoy the protection of academic freedom only because the university as a corporate entity is *not* committed to a political goal or does not act on its commitment, to the extent that unhappily it is still politically committed.

Secondly, the pursuit of the truth by the scholar, working alone or with his colleagues, does not entail withdrawal or isolation from society or aseptic purity from the grime, strife, and clamor of the marketplace. Even the purest scientist may have to dirty his hands. It all depends upon his project. The life of mind when it seeks truth of fact is a life of action. This must not be confused with the vulgar pragmatism, foreign to the philosophy of Peirce and Dewey, that thought necessarily exists for the sake of action. The astronomer who traces the course of the stars, the physicists and biologists with their electron microscopes—anyone engaged in controlled observation and experiment is engaged in activity.

In the house of scholarship there are many mansions. Society is a great laboratory in which scholars must and do involve themselves in the very interests of truth. The manner and degree of involvement do not warrant making any invidious distinctions. There are lonely thinkers who test their ideas by poring over dusty texts in the hush of libraries; others by manipulating dials in soundproof laboratories; others by working in the turmoil of cities, its welfare centers, clinics, courts.

We do not have to recognize an order of nobility here. So long as the choice of a problem is uncoerced and its conclusions not predetermined by the will to believe, by the dogmas of church or party, it is irrelevant whether the motivation behind it flows from a moral impulse or from sheer intellectual curiosity.

It is interesting to observe over the centuries the distrust that those committed to a saving cause have of "idle" curiosity and its works. The demand for relevance is often an expression of this distrust. That scholarly inquiry must be relevant to a problem to have significance is a truism. But why must it be relevant to a contemporary social problem? If the problem is a genuine one, the pertinent distinctions that bear on its analysis are between the trivial and significant; the obscure and illuminating; the superficial and profound; the barren and fruitful. These are attributes that can be objectively determined by the judgment of one's peers. On the other hand, the condemnation of a theme or inquiry as "irrelevant" is usually no more than a personal or group preference even when masked as a religious or political bull of excommunication.

Thirdly, the scholar can concern himself as a scholar with any problem within his competence. He doesn't need a philosophy of social commitment to justify concern with the social implications of any piece of knowledge. No one can be sure in advance what the quest for knowledge will bring forth. Not all things in the world are interrelated. Some obviously are. An electronic discovery may uncover ways of breaching privacy or controlling emotions; a biological breakthrough may make possible the control of population; a new chemical agent may upset the ecology of a region.

The study of the implications of the findings in any field on any other field, on human welfare, war, peace, or belief in God, freedom, and immortality is always in order if one is interested in it. It is just as legitimate a subject for scholarship as any other subject. To urge the study and clarification of the implications of discovery in any field for public policy is no departure from the ideal of scholarship but merely to extend its scope. It is banging on an open door of a room any scholar can enter. But it is demonstrably false as well as presumptuous to assert that one cannot properly pursue a

problem of scholarly research without *also* pursuing the questions: What are the implications of its findings for social welfare? Are they good or bad for man? The tangled complex
of issues involved in the alleged "indifferentism of *wertfreie
Wissenschaft*" have nothing to do with the point.

The findings of any science to the extent that they are
scientific are "value-free." To ask what bearing these findings
have on this or that human value, or aspect of human life or
policy alternative, is to ask another type of question, to
which the answer, if it is a scholarly answer, must also be
value-free. The historical relativity of scholarly judgments is
another red herring. Suffice it to say that no one can mean-
ingfully explain something as being historically relative to
human values or to anything else without committing himself
to a judgment of objectivity.

A simple illustration will do. I may study the growth of
automation in society out of fascination for the phenomenon
or out of loathing. That is a legitimate problem for a
scholar. I may, out of fear or in hope, investigate the social
consequences of automation on unemployment, vocational
education, leisure time, or what not. That is another legitimate problem. But I can study the first without the second.
And I can study the second without as a scholar committing
myself to a policy or program of social action that as a
citizen I may feel keenly about. Further, no matter what my
fellow citizens decide in the way of program or policy, if I
have a genuine intellectual interest in the subject of automation, no one has a right to forbid my continued inquiry.

There is a dangerous ambiguity in Schorske's statement
that the individual scholar can be protected in the pursuit of
truth only if the scholarly community recognizes "a *responsibility* [my italics] for the implications of its findings for
society and mankind."[8] No, the individual scholar deserves
protection in the pursuit of truth because of our commitment
to academic freedom.

As we have seen, academic freedom entails the right to

[8] Schorske. See note 1.

inquire into social implications of findings regardless of whether or not the scholarly community accepts responsibility for them. And what does it mean to say that the scholarly community must recognize "its responsibility for the implications of findings" any more than for the findings themselves?

Human beings are not responsible for implications. Implications are present or absent, logically valid or invalid. Human beings can be responsible only for *policies* and *decisions*. To take responsibility for policies and decisions affecting "society and mankind" is to take political action. It seems to me both dubious and dangerous doctrine to hold that the scholarly community or the university must take responsibility for public political policy other than the responsibility its members share with their fellow citizens.

Fourthly, I previously referred to one apparent exception to my view that the university as a corporate entity must not take sides in the clash of social goals, that although it extends its umbrella of protective neutrality to its scholar-teachers to investigate any problem within their ken or competence or to enlist as citizens in any campaign or crusade, it does not *as such* become embattled in any cause.

The exception is the defense of academic freedom. For this is integral to the *raison d'être* of the university and the calling of the scholar. To be sure, the common concerns of members of the university, as of members of all professional associations, require collective action that is outside the purview of the ordinary citizen and the individual scholar. For example, the university or scholarly association must decide what wages to pay its clerical staff; what, and where, supplies are to be purchased; what, and where, to build; and other housekeeping details. These are not *public* political issues in the first instance although they may have indirect political effects. To call all corporate decisions on these matters political is to broaden the meaning of the term "political" to embrace everything that may remotely affect man, and so empty the word "political" of any specific content. To argue in this connection that the refusal of a university or professional association to take a position on a political issue is, in virtue of that very refusal, taking a political position is completely without merit, for it in effect says that the distinction between the scholar and citizen is a political distinction. Under certain circumstances the refusal of citizens to act on a political issue, if it has determinate consequences that may have otherwise been avoided, might be characterized as a political action. But the responsibility of the citizen is not the responsibility of the scholar.

Were the university or professional association to refuse to take a stand on a religious dogma or commitment on the ground that such avowals are irrelevant to the life of scholarship, would any person seriously contend that therewith the university or professional association was making a religious decision, and conclude that therefore religious neutrality was impossible? The logic of this argument would suggest that the university or professional association by refusing to take a position on everything under the sun actually takes a position on everything under the sun[9]—which is absurd.

We are not restricting the university to an impossible purism and absolutism. The apparent "exception" to which we referred—the defense of academic freedom—justifies the university or scholarly association in taking public stands on issues that threaten or affect its educational ideals even if these have direct political consequences. A university committed to the free exchange of ideas will not feel called upon as such to condemn the foreign policy of Spain, Russia, Greece, China, or Brazil. But it is its legitimate business to condemn the suppression of academic freedom in these countries' universities.

It is obvious, or should be, that the preservation of academic freedom depends upon the survival of the free society of which it is a part. Therefore, the university may justifiably sponsor research in areas of military defense if its staff is willing and qualified to undertake it, and the nature of the research project does not interfere with its strictly educational functions, especially intellectual freedom.

[9] This seems to me to be the position of Richard Ohmann (note 5).

No hard and fast guidelines can be laid down. Each case should be subject to faculty evaluation. There are certain foolish views that plague the consideration of these complex and difficult issues. One is: if anything needs to be done, the university is the place to do it. There are other agencies and institutes that can do many things, especially of an operational nature, as well as or better than the university. This is probably true for large defense laboratories.

Another extreme view is that the university must refuse to sponsor defense research of any kind unless it approves of of the foreign policy of the administration of the moment. The university must take the long, the prudent, and the historical view. Until multilateral disarmament under strict control is introduced, it is not wise to risk the fate of free society and its free universities by a posture of naked defenselessness in a world of powerful totalitarian states.

No specific policy follows from these general considerations—only the right to engage in basic defense research, and the right of the individual scholar to approve or disapprove.

Fifthly, there is to be sure one constraint under which scholarship as well as sport, the university as well as the church must operate—and that is the criminal law. These moral limits are not relevant to the issue we are discussing, for there is no greater responsibility upon the scholar to be law-abiding than upon the sportsman or any other vocational group, whereas we are considering the alleged *special* obligation of the scholar to serve the cause of mankind.

Further, the constraints of the criminal law are negative, designed to prevent or punish certain actions, not to encourage "a moral or social passion" to advance progressive thought. No one therefore with a sense of proportion can claim that since the scholar is forbidden to kill or torture or steal to conduct his inquiry, he does not enjoy academic freedom; or that since such actions as experimenting on human beings against their will or without their knowledge are proscribed, therefore the expression of certain ideas in the academy should be proscribed and others encouraged.

It is as if someone were to argue that religious freedom did not exist because we do not permit human sacrifice; that such proscriptions proved that there could be no such theory as neutrality in religion; and that therefore where the religion of humanity is concerned, there could be no reasonable objection to the state, university, or professional association taking an official stand.

Finally, there is the question of the allocation of resources, where they are not unlimited, to one or another domain of scholarly research and inquiry. About this there are value judgments galore. The basic decisions, however, must be made by the citizens or their representatives on the advice of scholars and not by the scholars themselves. Whatever the decisions, scholars *must be free to determine their own field and line of inquiry.* Hardships are unavoidable for some when competing claims cannot all be granted, but they are less onerous when voluntarily borne to gratify one's intellectual passion.

In times of acute crisis we tend to disregard the distinction between citizen and scholar because a man can be both, and many other things besides. As a citizen he may become embattled on all public issues affecting his society to a point where he may permit his body to be conscripted. As a scholar in pursuit of knowledge he cannot permit his mind to be conscripted. He has an obligation to the integrity of his craft, profession, and scholarly community that is far from uninterested, and whose defense requires constant vigilance against Philistines, superheated patriots, impatient reformers, and revolutionists.

It is not an attitude of passivity but of intense intellectual activity that at its highest Spinoza calls *Amor Dei Intellectualis*, whose visions of excellence are among the glories of the human spirit, and whose fruits in virtue of the very indirection of its practical goals have lightened the burden of human suffering and ennobled the human mind. It is this dedication to disinterested knowledge that the partisans of social engagement under the slogans of "relevance" and "culture" and "humanity" scorn as "the traditional wisdom" and dismiss as "not adequate to our time."[10]

What do they put in its stead? An ambiguous and dangerous view. It calls upon the university and/or professional associations as corporate bodies to make scholarship serve the aims of the party of humanity or peace or progress with which they, of course, identify themselves.

This is done with a reckless disregard, or underestimate, of the dangers to the autonomy, independence, and critical detachment of the scholarly spirit, and sometimes with a crusading zeal that not only threatens intellectual tolerance but makes a virtue of intolerance. We are not dealing with a monolithic movement but with tendencies that shade into each other in a direction of growing extremism.

At one end of the spectrum are spokesmen hardly aware of the dangerous course on which they have set. At the other end are those who unflinchingly accept the costs of progress. They scorn, and in the light of history, justly, the virtue of barbarism. But they end up by countenancing, and sometimes advocating, practices that constitute a barbarism of virtue.

Consider, for example, the implications of the question asked by Schorske at the MLA plenary meeting in 1967: "Has the right to pursue the truth wherever it leads a more absolute justification than the right to pursue free enterprise wherever it leads?"[11] I do not know how one justification can be more absolute than another. But I do know that one right can have greater justification than another, that the right to pursue the truth wherever it leads is far and away of greater significance than the right to pursue free enterprise, that to regard them as comparable is as absurd as to assert that a man has no more right to think as he pleases than to hunt or shoot as he pleases.

[10] Lichtman. See note 2.
[11] Schorske. See note 1.

The right to pursue the truth has a prima facie validity because of its inherent qualities of delight and dignity as well as its beneficial consequences, whereas the right to free enterprise is narrowly limited by its consequences. The consequences of free enterprise may be—and sometimes have been —child labor, unemployment, hunger, and war. Can any reasonable mind lay such things at the door of the quest for truth?

To retort that the pursuit of scientific truth leads to war is a vulgar error, for war is a *political* action or decision taken by citizens and their leaders. It is not implicit in the hypothetical imperatives of knowledge. That the impact of scientific discovery has sometimes been socially disruptive is an argument not for making science responsible to existing morals inherited from the past but for investigating contemporary moral practices and assumptions with the same freedom and intellectual courage with which we pursue scientific knowledge.

To imply that because free enterprise must be subjected to necessary limitations therefore free inquiry must be subject to limitations is not only false but mischievously false. For it is an invitation to intellectual control and repression.

Shall we pass Truth in Opinion Acts comparable to the Pure Food and Drug Laws that curb rapacious profiteers, establish a task force to curb not only dangerous weapons but dangerous ideas?

Historically, all such attempts in the past have been based on fear—fear of the truth, fear that our inherited first principles may turn out to be prejudices, fear that our hopes of entering the Kingdom of Heaven may wither before the chill winds of scientific fact, fear that our Utopian ideals for the Kingdom on Earth may not withstand the acids of analysis. On such fears the seeds of persecution take root.

But why should we fear? Instead of censoring the truth to protect our ideals, is it not more intelligent, more courageous, more dignified, in the long run even more productive of human happiness, to revise our ideals in the light of truth?

The view that the dangers incident to the pursuit of truth justify some control can paralyze the nerve of intelligent adventure. It can do worse. It can undermine scientific integrity. In the spring of 1968, at a convocation called by the Polytechnic Institute of Brooklyn to consider "What Can Man Be?" the presentation of a paper by an invited Nobel Prize winner on "Human Quality Problems and Research Taboos" that *seemed* to challenge some biological assumptions concerning the equality of inherent racial capacities, mistakenly believed to have implications for liberal social policy, frightened the faculty into cancellation of the convocation.

As disgraceful as this action was, the rationalizations offered for it were even more disgraceful because they were disingenuous. Make human welfare or national security or the health of the revolution the criterion of permissible truth, then the gates are opened once more to the "Aryanization of physics" and the "Bolshevization of biology"—and comparable phenomena in the less rigorous fields of the humanities and social studies. Already throughout the country there is a growing tendency to judge scholars, award posts, distribute prizes and preferments not exclusively on the basis of professional criteria but on the basis of political criteria.

I know that Schorske is much too civilized to countenance such practices, and he explicitly disavows a desire "to subordinate scholarship to political criteria." The question is, however, whether once the primary allegiance of the scholarly community is declared to be not to the truth but to humanity—which is the citizen's highest virtue—can political criteria be extruded? Can we rely on Schorske's sensitiveness to check the excesses of those influenced by his unfortunate analogies?

For example, he believes that just as there are threats to the human body from our polluted atmosphere, so there are threats to the human spirit from our polluted culture, and that it is the community of scholars who must do something about it. He therefore proposes: "Not every scholar will engage in the task, but could not your community of scholars ex-

plore and report to the public on the problem of our polluted culture—including its flowers of evil?"[12]

Why, pray, must literary scholars as a body report on our
flowers of evil? Do we need another, more scholarly Legion
of Decency? To differentiate between flowers and weeds is
difficult enough. Why the pronouncement on good and evil?

Suppose the literary horticulturists of evil are found
among our colleagues. Once the contemporary Baudelaires
and others who are polluting our culture are identified, will
the next step be to propose the establishment of a cultural
sanitation squad? This is no work for scholars but, if necessary, which one may doubt, for the police.

Schorske's fearfulness that the republic of learning may be
invaded and swallowed by politics is commendable. It should
lead him to forswear analogies between the free market in
commodities and the free market of ideas, between disease
germs in the atmosphere and disease germs of the mind.

The existence of a polluted atmosphere can be established
with a fair degree of objectivity and scientific precision. A
"polluted" culture, when not an epithet of denunciation, is
an ideological construct usually elaborated for repressive purposes, which Schorske would be among the first to condemn.

A much less guarded and more forthright approach in
drawing the implications of this novel-sounding, great-souled
approach to the social responsibility of scholarship is found
in an eloquent article by a former Fellow of the Center for
the Study of Democratic Institutions and now a faculty
activist in reconstructing the University of California after
its recent earthquakes.[13]

For him neutrality is hypocrisy. The university as a corporate body must exercise its moral obligation for the uses
and abuses of knowledge. He is emphatic that the very "distinction [mark the term!] between pure and applied research
is disappearing" and that the most esoteric knowledge may
turn out to be hazardous to man. He thereupon concludes

[12] Schorske. See note 1.
[13] Lichtman. See note 2.

that it is not the citizens and their representatives who must take the responsibility for the applications of knowledge. The community of scholars as a group must check the scope, reach, possible use and abuse of the findings of its members, what may be investigated and what may not. Scientists cannot permit free enterprise in the life of the mind. They must take responsibility for its growth.

What about the threat to academic freedom in this ominous proposal? Lichtman replies:

> It is too late now to fall back on the platitudes of academic freedom: no biochemist can be sure that in pursuing the structure of an enzyme he is not perfecting a lethal form of warfare. This government will have to be disarmed before the clear and present danger now subverting thought can be dissolved. Until men of knowledge act to change the world, they cannot claim the unrestricted right to understand it.[14]

One hardly knows where to begin in analyzing these sentences. They move from a premise of hysterical exaggeration to a conclusion that is both intolerant and irresponsible. It is not the case that every theoretical position or discovery has practical consequences. It may or may not have. And if it has practical consequences, these may be for good as well as for evil.

The enzyme may be used to perfect a cure for cancer and not only to perfect a lethal form of war. Shall we therefore ban or hold up research in enzymes until we forever abolish war from the world? The responsibility for the use or application of truth is not the discoverer's but that of the citizen. To hold the discoverer or the scholar responsible for the practical uses of knowledge is viciously absurd. It is to hold the unknown genius who discovered fire responsible for arson; to blame Gutenberg for the lies that appear in type; Galileo for siege guns; Einstein for Nagasaki. It is to hold the founder of Chris-

14 Lichtman. See note 2.

THE BARBARISM OF VIRTUE

tianity responsible for Christian anti-Semitism and to brand
Nobel of the Peace Foundation a war criminal.

To place the responsibility on men as scholars for changing the world rather than on men as citizens is as sensible
and as moral as crucifying the bearer of bad tidings. This is
a Philistine, not pragmatic, view of the relation between
theory and practice.

Finally, to claim that "until men of knowledge act to
change the world [in the right direction, of course!], they
cannot claim the unrestricted right to understand it" is not
to dismiss academic freedom as a platitude but to move to
destroy it root and branch. For the right to understand
the world *unrestricted* by religious, philosophical, political,
social, or racial dogmas of any kind is what academic freedom is all about.

To deny the scholar the unrestricted right to understand
the world until he passes tests of good citizenship or virtue
is to reinstate in progressive form a system of intellectual
terror, to bring once more the priest or the commissar or
the tribune of the people, depending on where one finds
salvation, into the house of intellect.

Those who share this view have actually declared war
against the university as a community of scholars in the name
of the party of humanity. For that is the upshot of the in-
sistent demand that over and above the active commitment
scholars make to good causes in their role as private citizens,
*the* university as a corporate entity must espouse positions
on current issues of transcendent importance. This can
only embroil them *within* the academy as they are embroiled
without, and to transform university assemblies into political bodies.

If the university is expected to declare itself on basic
issues, what will be the position of those who are outvoted,
who see the road to serfdom in proposals their colleagues
proclaim as the highway to liberty, who cry counterrevolu-
tion where others cry revolution, who prophesy "1984" where
others welcome a planned and planning society?

"A university that will not speak for man," Lichtman solemnly intones, "has ceased to be a human enterprise." I find this assertion—and not the principle of academic freedom—a pious truism, for it excludes nothing that a free university does or says. The university speaks for man when it permits its qualified members to choose their themes for research; it speaks no less for man when it gives a home to those who suspend judgment, who refuse to speak, or refuse to speak like Mr. Lichtman.

The difficulty is that everyone who speaks professes to speak for man. All parties claim to be the party of humanity, with different views and voices about what is good for man but with equal sincerity. And although they cannot all be right, they can all be wrong.

Let us examine an issue on which Lichtman, and not he alone, believes that *the* university should take a stand, without thereby becoming political.

"Today," he writes, "the university is required to condemn the government of the United States for its barbaric crusade against the life and spirit of the people of Vietnam."

There are other scholars of Far Eastern affairs who are convinced that "barbarism" is the term to apply to systematic Vietcong terrorism against civilians, and that statements like those of Lichtman are not only wildly unjust but defamatory. I am not concerned now with the truth or falsity of his statement but with the likely consequences of requiring *the* university to take a stand on it.

Obviously anyone who disagrees with Lichtman's convictions about the barbarism of the U.S. government runs the risk of appearing as a barbarian of the spirit, unfit to enjoy citizenship in the university. It is not unlikely that just as he believes that the university that refuses to speak up for man is not a human enterprise, so he holds that the scholar who refuses to speak up for man is not a human being. Would not moral consistency require Lichtman to demand that the university condemn those of his colleagues who opposed his motion to condemn? And this is not political?

Even without overt political commitment the result would be disastrous. Imagine a situation in which *the* university is called upon to take a position on Vietnam. On the one hand are fanatics like Lichtman who assert that those who support the American presence in Vietnam are abetting murder. On the other there are his colleagues, equally fanatical on the opposite side, who hold that those critical like Lichtman of our presence there, and who would turn over innumerable thousands who fought on the assurance of U.S. support to the liquidation squads of the Vietcong, are traitors.

How long could a faculty survive in which one faction regards the other as guilty of complicity in murder, and the other faction regards the first as traitors and apologists for political genocide, and both require *the* university to choose between them?

Vietnam is not the only issue with respect to which *the* university is expected to take a public stand. Capitalism has been declared by Lichtman and the leaders of the SDS to be inhuman, too, and in no uncertain, if obscene, terms.

Must the university take a position on this, too? Is it not enough to permit its scholars to think and say whatever their pursuit of truth leads them to say about capitalism and socialism?

If this is not enough, then although economists who defend a mixed economy may be tolerated as half-human or half-civilized or mixed-up humans, one must fear for the fate of professors like Friedrich Hayck or Milton Friedman in any university dispensation that agrees with Lichtman. For they are unreconstructed and unrepentant believers in free enterprise who hold that all forms of socialism are necessarily more inhuman than capitalism. Although as a democratic socialist I disagree with them, I think any university or community of scholars would be poorer by far educationally and spiritually for their absence.

At any rate, whether we are inclined toward socialism or capitalism, we cannot intelligently believe that the mission of the university is to lead mankind to a new Jerusalem. Any attempt to do so would destroy, among other things, the university's historic function to serve as intellectual sanctuary when the winds of popular passion blow, and as a center for experiment, heresy, and reflective dissent.

To those unfamiliar with the growing literature of this philosophy of social commitment my analysis may appear alarmist and dialectically overstrained—all the more so as the writers from whom I have quoted seem to draw back from the rather extreme conclusions to which their principles, if applied, might lead. They know they are moving on a path toward a precipice even as they proclaim that there is no danger.

I conclude, therefore, with a brief analysis of the point of view of a writer who *has* the courage of his confusions, who starts from the same premises as his colleagues discussed previously, and is prepared to go to the end of the path without flinching. I refer to Dr. Herbert Marcuse.

Marcuse also belongs to the party of humanity. He is committed to "a human society" in which men live in loving tolerance of each other, free of fear and misery. Western capitalism, he tells us, has created an affluent society and the gadgetries of happiness; but he is not impressed by its rising standards of living and culture. He sees the spiritual nakedness of the masses under their fine clothes, and the gaping vacuity of their minds under the tinsel of popular culture. This explains why the powers that be extend a tolerance to all, both "to the party of hate as well as to that of humanity," for the masses, conditioned by the class education they receive, cannot identify the flowers of evil in our polluted culture.

The modern lords of the manor, in virtue of their control of press, courts, schools, and other media, can safely permit the freedoms of the Bill of Rights to flourish because they are not concerned with the truth. This is a false tolerance because "truth is the end of liberty and liberty must be

defined and confined [sic] by truth" . . . "The telos of tolerance is truth."[15]

The truth Marcuse is talking about is not the truth of
science. Science uses the methods of toleration or due process
to reach the truth. Marcuse believes that one must already
know the truth antecedently to permit toleration. The truth
Marcuse antecedently knows is that the ideal society, the
completely human society, is one in which there is no repression of human desire and no oppression of man by man.
It is a society nowhere in existence today but one whose
outlines our reason can grasp as well as the general direction
in which we must move toward it.

Tolerance of thought and expression is acceptable in order
to help us find our way toward the goal of universal human
liberation. But "this tolerance cannot be indiscriminate and
equal with respect to the contents of expression, neither in
word nor in deed, it cannot protect false words and wrong
deeds which demonstrate that they contradict and counteract
the possibilities of liberation."[16]

Let us pause for a moment to see just what Marcuse is
saying. Not merely that some forms of behavior are intolerable. No sane man can tolerate any and every kind of behavior. Not merely that certain words integral to criminal
behavior, that trigger it off, are objectionable. No reasonable man will disagree. Marcuse goes far beyond these reasonable limits. He believes that in the interests of tolerance
we must proscribe expression of false or untrue ideas about
what is good for man and society. Error is the enemy, long
before its fruits of conduct are manifest.

Marcuse is aware that this sounds grim to liberal ears.
And perhaps as a concession, he indicates that he would
exempt what he calls "the sphere of privacy" from the
watchful censorship of objective Reason and Virtue. He
should be given credit for this uncharacteristic liberal lapse—

[15] Marcuse, *Repressive Tolerance.*
[16] Marcuse. See note 15.

probably the effect of exposure to American life. But it is at the cost of a gross and obvious inconsistency!

For he is emphatic in his view that it is the whole that determines the truth—"the structure and function [of the whole]determines every particular condition and relation"— which explains why the dialectical eye of Reason and Virtue must search out all spheres of thought and action for error. But if only the whole is true and the truth lies in the whole, we cannot, alas! exempt the sphere of privacy.

What is said in private life, as every tyrant knows, spreads to public life. If the State or Party or Cause is denounced in the bosom of the family, it will be denounced in the playground, the schoolroom, in letters to the military. No, this disjunction between the private and public is no more tenable on Marcuse's view than the distinction between the scholar and the citizen, school and society.

Marcuse quickly recovers from his liberal lapse. Admitting that within existing democracy tolerance is widespread for right and left, for Communist and fascist, for black and white, for Marcuse and his critics, he denounces it as false *because* it is impartial. Until men become truly human, impartiality and neutrality in the presentation of all sides can result only in the triumph of the worse over the better. For men are not truly human yet, they cannot see with the eyes and understand with the mind of the future.

Consequently, objective Reason and Virtue must be given a handicap so that they can overcome the plausibility and temptations of what is not-Reasonable and not-Virtuous that subvert the half-blind majority. The best way of overcoming the plausibility and temptations of what is not-Reasonable and not-Virtuous, especially in an affluent society, is to silence them by "apparently undemocratic means" "apparently" because the future goal is democracy.

What are these means, concretely speaking? Marcuse spells them out clearly enough for even the brainwashed majority to understand.

> They would include the withdrawal of toleration of
> speech and assembly from groups and movements
> which promote aggressive policies, armaments, chauvi-
> nism, discrimination on grounds of race and religion, or
> which oppose the extension of public services, social se-
> curity or medical care, etc.

This "etc." is a little disquieting at a time in which some
publicists, economists, and educators are urging, in the interest of efficient postal service and better pay, better schooling, and better teaching, that the post office and the public
schools be transferred to the private sector.

Marcuse is not a man of half-measures. He continues:

> Moreover, the restoration of freedom of thought may
> necessitate new and rigid restrictions on teaching and
> practices in the educational institutions which, by their
> very methods and concepts, serve to enclose the mind
> within the established universe of disclosure and behav-
> ior—thereby precluding a priori a rational evaluation of
> the alternatives.[17]

One would have imagined that a rational evaluation of
alternatives proceeds by inviting alternatives to make themselves heard rather than by rigidly restricting them, but this
presupposes belief in academic freedom, which for Marcuse
is not even a platitude but a bourgeois illusion.

Reading Marcuse is like listening to a vehement denunciation of totalitarianism on the ground that it is the wrong
kind of totalitarianism; the right kind being the one that
declares itself democratic, for the party of humanity. If
only the party of humanity loved men, including scholars, a
little more, and humanity a little less!

Naturally Marcuse hesitates to do in the name of Marcuse
what he cheerfully does in the name of Reason. To escape
the appearance of imposing his personal and arbitrary views

[17] Marcuse. See note 15.

of what the future Society of the Right and Virtuous must be, with all its trappings of polymorphic sexuality, he must defend the objectivity of the liberating ideal in behalf of which he advocates systematic intolerance. If one asks him: who is qualified to make these decisions for society as a whole, he answers: "Everyone."[18] Everyone? Why this sounds as if he were moving toward a democratic consensus. But no! It is everyone "in the maturity of his faculties as a human being—everyone who has learned to think rationally and autonomously." But he has just argued that everyone cannot be mature or think rationally or autonomously until the world is completely transformed and human beings completely liberated.

By his own assumptions, he cannot now regard everyone as fit or sufficiently mature to make rational decisions. He has simply begged the whole question of rationality and redefined autonomy and rationality so that *his* iron whim becomes the criterion of objectivity. If one differs with him one differs with the party of humanity and its truth.

This is a far cry from democratic socialism in any of its varieties. It really is the Prussian socialism of Bismarck with a patina of Platonism. But this is a theme that cannot be pursued here.

Until now I have referred to this philosophy of social commitment as novel-sounding. It should, however, be obvious that it is novel in form alone. The logic of its position is identical with that of those Christian divines who, convinced that the end of learning was piety, censored science, art, and literature in the light of the revelations vouchsafed them.

There are obvious differences, of course. The felicities of the future life for the first had its locus in the Kingdom of Heaven, whereas Marcuse hopes for them on earth. There are also differences in the nature of the anticipated felicities. In the first, there is neither marriage nor giving in marriage but only the life of the spirit. In the second, marriage is di-

---

[18] Marcuse. See note 15.

alectically *aufgehoben*: everybody loves everybody. Nothing is repressed and no one is repressed. But for both, once the ideal is imperiled by heretical and retrogressive notions, it must be safeguarded by withdrawal of tolerance and all that this implies in the real interests of the victim as well as in the interests of the truth.

Nor is the logic radically different from that invoked by the cultural Babbitts and economic Bourbons of the American past who also believed that scholarship must be kept in leading strings to good citizenship, that institutions subsidized by the public purse or private largesse must not be permitted to undermine the reigning orthodoxies. It has required a difficult struggle to get public recognition of the principle of the unrestricted right of qualified inquirers to understand the world. That principle is under attack by those who are imbued with a sense of virtue, who under the banners of humanity want the temple of learning to become a fort from which they can sally forth to transform society with impunity.

There is a great and growing danger in this. In the unlikely event that they succeed, the temple may become a fort from which scholars who wish to serve humanity by seeking the truth rather than to seek the truth by serving humanity will be driven out. In the more likely event that they fail, the temple may be razed to the ground by the angry reaction of a society provoked by the usurpation of power by a self-selected elite.

The obvious rejoinder to all this is that the American university is not a temple of learning, not even a community of scholars in pursuit of the truth but—the litany of charges is familiar—only a bulwark of the established order, a public service station for industry, government, and assorted private groups, committed to imperialism abroad, and racism and reaction at home.

The rejoinder is largely false, and to the extent it is true, subject to correction in the light of the university's educational mission and the philosophy of academic freedom defended here. It is false in that the American university today is more of a center of dissent from, than of support for, government policy; false in that it has been, without any *Gleichschaltung*, a great laboratory of ideas for new social policies; false in that it has accepted no party line to guide its research; false in that the very presence in the university of those who utter these irresponsible statements, of the important posts they occupy, and the influences they exert, is incompatible with the burden of the charge.

Where the proliferation of services by the modern university threatens to take it far afield from its central task of scholarship, research, and teaching, it has been a consequence of pressures that should be resisted. To substitute other pressures for them is to intensify the trend toward the politicalization of scholarship, sometimes under the pretense of opposing politicalization.

Perhaps some words of amplification are necessary although the complexity of the subject of contract research and outside consultative or advisory activity requires more extended treatment than can be given here. As a scholar, I am free to criticize the pedantry, the "irrelevance," the careerist timidity, the hunger for publicity, the whoring after affluence—to list some of the unlovelier charges that critics of the current academic scene have made—reflected in the research projects of some of my colleagues, and they are free to reply in kind to me. But it would be intolerable presumption on my part as well as on theirs to try to *impose* by institutional decree or administrative methods our judgments in these areas, especially with tenured faculty members.

Almost a generation ago, lamenting the absence of great literary American achievements, a severe indictment was launched against Hollywood by some critics on the ground that it had seduced American writers by means of fat contracts into abandoning their dedication to the creative muse. Hollywood can be indicted for many reasons but surely this criticism was misdirected. The obvious fault, if any, lay with those who preferred the fleshpots to the uncertainties and torments of the creative life. Hollywood is a business and its function is to buy talent. Sometimes it seemed as if the denunciation came from those who lacked even the talent to tempt Hollywood, who couldn't "sell out" because they had nothing to sell.

Today we hear more widespread and bitter indictments of government and industry for seducing American scholars from the sciences and the social sciences into their research projects. By all odds government and industry are more important than Hollywood and their research projects usually are more integral to the expertise of the scholars than the munificently rewarded dawdling of writers in our modern Babylon to whatever genuine literary genius they possess.

Government and industry compete with the universities for talent, and if there were an absolute taboo against scholars engaging in projects in which they are interested and which government and industry are prepared and eager to sponsor, universities would be denuded of able researchers and teachers in many departments. Here, too, if criticism is in order it should be directed against the scholars who undertake this kind of research or advisory function. And each case must be decided on its merits, merits that have nothing to do with the motives behind the criticism, even when it is sheer envy, as is often the case among scholars in the humanities exploring esoteric intellectual terrain.

Ernst Renan somewhere characterizes the life of scholarship as one of genteel poverty. Those days are happily gone. Most scholars today earn a living wage, certainly beyond the level of genteel poverty. There are some, to be sure, some Philistines who imply that in the humanities, although scholars are well paid, they don't earn it—a view that would be disspelled if they realized that the work of a genuine scholar is never done, that it is a life-long pursuit that knows no hours and timeclocks or seasons. Happily, the life of scholarship and teaching is its own chief reward; otherwise, it would be difficult to explain the presence of so many able minds in the universities. There is no reason to begrudge scholars in *any* field an opportunity, if it presents itself, to engage in research and advisory services congenial to their talents, subject to the criticisms but not the proscriptions of their colleagues.

Nonetheless, the university as a community of scholars can exercise some restraints on the outside research and advisory activities of its members, and especially on the projects it agrees to house for which its members have found outside sponsorship. These restraints flow not from political commitment but from its adherence to the principles of professional ethics, implied by the principles of academic freedom.

These restraints, therefore, will not apply to the topics or themes of research, which should always be initiated by faculty members instead of outside agencies, but only to the manner or methods by which the research is conducted. The university has a right to a reasonable amount of the time of members of its full-time staff, and this must not be jeopardized by outside research or advisory functions. No university community should, as a rule, offer the hospitality of its facilities or the prestige of its auspices to any research activity undertaken to "prove" conclusions dictated by a sponsor or which is not open to challenge or the acceptance of whose antecedent validity is a *sine qua non* for its funding.

There are some projects that, because of their necessary secrecy or practical operational character, can be much more appropriately carried out elsewhere. There is no need for the university to give housing-room or the time of researchers to a project devoted to discovering a way to make better sausages or better guns or hosts of similar things. The individual scholar or teacher must be left free on his own time—and even here provided it does not interfere with his academic scholarly activities—to engage in research and consultative work that the university is unwilling to sponsor.

One of the virtues of a free society is that it permits plural avenues and opportunities for intellectual activity without giving a monopoly to any one sector of society. What a scholar or scientist may not do because of the limits set by the university on the range of its auspices, he may do as a private citizen. As Professor Don K. Price has put it in an essay reflecting expert knowledge, strong allegiance to academic freedom, and inspired common sense:

> A professor in the university may also be a consultant to a research corporation or a government agency and a member of a scientific society. His freedom to play different roles in these different institutions—and to defend the autonomy of each institution against the others —is one of the most important safeguards of freedom in modern society.[19]

In conclusion, we cannot and should not escape the world of politics. The wisdom of Aristotle and John Dewey are at one on this. But in a rational and humane society there must be some activities and institutions that are beyond politics. Our world, our politics, our lives will be the better for it.

They will be the better for it because of the indirect effects of a university and educational system in which the principles of academic freedom obtain. John Dewey was right in asserting that the basic problems of education are the basic problems of philosophy, too. For the latter center around the normative consideration of values. The educational system reflects society but in a democratic society it need not be a mere reflex of society, serving to perpetuate existing relationships of power.

Nor can the educational system rebuild or reconstruct the whole of society. To this extent the theory of historical

[19] From "Purists and Politicians," *Science*, January 3, 1969.

materialism is valid. But an educational and university system that enshrines the principles of academic freedom can rise higher than its source. It can generate the intellectual power and visions that gradually lift the level of social existence and social consciousness. These in turn help the educational process to reach greater heights.

# APPENDIX I

# SECOND THOUGHTS
# ON BERKELEY

The following analysis of events at the University of California, Berkeley, penned just a few months after their occurrence, was originally published in the October, 1965 *Teachers College Record* of Columbia University. I offer it here because the developments at Berkeley are widely taken as the *fons et origo* of the student rebellions that since then have broken out with such explosive impact, not only in the United States but in most European countries as well. Despite the existence of a small library of literature devoted to the happenings at Berkeley, there is an astonishing ignorance of the order and cause of events there that seems to grow thicker with the passage of years, and is reflected in recent commentary on the student and academic revolution.

There is little doubt that the student demonstrations at the University of California in the fall of 1964 that culminated in the seizure of the central administration building, mass arrests, and a student strike, marked a turning point in the history of American higher education. In several different areas of educational thought and practice, it has led to a reexamination of issues and questions that previously had been treated largely on an *ad hoc* basis, depending upon local traditions, the degree of institutional inertia, and the personalities of key administrators.

By far the most important of the questions *posed* by the events at Berkeley involve the relation between the liberal arts college and the university, between the size of class and the quality of instruction, between institutes, special projects, federal grants, etc., and the regular academic life within the complex multiversity. To imply that there was no or little discussion of these problems prior to the outbreak at Berkeley would, of course, be false. The writings of President Clark Kerr, among others, are concerned with these questions.

Nonetheless it is true to say that this concern was restricted, by and large, to professional educators and administrators. The scholars and teachers of the university cheerfully ignored them as outside their interest. Today a vastly greater number of run-of-the-mill professors, who in the past had been allergic to discussion of educational issues, find themselves involved with questions that a few years ago they would have patronizingly regarded as part of the dreary treadmill that, in the absence of genuine subject matter, presumably constituted the curriculum of schools of education.

Even those who have always busied themselves professionally with these questions—administrators and "educationists"—have been profoundly affected. Their deliberations are now characterized by a sense of urgency and crisis as if the entire future of American higher education depended on the immediate resolution of the questions discussed by them in recent years in academic and leisurely fashion. Their conferences in recent days are marked by frenetic pronouncements and Cassandra cries. It is as if biologists pursuing a long-standing research program on the bacillus of plague were suddenly to be told that the entire community is threatened by the disease.

The second area of growing concern among the college faculties of the country is altogether unprecedented. This is student-faculty relations, and obviously stems from the demands made by the so-called Free Speech Movement (FSM) at Berkeley for student rights and academic freedom.

To the average faculty member, the notion that the state of student-faculty relations, and the problems of student discipline, had any bearing upon his vocation as a scholar-teacher was just as foreign as the notion that the state of parent-children relations had anything to do with it. He left the latter to his wife, and the former to the dean. But since Berkeley, and the evidences of restiveness on many other campuses, those untroubled days have become a wistful memory.

The administrators have become so fearful of "another Berkeley" that they are hastening to put the problems of student-faculty relations and the definition of student rights and responsibilities on the faculty doorstep where it has, of course, always belonged.

Attitudes and styles of behavior are infectious among student bodies not only in matters of dress but of thought. It is indisputably a sign of educational progress that students are more concerned these days with the question of student rights within the university and in the enterprise of learning than with panty raids, swallowing goldfish, and, hopefully, football. The new attitude should be welcomed, and where it has not yet been felt, the faculty and administration should invite student participation, even when it has its amusing sides.

In some institutions students who have had no cause for complaint in the past are burdened by the feeling that they ought to be making demands on faculty and administration in order to keep up with the seas of change, and find themselves frustrated because of a failure to discover a plausible issue or cause. The best specific in such situations is an invitation to thoughtful student participation in joint meetings with faculty and administration.

A curious but widely held view has developed about the relation between the first set of educational problems, those involving the nature of the college curriculum and the organization of the university, and the second set of problems, the rights and responsibilities of students.

It has been asserted, with the very little evidence in support, that this second set of problems arises primarily as a consequence of the views taken with respect to the first, as if differing conceptions of the rights and responsibilities of students could be derived from the different conceptions of curricular and university organization. This view of the relation between the two sets of problems is regarded as a natural generalization of the causal relation between them, which, it is alleged, existed at Berkeley.

That is to say, it has been very widely and emphatically affirmed that "the mass lawlessness at Berkeley," a more accurate phrase than Governor Brown's "revolution at Berkeley," was a consequence of a failure "to solve," whatever that means, the problems of the multiversity. To make such a statement warrantably requires that one be familiar with what actually happened at Berkeley, what the issues were, and what events finally precipitated the mass lawlessness of the FSM.

I have read almost everything that has been published about the situation and have been astonished by the extraordinary amount of misinformation that prevails in many of the accounts. There is widespread ignorance both of the chronology of events and of key documents. And judging by what has been written by different members of the faculty at Berkeley, there is no agreement concerning some crucial points of fact and issues in dispute.

The academic battlefield in some ways is no different from an ordinary one. Even participants with trained minds have hardly better powers of observation and inference concerning the nature of the battle than the untrained soldiery. There is only agreement on the outcome.

This essay was undertaken primarily in an attempt to find out what happened at Berkeley. Such an inquiry seemed needed because of widespread bewilderment among college faculties, confusion among large sections of the nonacademic population, the hostility of the press, and politically naive administrators who welcomed the actions at Berkeley as the highest expression of American youthful idealism.

It was inspired partly by a reaction to my article on "Academic Freedom and the Rights of Students" (*New York Times*, January 3, 1965) devoted to a general discussion of the theme, but because it was editorially entitled "Freedom to Learn but not to Riot," assumed to be chiefly about Berkeley. In what follows, I shall state some of the relevant facts not known by many individuals with whom I have discussed the situation and by some who have written about it. I shall then analyze the chief issues in dispute, and assess in turn the role in, and responsibility for, what occurred of the administration, of the leaders of the FSM, and of the faculty.

The larger questions concerning the nature and function of the university that I have discussed elsewhere[1] I omit here since they do not bear directly on the events. Much that has been written about the nature of the university has no more specific

[1] Sidney Hook, *Education for Modern Man*, 2nd ed. (New York, Alfred A. Knopp, Inc., 1963).

relevance to what happened at Berkeley than a general discussion about the sociology of crime has on the specific question of who killed whom, when, where, and why.

There was not *one* civil disobedience sit-in demonstration at Berkeley but *four!* The first was on September 30 and followed the announcement by the administrative authorities of disciplinary hearings for five students who had manned tables for purposes declared illegal by sudden administrative edict on September 14. Some leaders of this demonstration were "indefinitely suspended."

The second sit-in occurred on October 1. This date is very important for the understanding of subsequent proceedings. Demonstrators surrounded the police car that contained Jack Weinberg—a former student and the arrested violator of the new university ruling—and threatened violence if the police attempted to remove the prisoner. Additional protestors stormed into Sproul Hall for another sit-in. When the campus police sought to close the Sproul Hall doors, a physical clash occurred.

The third sit-in took place on November 22. This followed the reversal and liberalizing by the Regents of previous university policy on November 20. Except on one moot point, it accepted every reasonable demand by the students, restored and expanded the area of student political action enjoyed in the past:

> The Regents adopt the policy effective immediately that certain campus facilities, carefully selected and properly regulated, may be used by students and staff for planning, implementing, raising funds or recruiting participants for lawful off-campus action, not for unlawful off-campus action.

The fourth and final sit-in of the year occurred December 2-3. This led to removal and arrest of students on the orders of Governor Brown *without* the approval of President Kerr.

There is reason to believe that if the last sit-down had not taken place, in the light of the Regents ruling of November 20, matters at the University of Berkeley would have composed themselves despite the plans of the leaders of the FSM. What sparked it?

Here several misconceptions prevail among those who have

not carefully studied the record. The popular view is that on November 28, Mario Savio and three other student leaders suddenly received word that disciplinary action was being taken against them for their peaceful actions of civil disobedience of September 30 and for setting up illegal tables prior to that; and that this action "reneged" on the agreement that President Kerr had made with students on October 2. The student leaders appear as victims of vindictive administrative persecution for exercising the peaceful right of petition.

This is false. The agreement President Kerr had made with the students called, among other things, for the dropping of university charges against the ex-student Weinberg, the arrested man in the immobilized police car, and for turning over the cases of the suspended students to a Committee of the Academic Senate of the Faculty. These provisions were carried out. The faculty committee was formed (the Heyman Committee); and, after elaborate hearings, it made its report on November 12.

In its report it pointed out that, with the assent of all parties, it "has considered only those events occurring up to the night of September 30, 1964, when the students here involved were indefinitely suspended by the chancellor."

The Heyman report is couched in very mild and gentle, almost apologetic, language. Nonetheless it is quite critical of some aspects of administrative policy. At the same time it concludes that the students did violate university regulations. The penalty for each of six students was "censure" to take the place of the penalty of "indefinite suspension," which was to be expunged from their record. The suspension of Messrs. Goldberg and Savio, however, was *upheld* but limited to six weeks.

One key paragraph of the report of this *ad hoc* faculty committee on student conduct reads with reference to events on September 30:

> While we are not prepared to condemn on moral grounds the device of demonstration by peaceful and orderly sit-in, we recognize that those who organize and participate in a sit-in which is judged to violate valid regulations must be prepared to pay the price for such conduct. In this instance (September 30), we believe that the price must be higher than [for] the manning of card tables, another form of civil

disobedience, not because of any discernible difference in
motivation, or moral position, but because of *the potentially
more serious consequences of the action* [my italics].

This closed the matter, for all practical purposes, of the September 30 demonstration. What then sparked the fateful sit-
ins of December 2 and 3? It was a resolution adopted by the Regents on November 20, the very day it liberalized the Rules for
Political Action on Campus. This second resolution on Disciplinary Action read in part:

> New disciplinary proceedings before the Faculty Committee
> on student conduct will be instituted immediately against cer-
> tain students and organizations for violations *subsequent* to
> September 30, 1964 [my italics].

The actions subsequent to September 30 covered the incident of the entrapment of the police car on October 1 and the
fracas in Sproul Hall on the occasion of the second sit-in. The
Regents' resolution was a directive to Chancellor Strong who, on
this matter at any rate, cannot be regarded as responsible for the
action. His letter to Savio and Goldberg did *not* announce any
punishment. It merely requested them to attend a hearing before
the faculty committee on student conduct. It did not charge
them with *peaceful* sit-in demonstration, even of the kind the
Heyman Committee had condemned.

It charged them with acts of violence—forcefully resisting the
efforts of police officers who attempted to close the main doors
of Sproul Hall, assault (specifically Savio) for biting a police
officer in the thigh, entrapment of the police car, and threats of
violence. In addition, they were charged with organizing the
invasion of Sproul Hall on October 1 and, by deliberately blocking the exits, compelling personnel from the Dean of Students
office to flee through a window and across a roof.

Obviously the leaders of the FSM were *prepared* to riot, did
riot in Sproul Hall, and technically were guilty of riot in preventing an arrest of an individual charged with breaking the law.
Even staunch faculty friends of the FSM admit that if the administration had not yielded October 2 and withdrawn the police, there is every likelihood that bloodshed would have oc-

curred. For had the police attempted to move the car or remove the demonstrators, the latter would have resisted them. Under the circumstances, the indignation of the FSM leaders over the title the editors of the *New York Times* placed on my original article is synthetic. Subsequently, by his fierce diatribe against Dr. Martin Luther King and his ridicule of the philosophy of passive resistance, Mario Savio revealed that he was not in principle opposed to the use of violence in resolving problems of civil and educational rights.

When one examines the actual *issues* in dispute at Berkeley one must conclude that, to the extent that the students in the FSM were primarily concerned with organizing *civil-rights* demonstrations, legal or illegal, *off campus*, their request that they be free of administrative or faculty disciplinary jurisdiction was morally and educationally justified. What they failed to see, and the great majority of the faculty with them, was that, in the nature of the case, one cannot formulate a *rule* to the effect that *all* illegal off-campus activity, whether political or not, falls within the *exclusive* province of the civil authorities. The action of the faculty, for reasons I shall try to make clear, can only be *ad hoc* depending upon the nature, the place, and the attendant circumstances of the activity of the students.

The administration itself had recognized that there were certain permissible off-campus demonstrations in which students had participated in which they had been arrested for flagrantly violating the law, *e.g.*, the sit-ins at the Sheraton-Palace Hotel, and before that, the disruptions of the San Francisco hearings of the House Committee on Un-American Activities.

Although President Kerr took the position that they had been organized off campus, and hence were altogether a citizen's activity, actually both demonstrations were at least partially mounted on the campus. Yet the administration had courageously refused to add educational punishment to the civil punishment. For obviously, whether ill- or well-advised, there had been no educational interest of the university affected. Nor could one sensibly say that the organization and support of student activity in behalf of the extension of the democratic process in Southern states or in behalf of the unorganized migrant workers, even if they were illegal under a local or federal statute, in any way were prejudicial to the ethos of the educational community.

During the thirties we helped students go to Harlan County, Kentucky, and arranged for them to accompany Norman Thomas when he went to Jersey City to violate the decree against freedom of speech by "I-Am-the-Law" Mayor Hague. There was no demand even from reactionary elements that these activities be subject to university restriction.

Nonetheless one can easily imagine situations in which student off-campus activity, legal or illegal, might very well have a definite bearing on values and standards regarded as precious to the educational community. That the students involved are more likely to be reactionary than radical does not affect the principle. And I have seen radical students sometimes act toward other students (usually other radical students) in the same way as they are sometimes treated by the reactionaries.

Suppose a group of students, in order to prevent the policy of desegregation at a college or university, waylay and violently haze the black students, being careful to carry out their attacks off the campus. Would it be wrong for the university community to be concerned about such activity and take action against those who by their illegal (or legal) off-campus activities were destroying its educational ideals?

American universities have not yet become as politicalized as universities in India and Japan although some members of the University of California have expressed the fear that they are well on their way. I have been at universities abroad where students, dissatisfied with their grades or disagreeing with the *political* views of their professors, have mobbed them off campus. Suppose some students of the FSM, instead of jeering at Professors R. and L. or calling them "fink," were to mob them (making sure they were not on university ground) because they disagreed with their political or educational views. Would this be of no concern to the university community? Would it be morally or legally wrong for the university to take disciplinary notice of this off-campus behavior?

A day may come in this country when those who presently fawn on the students who share their views may face another and more hostile generation of students. Those who have any memories of the First World War in this country, or have read about it, will know what I mean.

But if students were ever to be punished by a faculty for an action that had already been punished by the sanctions of the civil authorities, would that not be placing them in "double jeopardy"? This is another thought-stopping phrase when introduced in an educational context. It is curious that so many able minds in the academy in a crisis fail to reflect on their own experience. Almost anyone exposed for some years to reports of faculty discipline committees can match the following cases.

A student steals examination papers, usually an off-campus job, sells them, is arrested, and punished. His case comes before the faculty. I have never known anyone who, whatever his recommendation for action, even protested that this placed the student in double jeopardy. Or a student is arrested for rifling lockers or stealing books from the library or dipping into the till of the college bookstore and the law takes its course. Is the faculty guilty of violating the constitutional rights of the student if it concludes that in the educational interest of the community some disciplinary action is justified?

Actually, there are many actions that, strictly speaking, are not illegal and yet are a legitimate concern of the academic community, e.g., plagiarism, especially of something in the public domain, and other forms of cheating that are not illegal. Indeed, students have a *constitutional* right to join any fraternities they please. Yet who would deny the right of faculties to declare on educational grounds that fraternities would not be tolerated on the campus?

When a university faculty disciplines a student, it does so or should do so on *educational* grounds, irrespective of the legal aspects of the student action. When a court punishes a student, it is *not* primarily on grounds of educational policy. If off-campus fraternity hazing or other off-campus student activity seriously imperils the educational goals and ideals of the academic community, the freedom of students to learn and of the faculty to teach, it falls within the area of academic concern.

One further objection: The off-campus student activities that are legitimately subject to regulation, it may be retorted, are not political. Both the Regents' rule forbidding unlawful off-campus action and Point 3 of the faculty resolution of December 8, denying the right of the university to forbid or regulate such action, are aimed only at political and social action. Even if true, this is irrelevant.

People can get hurt just as much in political and/or social action as in any other. What is political and/or social action, anyhow? Is a lynch mob a form of social action? Is a nonpolitical off-campus raid of a rival campus, in which property is destroyed and students hurt, a legitimate concern of the faculty of the raiders but not if the raid is against a Socialist club on the raided campus? Who is to determine what falls within the purview of privileged political and social off-campus action?

On March 5, 1965, after the hubbub at Berkeley had subsided somewhat, Stephen Weissman, one of the leaders of the FSM, declared at a Plaza rally that obscene speech was an integral part of the civil-rights movement, and demanded immunity from university regulation in terms of the faculty's own resolutions. It is obvious that the faculty must decide issues of this kind from case to case. The term "political" designates a rubber-band concept.

If my analysis is sound, then *both* the Regents' rule of November 20, and the flat faculty statement of December 8th, "Off-campus student political activities shall not be subject to University regulation," are equally objectionable from the point of view of enlightened educational policy and common sense, a resource, alas! that seems to have been in short supply at Berkeley during this period.

More extraordinary is the very first sentence of Point 3 of the faculty statement of December 8. "The content of speech or advocacy should not be restricted by the University." What makes this sentence extraordinary is the word "content." It is *not* synonymous with "advocacy." It goes far beyond anything referred to by "advocacy." It makes sense to contrast "advocacy" and "incitement." But it makes no sense to contrast "content" with "incitement."

The content of speech may have nothing to do with either advocacy or incitement. In actual fact, the content of most of our speech has no bearing on either advocacy or incitement. What the faculty at Berkeley voted is that the content of any speech should be free, not merely of prior restraint, but of *any* kind of restriction. Such a position is not only legally untenable but morally irresponsible.

Let us test this by a few examples. Here are a few statements that have been circulated on the campuses of some American institutions of higher learning. I use letters for names.

> X is an anti-Semite and notorious politician whose change of religion facilitated his advance in the school system, and who is now under surveillance of the Commissioner of Accounts' office for possible fraud . . . (He once sent a circular notice to his department chairmen asking them not to hire Jewish workers if they could help it).

> Y is a New Jersey stooge. Apparently Professor Y has decided to take the cue from his colleague Professor W, who by dint of loyalty to his president has risen to a professorship despite his limitations as a scholar in mathematics . . . A certain W.S., a stooge of Y, who as an alumnus illegally participated in Student Council activities, has already reaped the harvest of his proadministration stand. He has been appointed as a personnel director.

> Z is a charlatan, a ruthless exploiter. He also stands indicted on many other charges. He has appropriated Prof. M's Personality Rating Scale, changed the name of the scale to index, and "neglected to mention in his publication of the scale that the index was Prof. M's Personality Rating Scale with Prof. M's name omitted. He has had mimeographed, on college supplies by college employees at the expense of the college, a great deal of material that he has been using, for his private practice . . . A persual of some of Dr. Z's contributions to the pseudopsychological magazines such as *Modern Psychology* justifies the nomination of him by prominent scientific psychologists as Public Charlatan No. 1. . . .

There are other statements that have been circulated that are even more rank, broadly insinuating that certain faculty members have been guilty of seduction, trafficking in grades, and defalcation of university funds.

What would the Berkeley faculty of the University of California think of the "content" of these remarks, were they printed and widely distributed on and off the campus? This is no fanciful assumption since they actually appeared in leaflets and publications on an Eastern campus in a campaign to discredit X, Y, and Z politically. Would similar content of speech be privileged?

I am informed that some Berkeley students have paraded with signs "Kerr is a cur!" Some of them apparently regarded this as a contribution to free speech. "Content" takes in a lot of ground. It covers *anything* that may be said. But how long would the educational processes of a university remain unaffected if students could with impunity slander and libel whomever they pleased? What remedy has a teacher falsely charged with plagiarism or with having passed a failing student for a bribe? A public disavowal? Some slanders are spread by the very acts of disavowal. Should a faculty woman taxed with having slept with the chairman of the department to get a promotion write to the student newspaper denying that she slept with him—for that reason?

What is presupposed here is that a faculty has no right to require of students (or for that matter its own members) a standard of conduct in speech or behavior higher than what will enable students to stay out of jail. This is preposterous on its very face. For a university is fundamentally a community of scholars dedicated to the discovery and teaching of the truth. No one is compelled to seek entry to it. It has not only a legal and moral right but an educational obligation to raise its standards *above* that of the community whose law often expresses no more than the lowest common denominator of what is necessary to prevent men from breaking the social peace. It can therefore require both of its students and faculty conformity with a code of manners, speech, and conduct, provided it is not unreasonable or unjust, *higher* than what obtains in the marketplace.

In any event, it is impossible for any intelligent faculty to *act* on the principle explicitly affirmed by the overwhelming majority of the Berkeley faculty that the *content* of speech should be beyond any restriction by the university. There need be no prior restraint, but morally there cannot be impunity for *any* kind of utterance.

The obvious truth of the matter is that after the Resolution of the Regents on November 20, a false issue bedeviled the situation. The students were granted everything that had been taken away from them when the strip of sidewalk outside the campus had been yanked from under their feet in September.

It is simply not credible that, if *after* November 20, the students had, say, collected funds for antisegregation sit-ins in the South or even in California or enrolled volunteers for such actions, that the administration would have taken any action against them. And as a matter of fact, the FSM did set up its tables once more on November 24 without let or hindrance by the administration! Even the adherents of the FSM realized this.

In effect the *status quo ante* September had been restored and liberalized by the elimination of some ambiguities in the administrative rulings. This explains why the third student sit-in on November 23 fizzed. Only the hard core of the FSM kept up a half-hearted ranting, and even it was split. It was at this point, when the FSM agitation would have petered out, that the notices to appear for hearings before the faculty committee on student conduct were received by Savio and the Goldbergs.

The issue then shifted radically from one of *policy* to one of discipline and the justice of the proposed disciplinary action. Who would have imagined that a proposed disciplinary action involving four individuals would have convulsed the largest university in the country? The outcry of the FSM leaders was that this was a betrayal of the agreement with President Kerr reached on October 2 that prevented bloodshed on Sproul Plaza. Could they have been really ignorant of the Regents' specific directive of November 20 to bring this disciplinary action?

Assume that the student leaders were persons of good faith, indignant at the betrayal of what they sincerely believed to have been the signed understanding of October 2. What would be their normal reaction to a notice to appear for a hearing before a *faculty* committee? They would jump at the opportunity to demonstrate the injustice of the charges and to denounce the administration for double-dealing.

They could have called as witnesses in their behalf the members of the faculty who had negotiated the agreement with the president and who would gladly have testified for them. They could have even pleaded that since they were under suspension after September 30, they were not bound by university rules. At the very least, they could have waited to see whether the faculty committee on student conduct would dismiss the charges against them *before* resorting to direct action, which, even when it is justified, is always an instrument of last resort.

But the student leaders did nothing of the sort. They weren't interested in exoneration from the charges. They issued an ultimatum, carefully couched in language certain to provoke the administration, demanding on pain of "bringing the University machine to a grinding halt," to use the words of Savio, that all charges be dropped by noon December 2. This was a clear threat of a student strike! And as Stephen Weissman relates in his article entitled "What the Students Want" (*The New Leader*, January 4, 1964) the decision and vote to call the student strike were taken even *before* the final sit-down was called that led to subsequent police action.

He has admitted even more. Had the administration not sent out the notices to four FSM leaders to appear for a hearing, Weissman and his group were prepared to provoke the administration into bringing the police on campus by a public showing of obscene films against the walls of Sproul Hall. The importance of this can hardly be exaggerated because it shows how far the student leaders were prepared to go independently of the manner in which the sit-in terminated. It shows they were intent on bringing about the very state of affairs that they pretended subsequently to deplore—a state of affairs that they cleverly exploited to enlist both student and faculty sentiment on their side.

And the administration played right into their hands—as it had done all along!

Everyone seems convinced, with reason, that the administration made errors in handling the situation at Berkeley. But I have found no analysis of the nature of the errors. Even Dr. Kerr, who frankly avows that the administration fumbled and floundered, remained puzzled about the situation.

"The worst thing is," he acknowledged, "that I still don't know how we should have handled it."

There is no space to go into the matter in depth. But his first great mistake, on his arrival at the campus from his trip abroad, was his failure to rescind the order barring the use of the Bancroft Strip, since he realized that the decision was wrong "both in the action itself and the way it was done." A man of his intellectual candor and moral courage should not have hesitated out of fear of losing administrative face. He endured much greater humiliation later, and everyone knew that the order did not emanate from him. To be sure, the situation was complicated by the division of authority, by the fact of campus autonomy, and the primary role of the chancellor in administering the rules of discipline.

I am not minimizing the difficulties; but in a crisis educational statesmanship must find ways of coping with the rules and, by the proper use of psychology and authority, of inducing those involved to undertake proper action.

His second great mistake was in not drawing the proper lessons from the first sit-ins and the narrowly averted mass violence and bloodshed on Sproul Plaza at the time of entrapment of the police car. Dr. Kerr has been criticized in some quarters for capitulating to the student leaders. Instead of criticisms he deserves the highest credit for yielding at this time, instead of insisting on law enforcement and thus giving the student leaders the martyrs they so obviously wanted.

His error lay in not grasping the enormity of what he was now up against, the intransigence of a skilled group of organizers of dissent prepared to go to almost any length to get their way. He underestimated his opponents, and the effectiveness of the combination of intense fanaticism about goals and maximum flexibility in the means of fighting for them. When he did identify them, he overestimated the willingness of faculty moderates to dissociate themselves from the radical student leadership.

It is at this point that he should have brought the Faculty Senate into the picture focally, entrusting to them the negotiation and implementation of the rules governing student behavior. This could have been achieved by a series of special meetings with the faculty acting as a committee of the whole. Had faculty committees taken over discussions with all student groups, the duly elected, like the Associated Students of the University of California, as well as the FSM, their reports would have given the faculty a better idea of what the leadership of the FSM really sought. Even if matters had developed to a showdown, the faculty, except for a small group sympathetic with the ideals of the student leaders—instead of condoning the final mass illegal sit-in—would have strongly condemned it, and imposed appropriate disciplinary penalties on all who engaged in it. Strictly speaking, however, this was a problem for the chancellor working with the Berkeley faculty. Dr. Kerr could have inspired these activities without taking a more conspicuous public role than he was later forced to assume.

Dr. Kerr must have done yeoman work in restraining the Regents from taking further disciplinary action against the suspended students, inducing them to approve their reinstatement, and to authorize opening up the campus to all student political activities except organization for illegal off-campus activity. (This last phrase, as we have seen, is a mistake. But it need not have been enforced unless and until the off-campus illegal activity affected an educational interest of the university.)

With respect to the second resolution in which the Regents *instructed* the administration to bring disciplinary actions for rowdy and violent behavior connected with the events of October 1-2, Dr. Kerr's position is not clear. If the agreement with the students promised them immunity for *all* actions through October 2 and not September 30, he should have pointed that out to the Regents. If he had done so, it is not likely that they would have repudiated him. Since apparently he did not protest, he must have been honestly convinced that the agreement exempted actions only through September 30. Even so, it is hard to believe that Dr. Kerr was so unimaginative as to fail to calculate the effect of this directive, however mild and morally justified it appeared to him, on the extremist leaders and their followers, now in disarray.

So far as I have been able to discover, two of the faculty members who drafted the agreement, Professors Feuer and Glazer, were under the impression that its provisions in all likelihood promised immunity for the students through October 2. This was not written into the agreement, and they can recall only the verbal assurance of the likelihood.

This, however, is not confirmed by other participants in the negotiations. Almost no one knew at the time that the charges against the students involved acts and threats of violence by them. They thought that the offense charged was solely a violation of university regulations. Under the circumstances the students, it seems to me, were justified in believing that the immunity extended through October 2; and, if they had pleaded their cause to the faculty committee, I have no doubt that the charges against them would have been dropped despite the Regents' resolution.

The next great error was committed not, as I originally thought, by Dr. Kerr but by Governor Brown, who has long suffered from a constitutional ailment known as foot-in-the-mouth disease. As a rule the best way to handle a student sit-down is to let it run its course except where destruction of life and property is imminent.

The longer the sit-downs, the greater the hardships imposed on the other students. Sooner or later the students who had seized Sproul Hall would have been driven out by their own stink. Instead of dragging them out, the buildings should have been cordoned off, preventing for the sake of safety any further ingress after the students were in.

Just as soon as the students marched on Sproul Hall, the president should have called an emergency meeting of the Faculty Senate and the students put on notice by appropriate resolution of the faculty to vacate the premises on pain of expulsion. Perhaps this would have induced the governor to hold off bringing in the police.

Two further errors, if avoided, even after the students had been removed, might have prevented the rout of reason and the triumph of fear at the final faculty meeting. Instead of addressing the huge outdoor gathering at the Greek theater, Dr. Kerr should have called an emergency meeting of the faculty and presented the proposals of university chairmen headed by Professor Scalapino for faculty action. Negotiations with student organizations could have followed.

As Dr. Kerr knows from his labor experience, *details* cannot be worked out at a mass assembly of fifteen thousand people. Finally, Dr. Kerr should have attended the final faculty meeting and actively participated in the critical discussion of a set of proposals that a considerable section of the faculty voted for on the strength of false but artfully disseminated rumors that the proposals—which were in effect a stinging rebuke to him and an endorsement of the student action!—had his approval. He should not have been deterred by the fear that some members of the faculty might have regarded his presence as supererogatory or been discouraged by the evidence that in reaction to the police intervention a sizable portion of the faculty, by far not a majority, had turned against him. For he was defending the common cause—the integrity of the educational process, the relative autonomy of the university, and its independence from threats of coercion.

Whatever the mistakes of President Kerr and Chancellor Strong, they have suffered punishment far in excess of anything warranted—and at the hands of a faculty whom they have served better than previous administrations. President Kerr's activities have been sufficiently notable in the defense of academic freedom to earn him an award from the American Association of University Professors (AAUP), an organization so jealous of the prerogatives of faculty members that, according to one of its founders, Arthur Lovejoy, it has neglected to uphold proper *professional* standards of conduct.

One need only read the extravagant language of the resolution adopted at the national St. Louis meeting of the AAUP in the spring of 1964, praising Dr. Kerr's liberalism in thought and practice, to realize how unjustly he has been characterized by the FSM leaders and their faculty supporters.

"No man," said the Romans, "suddenly becomes base," and a "great liberal" does not become a "foul reactionary" overnight. Chancellor Edward Strong obviously made errors of judgment in September, but like President Kerr, far from being the snorting bureaucratic ogre lampooned by student leaders, he can be classified with more justice as a person with strong liberal convictions. Neither one waited until the civil-rights movement became popular to support programs extending democracy in the fields of labor, education, and public housing. That they should become the target of envenomed attack as illiberal and reactionary seems strange until we examine the position of the leading attackers.

There has been a great deal written about the generational conflict, about the sense of alienation, the absence of meaning and the meaning of its absence in an attempt to explain what happened at Berkeley. Much of it seems to me to be sheer mythology, written with a breezy dogmatism about matters of dubious relevance to the actual events and the responsibility for their occurrence.

Ideas and friendships are sufficient to sustain most students as they mature into persons. The college can supply only the first by effective teaching; students must find their own friendships. Neither one nor the other is a function merely of size. Students can be bored at a small college, and inspired at a large one, and conversely. It is the caliber of members of the faculty—their interest in teaching, and in the students as human beings—that is decisive.

What happened at Berkeley, of course, did not occur in a vacuum. But those who played the greatest role in making things happen were the leaders of the FSM. They made no bones about the fact that their aim was to bring about a situation on the Berkeley campus very much like the one that resulted in consequences of the sit-ins and strike.

They consistently refused to use available opportunities to bring about "a peaceful and orderly change" in existing regulations deemed either unnecessary or unjust. They could have petitioned the Faculty Academic Senate to hear and act on their appeals. Instead they resorted to organized illegal action, to threats of violence and some actual violence, to boycott and mass picketing that threw the university into turmoil for almost the entire fall semester and made normal educational activity impossible.

It was clear that the leaders of the FSM had hoped to get their martyrs at the time their followers put up mass resistance to the police arrest of Weinberg. They were jubilant when the police were finally called in to clear Sproul Hall.

Savio declared at the FSM rally of December 1, "We will march into Sproul Hall tomorrow and stay there until they take us off to jail."

The sit-in was to have no limited duration. In addition, a strike was proclaimed to bring "the university machine to a grinding halt" barring capitulation by the university, which Savio himself had declared would be naive to expect.

Once the police action had been taken, Savio astutely used this fact to rally additional student support. In FSM leaflets, distributed December 3, calling for "Strike!" students who opposed the sit-ins were told: *"It does not matter whether you support a particular tactic—the matter is that the police are on our campus . . . there are only two sides . . . you must choose yours . . . support your fellow students."*

The leaflets did not say, of course, that Savio's tactic was designed to bring the police on campus. This was his real hope. For it alone could bolster up the sagging morale of the FSM. No wonder he cried: "This is wonderful!" when the police began to clear Sproul Hall.

The strategy of the FSM leaders was obvious to anyone who is informed about the psychology and practice of some irresponsible factional radical groups in the United States. In broad outline, it runs something like this: Organize a Committee for Free Milk for Babies of Indigent Mothers. Couple this demand for free milk (already available through welfare agencies) with a series of *political* demands not related to free milk, like Hands Off Cuba! or Unilateral Nuclear Disarmament! or Withdraw from Vietnam! Organize a noisy sit-in on the busy premises of some office building, and arrange for maximum publicity. Refuse repeated requests to leave the seized premises. When police finally arrive to remove the demonstrators, make a great outcry that those who ordered the police in, or approved their action, are monsters opposed to free milk for babies, and to indigent mothers, too! Sometimes the slogan employed as a decoy is "Peace!" or "Free Speech!" to the embarrassment of those groups that genuinely believe in peace and free speech.

Judging by what could publicly be heard on campus, there was no basic issue of free speech at Berkeley. Speech was so free that some members of the FSM, having exhausted the vocabulary of political extremism, felt they could only enjoy their freedom by publicly reveling in the obscenities of filthy speech. And certainly after November 20, there was no doubt that all the constitutional freedoms recognized by the highest court in the land obtained. Obviously, the organization and agitation for illegal off-campus activites in the nature of the case can have no constitutional protection. The issue here is mainly who exercises the regulation. This has nothing to do with free speech.

As has been pointed out by Professor Lewis Feuer and others, the main problem of the leaders of the FSM was to find issues that would enable them to keep the situation embroiled even after the administration and Regents had made concessions retrieving their original errors. What the leaders of the FSM were obviously seeking was to bring the university to a halt not in the interests of free speech but for other reasons.

What are those reasons? The answer to this question is not simple. Listening to Savio denounce "the military-industrial complex" that allegedly dominates the university, and repeated outcries against the educational establishment, it is obvious that neither free speech nor civil rights was the basic issue in the eyes of the leaders of the FSM.

We are again indebted to Stephen Weissman for spelling this out in his article in *The New Leader.* The FSM, we are told, is making a "very complex political demand." This demand goes beyond the power to use university facilities "to organize illegal acts in the community at large." It is related to a whole series of other demands to reform and reconstruct the University of California, whose educational process has been perverted by the "contradictions" (objective, of course!) of capitalism, and of capitalism in the era of the cold war. "Big business buys researched knowledge as well as the two batches a year of technicians and intellectual servicemen needed to manage and operate the economic establishment." That is why "training replaces education" and threatens the intellectual and academic freedom of the teachers and students as well as civil rights.

Kerr is the ideologist of this system—a system whose contradictions must be "related to the more pervasive contradictions in the society at large." The faculty and students must join forces to change this system. At the very least they must "participate in making those decisions which affect them." As for the students, "they will be reluctant to advise when they have the power to bargain."

Since the Regents have refused to accept the faculty stand endorsing the FSM position, "further demonstrations are a distinct possibility," and "if this obstacle is hurdled, there is still the problem of weakening the structural ties between university and industry." (The word, "industry," is a slip. It should read "capitalism." After all, the young comrade has forgotten that "industry" will exist under socialism, too.)

Mr. Weissman concludes: "In place of a board of regents selected from and responsive to the economic establishment, the university community should be governed by persons selected by and responsible to the faculty, and where appropriate, to the student body. Only with structural changes of this type can the multiversity be resisted."

For the moment let us not assess the validity of these ideas—it would be less cruel to ignore some of them than to take them seriously—but appraise their significance for the FSM as a movement. Mr. Weissman is the Chairman of the Berkeley Graduate Co-ordinating Committee—the largest single group in the FSM. This is an official leader's view of what the FSM is after!

I doubt whether more than a handful of students and faculty members are aware of these goals of the FSM—goals that in the eyes of the FSM leaders are furthered by any actions that bring the educational "establishment" into chaos. But in their sectarian zeal they forget that one can still oppose capitalism and war—after all, the only valid reason for supporting the cold war is to prevent a hot one!—without destroying the hard-won ideals of academic freedom.

Anyone who understands the meaning of a university and the meaning of an ideology, either in the Marxist or the more popular sense, knows that the American university has no ideology. It has mostly problems—and deficits. The greatest of its problems is to win, sometimes to preserve, its educational autonomy from all sorts of pressure groups in religion, politics, agriculture, and business—happily, not yet from politicalized student bodies. Clark Kerr is not the ideologist of the American university or even of the University of California.

The FSM, on the other hand, definitely has an ideology both in the Marxist and in the popular sense. In the Marxist sense, it imagines it is fighting a great battle for free speech, and deceives itself and others in the belief that any restrictions on act or utterance, except those imposed by a court, constitutes a denial of the sacred rights of a citizen. As well say that compulsory chapel or R.O.T.C. or Gym I violate the Bill of Rights! The leaders of the FSM also have an ideology in the popular not the Marxist sense, since they are not deceiving themselves but only their followers with their talk about free speech.

This ideology is expressed in the article by Stephen Weissman and in Mario Savio's speeches. But the fount of its soapbox puerilities is the more than fifty-year-old youth, Hal Draper, the gray eminence of the Steering Committee of the FSM.

It would not be necessary to mention Mr. Draper except for the fact that the student leaders take so much of their line from him. His pamphlet, *The Mind of Clark Kerr*, is distributed by the FSM and has been called the source book of its diatribes. It is as faithful an account of Kerr's educational ideals as Julius Streicher's caricatures of the Jews. Draper was a Trotskyist who left the Socialist party when the Trotskyists were exposed as a faction conspiring to take over the party in flagrant violation of the pledged word of their leaders to refrain from factionalism—the condition of their acceptance.

I do not know what his current political views are except that he is not an orthodox Trotskyist and no longer regards Russia as a worker's state. I recall that, like the Trotskyists, he opposed the war against Hitler. The Trotskyists offered several grounds, one of them that Roosevelt was as great if not a greater enemy of the American working class than Hitler. Whatever the grounds for Draper's position, it would have led to the enslavement of the free world, including the American working class; and whatever his political views are today, his polemical manners and style of thinking are like those of the Trotskyists. The student leaders of the FSM are indifferent or confused about doctrines—theirs is the radicalism of mood and violent gesture—but they obviously have been influenced by Draper's polemical manners and style of thinking.

The phenomenology of the Trotskyist mind reveals two compulsive tendencies. One is a desire to prove to Stalinists (today to the officials of the Communist party) that despite the denunciation of Trotskyists as counterrevolutionary traitors, they are the purest and most revolutionary of all. In consequence, in every concrete situation the Trotskyists will take the extremest position possible, always the leftest of the left. The reconstructed "Stalinists" can always be relied on for a certain degree of responsibility—to the interests of the Soviet Union; but the Trotskyists are proudly irresponsible since all they need do is trump the Stalinists with a more daring proposal.

The second compulsive tendency of the Trotskyist mind is to concentrate most of their attacks, whenever they are part of a radical coalition, on liberals and democratic socialists in order to prove that the latter are preparing the ground for fascists, or proto-fascists, or almost-fascists despite their "subjective intentions." Normally this makes for hilarious reading. This second tendency is apparent in Draper's pamphlet. According to Draper, the world view behind Kerr's book, *The Uses of the University*, is Orwellian 1984. Kerr professes that he is just a historian describing the tendencies that make for 1984. But this candor, says Draper, is a fake. It is "an intellectual imposture." Indeed, "by *adding a single sentence, Kerr's book would become the work of a proto-fascist ideologue.*" (Italics in original.)

Draper does not tell us what the sentence is and how long it would have to be but since the sentence is not there he admits that Kerr is not a proto-fascist ideologue. *But*, insists Draper, any man who accepts the future on the basis of a "scientific" prediction (even if he *doesn't* approve it) is taking a political stand. He is helping to bring that future about. Kerr, in the introduction to a book on an altogether different subject, *Industrialism and Industrial Man*, in 1960 wrote that he was presenting his views to aid understanding of this moment in history and possibly "as a guide to the next stage." This proves, says Draper in a typical abuse of context, that Kerr "is seeking to *assist* the transformation toward the New Slavery." (Italics in original.)

It turns out that even though Kerr doesn't approve, his very "mode of being" makes him a proto-fascist after all, consciously *assisting* to bring about the New Slavery. Draper gravely declares: "There is no academic right to grease the road to fascism in the name of 'scientific' detachment."

No academic right means that Kerr cannot even claim academic freedom to peddle these dangerous intellectual wares in a university. Communists, of course—even members of the Communist party, which gives instructions to its teacher members to abuse their educational trust—have a right to teach in the university. Clark Kerr, greasing the road to fascism, has not!

Mr. Draper is a librarian in a university in which Clark Kerr as president protects him from those who have the same conception of academic freedom as Mr. Draper. How lucky for Clark Kerr that he is not a librarian in a university in which Mr. Draper is president!

This is the mind that nourishes the leaders of the FSM movement. I do not wish to imply that Draper is the only influence that has played on them, even if he is the most important. Other extremist tendencies have also been present.

It is not the minds or ideas of the FSM leaders, however, that are dangerous. They need only be exposed to critical discussion. Their *actions* deserve the strongest condemnation, and on two grounds.

The first is their systematic attempt to bypass the duly constituted and democratically elected heads of the student body, the Associated Students of the University of California (ASUC), who, although sympathetic to the specific demands of the FSM, disapproved of their tactics and wished to negotiate with the administration and faculty. The student leaders of the FSM, who talked about democracy but did not practice it, in response to this criticism denigrated the ASUC as a company union.

When this response failed of its effect, they claimed that the ASUC was not representative, that the graduate students had been "disfranchised from the Student Government in 1959." ("Disfranchised" is the word also used on page 13 of the preliminary report, "The Berkeley Free Speech Controversy," prepared by a self-styled Fact-Finding Committee of Graduate Political Scientists that contains no facts prejudicial to the FSM.

The actual facts turn out to be that, far from being disfranchised, in April, 1959, the graduate students were allowed to withdraw after thirteen hundred of them had petitioned for "disassociation" from the ASUC and for relief from paying the fees involved. The move was upheld in a poll of graduate students. Finally, when the student body, misled by the leaders of the FSM and angered by the mistakes of the governor and administration, was aroused, the leaders of the FSM set out to contest the posts of the ASUC in the student elections in order to capture what they had labeled a company union.

The second, and morally the gravest, dereliction was the abuse of the principle of civil disobedience in a democracy, the needless risk of mass violence and bloodshed, thus opening the door to a politicalization of the university, which may weaken and compromise the degree of university autonomy achieved in the past. Whatever the gains of the FSM, and the situation is now back to where it was before the first ruling, they could have been achieved without the sit-downs and sit-ins.

Civil disobedience, since it violates the democratic rule that abuses in a democracy must be remedied by legal means, should be employed only in extreme situations, where no legal remedies are available, and in behalf of a great and noble cause like national freedom in India or civil freedom in the United States.

The doctrine that inspired Dr. Martin Luther King, Jr., was drawn from the teachings of Gandhi and Tolstoy. "I am here," said Gandhi before the British Court in Ahmedabad, "to invite and cheerfully submit to the highest penalty that can be inflicted upon me for what in law is a deliberate crime and what appears to me to be the highest duty of a citizen." And later to his own countrymen: "Rivers of blood may have to flow before we gain our freedom, but it must be our blood."

In summarizing the rationale of nonviolent resistance to evil, Dr. King said at Oslo:

> We will not obey unjust laws. We will do this peacefully, openly, cheerfully, because our aim is to persuade. We adopt the means of nonviolence because our end is a community at peace with itself. We will try to persuade with words, but if our words fail, we will try to persuade with our acts of civil disobedience. We will always be willing to talk and seek a fair compromise, but we are ready to suffer when necessary and even risk our lives to become witnesses to the truth as we see it.[2]

Both Gandhi and Dr. King stressed the fact that while they would not submit to unjust laws, they were prepared to submit to the penalties provided by those unjust laws.

[2] I am indebted to the writings of Dr. Milton Konvitz for these quotations on civil disobedience.

These doctrines and practices are not to be lightly invoked and trivialized by being irresponsibly injected into situations to settle complex questions on which reasonable men of goodwill can legitimately differ. Whether a rule should be formulated to forbid or command university authorities to restrict on-campus organization for off-campus illegal activities is such a question. It is a question, I have argued, on which both sides are wrong.

To throw a university into turmoil, to risk violence and bloodshed, over issues of this sort is the height of irresponsibility. Those educators, including some administrators, who have condoned these student actions, or remained discreetly silent about them while praising the rhetoric of the FSM movement as expressions of the language of social idealism, have become accomplices in educational irresponsibility.

To make matters worse, the leaders of the FSM fail to understand that the techniques of civil disobedience and the site of its action, according to Gandhi and Dr. King, must be related to the specific evil being opposed. If it is wrong to discriminate against blacks or untouchables at lunch counters or temples, it is at those places that the law must be disobeyed.

If a board of education refuses to desegregate its schools, the sit-in may be justified on its premises but not on a bridge or highway miles away used by out-of-town motorists. If a university refuses to register black students, a sit-in may be justified in its administration building, not in its boiler or fire-control rooms. If students regard the setting-up of tables on campus as a nonnegotiable issue comparable to the great causes of civil freedom and independence, their civil disobedience would be expressed by setting up tables, not by seizing the administration building or striking classes to close down the university.

And once the FSM leaders bravely defy the dreadful rules of the university and chase the administrators from their offices, the ethics of civil disobedience require that they cheerfully accept the punishment they voluntarily invited instead of making loud lamentation or whining complaint about the enforcement of the law. When Thoreau refused to pay his tax, he didn't run for the hills or refuse to plead.

It is obvious that for the FSM leaders, the sit-in as a form of civil disobedience is just a tactical "gimmick." They are not pacifists; their mentor agrees with Lenin and Trotsky about the role of pacifism in the struggle against capitalism. Aware that the trivialization of the civil-disobedience movement can only end in making them absurd, they strive with desperate rhetoric to identify their cause with the cause of the civil-rights movement in Mississippi, their danger in California with the dangers of the Mississippi martyrs; and their opponents, Kerr, Strong, and the faculty critics of the FSM, with the conscienceless Mississippi officials who have trampled the Bill of Rights into the dust. Savio's contemptuous remarks about Dr. King's principle of nonviolent civil disobedience speaks volumes about his real views on the use of violence.

What adds to the moral offensiveness of the behavior of the FSM leaders is their unexampled effrontery and arrogance. One reads with astonishment in the Heyman report of their invasion and interference with a university function as early as September 28, 1964. I know of no other faculty that would tolerate behavior of this kind, a disruption of an official meeting carried out in open defiance of requests to leave. Whoever heard of negotiations with students prefaced by ultimata from them—"Yield within twenty-four hours or else—"? Where except at political meetings is a microphone grabbed in the way Savio grabbed the microphone at the ill-fated Greek theater meeting?

"Horrendous!" he proclaims of the Regents' declaration of December 18 that even the Emergency Executive Committee of the Academic Senate, after the Senate had capitulated to the FSM at its meeting of December 8, professed to find quite encouraging on the whole.

A "sell-out" and "a violation of the spirit of the December 8 resolution," declares Miss Myra Jehlem, a member of the FSM Executive Committee, of the Report of the Academic Freedom Committee on how to implement the surrender to the FSM.

"We will sue the *New York Times*," threatened leaders of the FSM, these impassioned advocates of free speech, in their interview with Mr. Raskin of its editorial staff, for printing my original article on "Academic Freedom and the Rights of Students" (January 3, 1965).

The Berkeley episode was not only unprecedented in the history of American education; unprecedented were the gall and tone of contemptuous arrogance the leaders of the FSM took toward the administration and faculty.

"We made monkeys out of them!" crowed one of their supporters in an abusive but revealing letter to me.

And actually the leaders of the FSM were acting on a maxim that can best be rendered in a Jewish idiom: "When dealing with *yolden, chutzpah* becomes *chochmah!*" When dealing with the simple-minded, nerve becomes wisdom! Who were the simple-minded in the Berkeley situation? To answer this question we must examine the sad, sad role of the faculty at the University of California.

The role the faculty played is described by Mr. Draper in a speech (January 9, 1965) defending the leaders of the FSM, acting under his tutelage, against the charge that the FSM could have done as well or better by different methods, methods more "reasonable" and less "intransigeant."

> But it's not true. And the proof that it was not true came on December 8th, when the "intransigeants" were satisfied—weren't they, that day, when the Academic Senate's resolution was adopted, which adopted the position of the FSM. Now remember, this is what it was all about. It was this—the question of "free speech" and the rights of social and political activity—which the Academic Senate adopted. That was it. . . . And it was on this issue that, at this time, the FSM smashed the "nonnegotiable" position of President Kerr and the administration, and won the faculty to support its position.

> Now I tell you that this was a titantic achievement. It had never been achieved before by any student movement in this country. I say that as an expert on the subject. . . . I was, in the 1930s, a member of the first national committee of the American Student Union . . . In 1934 and '35, I and another chap organized the very largest of the student anti-war strikes of these years. [At these strikes, students took the Oxford Oath never to bear arms in defense of their country. Hitler was already rearming!]

And I tell you solemnly that nowhere, at no time in this
country, has any student protest ever scored such a smashing
achievement [as this one] over a hostile administration.

Mr. Draper is wrong in his dogmatic contention that no other
method but the violation of law would have succeeded in modify-
ing university policy. After all, community and legislative opposition to Communist party speakers on campus was much more
vehement than to illegal student picketing for civil rights for off
campus. Yet Dr. Kerr had been able to reverse Regents policy
without benefit of student sit-ins. Had they occurred, the ban
probably would never have been rescinded. And even before
that, under President Sproul in 1956, faculty and students had
been able to revise Rule 17, the regulation that barred political
activity on campus, *without* any sit-ins.

Nonetheless, Draper is justified in claiming a smashing victory.
It was a victory that, with the help of the overwhelming majority
of the faculty, smashed the traditions of orderly educational
process and opened the gates to the politicalization of the American university system. Although the leaders of the FSM may not
press their luck further, their actions will probably inspire others.

How did all this come about? Certain relevant facts must be
considered. The first is that the Faculty Senate was originally
vested by the state legislature with disciplinary authority in enforcement of university rules. It subsequently relinquished this
power formally to the Regents, who then entrusted it to the
administration.

The faculty, however, could always express its position on
matters that had a bearing on educational policy, which is still
officially in its province. The issues of substance and discipline
created by the conflict between the FSM and the administration
were definitely within the purview of educational policy.
There was nothing to prevent the faculty from taking a stand
on these issues or considering appeals made to it. And it did take
a stand!

On several occasions before the final FSM sit-down, it condemned the use of "force and violence" on the campus but
without specific reference to the FSM. It also failed to repudi-

ate the action of the administration, which it could have and
should have done, at its October meeting. It referred the issue
and problems to its Academic Freedom Committee. At its
meeting of November 24, it *defeated* two resolutions. The first
motion, defeated by a vote of 274 to 261, proposed to limit university regulation of student speech and activity only to the
extent "necessary to prevent undue interference with other university affairs." The second resolution defeated sought to establish a new faculty committee to deal specifically with student political conduct.

Up to this point, the majority of the faculty, whatever its
doubts about the administration, seemed opposed to the FSM
primarily because of its resort to the disorderly and illegal tactics
of campus sit-downs.

After the students were removed by the police from Sproul
Hall, an agreement was reached between the department chairmen and President Kerr to restore educational peace and order on
the campus (the so-called Scalapino proposals). These were presented at a Convocation of Faculty and students at the Greek
theater on December 7. The chairmen were overwhelmingly behind the Scalapino proposals and discussed them with their re-
spective departments before the convocation. Although there was
some disagreement with these proposals expressed in some departments, there is little doubt that they were acceptable to most
of the faculty.

Of the five points in the Scalapino proposals, the two that are
most relevant in understanding the nature of the subsequent
triumph of the FSM leaders are, first, the promise of complete
disciplinary amnesty for the actions of all students involved in the
events prior to and inclusive of December 3, and, second, the statement that *"the Department Chairmen believe that the acts of
civil disobedience on December 2 and 3 were unwarranted and
that they obstruct rational and fair consideration of the grievances brought forward by the students."* [My italics.]

What the mass meeting in the Greek theater was supposed to
accomplish has remained mystifying to me as well as to others
who have described its proceedings. And once Savio had reached
the microphone, he should have been permitted to talk and not
been dragged away and then given access to it again—an opportunity he cleverly exploited by substituting a brief announce-

ment for his intended harangue, thus giving the impression to some naive minds that all he had desired in the first place was to cooperate with the purposes of the meeting. He had made no request to be permitted to broadcast an announcement.

At the final Academic Senate meeting the next day, not by so much as a word did the adopted resolutions condemn the tactics and behavior of the FSM. On the contrary, a motion to amend these resolutions, which was interpreted as a minimal rebuke for the FSM, was overwhelmingly defeated.

The faculty thus explicitly refused to condemn "the lawlessness" of the FSM action. Coupled with the demand for a complete amnesty for the arrested students, this was tantamount to an *approval* of the sit-in actions. What was condemned, in effect, were the policies of the Regents, President Kerr and his entire administration, the past policies of the faculty itself, and the position of the hundred-odd members of the faculty who opposed this capitulation to the demands of the leaders of the FSM. Draper was justified in crowing over the smashing victory he and his disciples had won.

The mechanics of the victory depended upon a hard core of about two hundred members of the faculty who were in complete sympathy with the FSM from the very beginning and whose leaders were obviously in touch with the leaders of the FSM. This group met the day before the meeting at the Greek theater to plan the strategy to win the Academic Senate to endorse the FSM position.

After the meeting at the Greek theater, "word is spread that he [President Kerr] has endorsed the resolutions of the two hundred," says "The Report of the Fact-Finding Committee of Graduate Political Scientists" (page 9). The report does not say that the "word" about Kerr's approval was false, and that those who spread it were leading members of "'the two hundred." The teachers were learning factional political tactics from their students.

At any rate, the Academic Freedom Committee of the Senate accepts the resolutions. At the meeting of the senate, the next day, one of the leading members of "the two hundred" gives his colleagues the definite and uncontradicted impression that the administration itself is behind these proposals! The department chairmen sit silent. President Kerr is not present to speak for himself or his administration. The vote rolls in to the cheers and jeers of a huge crowd of students and nonstudents massed outside the assembly hall of what must be regarded as the strangest faculty meeting in the history of American education.

It is this *approval* of student lawlessness on the part of the faculty, no matter what its alleged causes—ignorance of the facts, resentment against the administration, weariness with the whole business, conformism, desire to curry favor with students —that constitutes the most shocking aspect of the role of the faculty in the Berkeley episode.

The misled students have the excuse of youth; and the administration, that it didn't understand until too late the fundamental political orientation of the FSM leadership. But the faculty took its position on the only issue that was clearly defined in the situation, *viz.*, whether the complex of problems arising from the effects of speech and action, on campus or off campus, on the educational objectives of the university, should be resolved by educational means or by student resort to civil disobedience. Its vote can only serve to encourage further lawlessness.

Unfortunately there were even some individuals among the faculty who abused their position of academic authority. to help the FSM. Some called off classes to make the student strike more effective. One assistant professor listed the term "civil disobedience" among the main topics to be discussed in his course on biochemistry and coolly defended its relevance to the subject matter on the grounds that he was concerned with the "social" organization of cells.

Another professor of biochemistry included as one of five questions on his final examination: "In your opinion, what were the events, conditions, acts, and other factors that led to the campus turmoil of the last few months and, in particular, to the sit-in at Sproul Hall and the campus-wide strike?" The professor explained that he had included this question because some students had told him they were behind in their studies in consequence of the FSM activity.

He defended himself against criticism on the ground that the question was optional. Those who could answer the other questions based on their knowledge of the course work were not compelled to answer it.

It is difficult to tell which shows greater contempt for the standards of academic integrity—the actions themselves or the justifications offered for them.

In view of this behavior, I have been asked on what grounds I can justify my educational philosophy that the faculty should have the ultimate authority to determine all basic policies of education and discipline in the university.

I can only reply by paraphrasing a remark of Justice Frankfurter—the appeal from the decision of an unenlightened faculty must be made to the decision of an enlightened faculty. There is no need for administrative or political action that would further undermine the relative autonomy of the university. The need is for further reflection by the faculty.

Nonetheless, if and when a faculty persistently refuses to exercise its responsibility, or systematically abuses it, it runs the risk of provoking representatives of the public, which after all underwrites its cost heavily, into actions directed against the abuses.

In what follows, I shall attempt to contribute to the process of reflection by examining not the causes of the actions of the Berkeley faculty but the grounds offered in defense of them.

A considerable mass of literature by members of the Berkeley faculty justifying their actions already exists. That they should have felt it necessary to explain and to defend their refusal to condemn student lawlessness is natural enough in view of the bewilderment of their colleagues elsewhere. But the character of the explanations only increases one's bewilderment.

I restrict myself to a series of statements published by some leading members of the faculty to explain matters to "the troubled friends of the university" and to the plea submitted to the justice of the municipal court by approximately two hundred members of the Berkeley faculty urging that the legal action against the students—not university sanctions, which had all been lifted— be dismissed on simple grounds of *justice*.

A lengthy statement by Professor Charles Sellers flatly states that "the great majority of the faculty heartily disapproved the methods and tactics of the FSM." Why, then, didn't the great majority say so? Because "seeing faults on both sides, [it] nevertheless scrupulously sought to avoid praise or censure." But this is a complete non sequitur.

First, the faculty could have condemned *both* administration policy and the FSM behavior; second, its resolutions constituted a sharp repudiation of administrative and previous faculty policy, and a complete vindication of the FSM, whose cries of total victory could be heard as the vote was tallied (the very fact that Professor Sellers explains at such lengths is an indication of how the faculty vote was interpreted); and third, there was no evidence that the FSM leaders cared a farthing whether their tactics were condemned, provided they received their amnesty and their policy was approved (even after their victory, Draper, Savio, and Weissman spoke with utter contempt of the faculty as frightened into agreement by the shock tactics of sit-in and strike).

Professor Sellers then adds that the policies expressed in the resolutions adopted by the faculty "do not condone and would not permit the kind of student demonstrations that have occurred on the Berkeley campus this semester."

If this is true, it could and should have been said as part of the motion or in a preamble; it would be merely dotting the *i*'s and crossing the *t*'s of the motion. But it is not true! What his words suggest is the hope of a sizable section of the faculty that if the university yielded to the FSM, their leaders would be surfeited with their success, and cease from further disorders.

The next statement is by Professor Henry Nash Smith. This one is entitled "Why Has the Berkeley Faculty Failed to Condemn Violations of the Law by Students?" I wish I could quote it in its entirety. It is like the story of the man who maintains he has returned the same borrowed pot three times and then ends up denying he ever borrowed it.

First, the faculty did not want to condemn the FSM sit-in at Sproul Hall because the country might think that Professor Smith and his colleagues were opposed to civil rights in the South! As if a clear statement of the distinction between a sit-in in behalf of sacred human rights and a sit-in to oppose a request to appear before a civilized faculty committee for a hearing were beyond the rhetorical powers of a distinguished faculty!

Second, the idea of "law" has become in the eyes of many

respectable citizens "problematical." One cannot answer the question: "Do you condemn all violations of law?" with a simple "Yes" or "No"! But no one proposed that the faculty declare that it condemned *all* violations of law! The question was a *specific* violation of a *specific* law with respect to a *specific* issue, the consequences of which disrupted the entire university.

Thirdly, "some men learned in the law believe that present university restrictions on advocacy are probably unconstitutional." Some men who are even more learned in the law emphatically deny it—but the whole issue of constitutionality is here irrelevant because the question Professor Smith started out to explain is not why the faculty voted to abandon the restrictions but why it failed to condemn what he himself calls violations of law!

Is he suggesting that some men learned in the law believe that the seizure of a university building, in reply to a summons to a hearing from a faculty committee, is constitutional and that to condemn the seizure is not?

Finally, although admitting that a "judicious condemnation" of *both* administration policy and student illegal behavior is "perfectly comprehensible and has a certain moral grandeur," he believes the faculty is justified in begging off from doing this understandable thing because judicious condemnation, even when austerely phrased, can only be expressed in this situation as "invective."

What extraordinary things can be heard in California! Why "invective"? After all, the policy of the administration was condemned by the faculty without "invective" or even explicit mention? Yet everybody knew who was meant. Why could not lawless behavior on campus also have been condemned, even without mention of the FSM? Everybody would have known who was meant. It did not require "moral grandeur" to condemn the FSM and the administration. It required only a little wisdom, a sense of fairness, and courage!

This brings us to a printed flyer, widely circulated, from eight faculty members of the University of California at Berkeley and addressed to colleagues and friends in the state-wide university, to members of other colleges and universities, and to fellow citizens. It lists the propositions adopted at the Academic Senate meeting of December 8 and tells what they mean.

The collective statement is followed by eight individual statements. The collective statement is a gem of modesty—almost humility—designed to reassure everyone that nothing very important has happened. "Very little change" in the current Regents rules governing political activity is involved. "It is meant to apply only to the Berkeley campus." No need to take alarm elsewhere. The faculty has merely "suggested one small but important procedural change—that disciplinary jurisdiction over breaches of regulation concerning the time, place, and manner of student political activity be transferred to a committee of the Academic Senate." Just a big bang—over an important trifle!

I regret to observe that this simply does not correspond to the facts. There is no reference whatsoever in the collective statement to the meaning of the all important, the key proposition Number 3, the first two sentences of which read:

> That the content of speech or advocacy should not be restricted by the University. Off-campus student political activities shall not be subject to University regulation.

Both are flatly contrary to the Regents' statements of November 20 and December 18. The first Regents' statement proscribes student advocacy of unlawful off-campus political activity—which illustrates a favorite maxim of F. H. Bradley that the opposte of an absurdity may be every whit as absurd. The second Regents' statement, of December 18, asserts that no restrictions beyond the purview of the First and Fourteenth amendments are envisaged, but there are plenty of restrictions *within* the purview of these amendments. Some of them were spelled out in Professor Lewis Feuer's amendment (which was defeated) to Proposition 3.

Professor Philip Selznick claims that the action of the Berkeley faculty upholds "the highest ideals of university education and educational life." He fails, unfortunately, to relate those ideals to the FSM sit-ins and student strike—which he elsewhere characterizes as "direct action, pressure, and intimidation." (*Commentary*, March, 1965.) "A great many rules and some state laws were broken," he admits. Regrettable, to be sure, but, he adds, we must "get at the root of the trouble." He leaves the matter there.

*One* of the roots of the trouble is a mode of thinking that he himself illustrates and that seems to be shared by others. It is expressed in one of the most remarkable sentences to have come out of the situation at Berkeley. "He who insists on obedience to rules should be ready to justify the rules themselves." The context suggests that Selznick interprets this to mean that unless a rule or law seems justifiable to us we are under no obligation to obey it.

This is the formula of anarchy. No ordered community life is possible on this basis, for it means that if a minority is outvoted on any proposed law, it is absolved from any obligation to obey it. This goes beyond the extremism of those who say that *unjust* laws should never be obeyed, for it implies that *foolish* laws, which we are not prepared to justify, should also be disobeyed. It was thinking of this kind that contributed to the self-righteous intransigence of the FSM leaders and their faculty supporters. From a moral point of view, one cannot take an unqualified position here. If we distinguish between a substantive law and a procedural rule, we may obey some substantive laws that are unjust or foolish or both because the violation of the procedural rule may lead to morally worse consequences.

Sometimes the substantive law is so morally outrageous that we are prepared to accept the consequences to ourselves of violating the procedural rules. Selznick does not say which laws or rules he believes the FSM students were justified in breaking. Setting up the tables on campus in defiance of a foolish rule or seizing the administration building or resisting the police arrest of Weinberg? One could make a case for the first, for had Selznick and the faculty taken a firm stand in October, instead of December, against the first administrative order, events would have taken a different turn. That he is now compelled to justify disobedience to *any* unjust or foolish law indicates the desperate intellectual straits to which he is reduced in his attempt to gloss over the real contempt by the FSM leaders for the democratic process, concealed beneath their ritualistic invocations to principles of free speech.

Professor Carl Schorske must be applauded for the brave opening sentence of his *apologia*. "The primary task of the University of California has always been and must always be teaching, learning and research—*not* political activity.'" But alas!—with this effort he falls back exhausted. He, too, repeats mechanically that the university cannot regulate "the content" of expression, from which it would follow that, *e.g.*, if a student falsely charges that his teacher demanded a bribe for passing him or her, "the content" of the statement presumably is no business of the university.

His common sense reasserts itself in his final sentence: "Offenses against the University community should be punished by the University."

Excellent! Now suppose these offenses are committed off campus! But he has just voted for a resolution that *forbids* the university to regulate any off-campus political activities. "Political" is an umbrella word under which almost any kind of activities can be brought, from hazing Jewish or black students, to destroying the books and papers of politically unpopular teachers, and all sorts of things one reads about in the press concerning the off-campus behavior of students in the politicalized universities of other countries.

Professor Schorske surely cannot rule out the possibility of the occurrence of off-campus student activities, offensive to the university community. Some of these offenses may not even be technically illegal. Students may organize fraternities based on principles of segregation the faculty declares harmful to the common educational interest. These off-campus derelictions, according to the resolutions for which he voted, are not subject to university regulation.

Professor Tussman's *apologia* is even more disappointing because as a political philosopher one expects a little more intellectual sophistication from him than from his colleagues concerning the key Proposition 3. But he blandly says it is a "sensible" rule that "obviates most of the difficulties in this sensitive area."

It is a pity he leaves the difficulties unmentioned. There are many ways of obviating difficulties. What is wanted is a rule that will help solve difficulties that cannot be properly obviated. What is not wanted is a rule that will create additional difficulties. And this rule does.

Tussman concludes by saying that this rule "expresses the conviction that ours is an institution whose *proper* mode of dealing with the mind is *educational,* not coercive." The conviction is commendable but unfortunately the rule does not express it, since it is obviously concerned with parceling out the sphere of disciplinary *coercion* over student *activities*, on campus and off campus. Tussman's conviction would be relevant as a ground for the condemnation of "radically inappropriate means" of dealing with "problems of mind and spirit," means such as those used by the FSM—sit-downs and student strike, in answer to a request to appear for a *hearing*.

Tussman should agree because he supported the Scalapino proposals that declared the acts of civil disobedience of October 2 and 3 unwarranted in that they obstruct "rational and fair consideration" of the issues. He therefore owes his colleagues an explanation of why this proposal or some variant of it is absent from the list of propositions whose adoption he justifies. Not only is his position inconsistent but his efforts, as reported in the press, to ingratiate himself with the leadership of the FSM, seem highly unedifying.

Professor Miles gives the faculty three *A*'s for supporting three principles; Advocacy, Academic Responsibility, and Amnesty. Since the faculty made no mention of the students' "lawlessness," she could have added Amnesia. The principle of Advocacy is simple. It is "the citizen's constitutional right to *speak* and be heard without the limitations set upon *action*." Professor Miles undoubtedly is aware of what happened to the dean of women at Stanford who did no more than *speak* about the purported behavior of the young male English teachers toward their attractive coeds. And what the dean spoke about wasn't a capital offense either! And yet if she hadn't resigned, since her speech was deemed false, she would have suffered from some "limitation."

The joint declaration of Dean Maslach and Professor S. A. Schaaf makes one wonder what the faculty voted for so overwhelmingly at their final meeting. Is it possible that the excitement inside and din outside were so confusing that a considerable number didn't understand what they were voting for or against? I realize that this is a startling suggestion to make about an assembly of distinguished minds. But my justification is the final paragraph of their joint statement:

> The Berkeley Senate's policy recommendation is the direct
> followup of the substance of the interim administrative

agreement made between all Berkeley Department Chairmen and President Kerr, which was announced to the entire Berkeley campus community at the Greek theater meeting on Monday.

As far as the plain English of the texts of the two sets of propositions goes, it would be far more accurate to say that the second constituted a repudiation of the first.

We need not consider in detail the statement of Professor Henry Nash Smith because we have already analyzed a longer one by him. He gives three reasons for voting for the propositions: (1) *They are in conformity with the United States Constitution.* But so were the Scalapino proposals. So are the Regents' rules. Constitutionality is not relevant here, only unconstitutionality. (2) *Alternative policies are unworkable.* This is false. The *de facto* policy in existence before Dean Towle's arbitrary administrative ruling was workable. It could have been reinstated without the proclamation of the silly and doctrinaire key proposition Number 3. Finally, (3) *the civil rights movement expresses the moral idealism of a whole generation of young Americans.* True, but irrelevant.

It was not the moral idealism of the FSM that was objectionable but what they *did* on October 1-2 and December 3-4. Surely even Smith cannot believe that moral idealism is a justification for any or all actions, although he sometimes gives that impression. Nor can the support some leaders of the FSM gave to the Filthy Speech Movement, on the ground that under the faculty-approved resolution the content of speech was beyond control, be considered an expression of moral idealism. If Mr. Smith has condemned the Filthy Speech Movement, which developed after the above pronouncement, it has escaped my attention.

Professor Parkinson is another English scholar who also cuts difficult Gordian knots of constitutional law with simple, straightforward speech. "There is no such thing as more or less freedom; men either have freedom or they do not, and limitation of the content of speech destroys freedom." Since there is no legal system in the entire world that does not limit to some degree the content of speech, we must conclude that men are nowhere free. Fortunately for mankind, however, freedom is not like pregnancy. There *are* degrees of it.

Professor Parkinson's second point is that there should be an amnesty for everybody on the Berkeley campus—administration, faculty, and students. Few would contest this. He should, therefore, have moved an amendment to Proposition 1 that amnestied *only* the students. Since this proposition provides for the remission of punishment for the students' lawlessness rather than for the extinction of their offense, the amendment could have contained an expression of disapproval of the offense without curdling the charity that inspired the original motion.

I have left to the last the statement of Professor Chamberlain, the eminent physicist and Nobel Laureate, because of a reluctance to criticize the words of so distinguished a scientist. They provide a paradigm case of the phenomenon of nontransference of training from one field to another.

Constitutional law and politics are fields in which apparently everyone is an expert. There are so many independent variables involved that many worthy persons imagine that neither study nor thought is necessary to discuss problems in these fields intelligently. What adds to one's acute embarrassment is that Professor Chamberlain's nontransference of scientific training extends to a field in which most parents on the basis of experience acquire some expertise—*viz.*, child psychology. Professor Chamberlain voted for the resolutions because, as he interprets what he heard the FSM students say, it went something like this:

> Show us you do not have to treat us always as children, but more as adults when we achieve adult skills and facility. Show us that you can, if we insist, treat us like men and women, each responsible for his actions. Show us that we do not have to be treated as children who now and then follow some "insidious" leader.

But surely Professor Chamberlain knows as a parent that the first principle in treating children who want to be regarded as adults is actually to hold them responsible for their conduct, not to apologize or extenuate what they do on the ground that they were children who really meant well; to apply the same rules to them as to other adults in the same relevant situations; to expect them to take the consequences of their deliberate conduct, not necessarily always to punish them but to make them understand when they violate laws that their acts are punishable, and that, even when amnestied, they cannot be continued with impunity.

I agree with Professor Chamberlain that the leaders of the FSM were responsible according to their own lights, that they were prepared to accept the appropriate punishment for their actions in breaking the law. The question at issue is the responsibility of the faculty in letting them get away with it. To this Professor Chamberlain does not address himself.

On the question of responsibility, Professor J. ten Broek, and others, have taken up the gauntlet. In their statement to the court before whom the FSM students were brought for violating the law, they claim that all the charges against the students should be dismissed on grounds of *justice*. The "lawlessness" of the FSM is not denied but the responsibility for it is laid completely at the door of the administration. The FSM students are idealized in glowing language that goes beyond the encomiums their leaders pay themselves. They are hailed as an expression of the highest idealism and promise of American life—as inheritors of the legacy of a martyred President, "answering in force but not in violence" his trumpet call for struggle against the enemies of mankind.

The rhetoric of the document is very strong but it is correspondingly weak in factual accuracy and in the analysis of the key issues. Its most original feature is its discussion of academic freedom and its conclusion that its rights and privileges extend to students as well as teachers. This is reached by an elementary but eloquently expressed confusion between what is desirable on educational grounds and what is entailed by academic freedom.

The factual inaccuracy of the report is manifested as much by what is omitted as by what is misstated. Omitted is the fact that the student leaders were summoned on authority of the Regents to answer charges of *violent* lawlessness. Omitted is the record of the Academic Senate motions of November 24 that in effect voted down the demand of the FSM. Omitted is reference to the behavior of the FSM to the ASUC. Misstated is the truth about the policy of the administration, which for all its errors was not one of consistent "vindictiveness" but of compromise, concession, and retreat from its foolish positions. Misstated is the implication that all the gains won by the FSM, gains that had almost restored the situation in September, were suddenly snatched from it by the summons of its leaders to a hearing. Misstated crudely is the position of the United States Supreme Court on the illegality of sit-ins in *defiance* of laws that are constitutional.

Sit-ins in defiance of local laws that are unconstitutional is one thing; sit-ins in defiance of constitutional law, quite another. Even the FSM leaders do not go so far as to say that the state laws that forbid the seizure of public buildings are unconstitutional. And misstated to the point of daring invention is the reference to the alleged action of the state legislature in amending the trespass provisions of the state law and which would make the FSM sit-ins legal!

These omissions and misstatements—and I have not listed them all—are extreme even for a partisan brief. They have one purpose, to indict the administration as totally blameworthy for the events at Berkeley, to exonerate the faculty from any blame, and to present the FSM as completely innocent of wrongdoing, as harnassed into lawlessness against its will.

The truth is that the administration's faults are very grave, the students' behavior out of all proportion to them, and the conduct of the faculty, in what it at first failed to do and in what it finally did, the most irresponsible of all.

What is odd to the point of being bizarre is the attempt of the signers of the brief to describe the behavior of the students as motivated by a concern for academic freedom:

> The recent events on the Berkeley campus were an expression of the deep concern of students for their rights of membership both in the university community and in the larger political society. It is a concern intimately connected to academic freedom.

But academic freedom cannot exist if the teaching, research, discussion, or dialogue is disrupted by pressures, demonstrations, and strikes. The faculty is on record as deploring actions threatening the integrity of the educational process. No one interfered with the student's freedom to learn. There was interference with the freedom to teach. There was no interference with the students' freedom to learn, even with their "freedom to learn by doing," after the Regents' resolutions of November 20, unless the freedom to learn by doing means freedom to do as one pleases.

The writers of the brief not only falsely invoke the decisions of the Supreme Court and the memory of a martyred President to justify the lawlessness of the FSM, they cite some words from Justice Frankfurter, the great opponent of absolutism, for the same purpose:

> It is the special task of teachers to foster those habits of open-mindedness and critical inquiry which alone make for responsibility in citizens, who in turn make possible an enlightened and effective public opinion. . . . The unwarranted inhibition upon the free spirit of teachers . . . has an unmistakable tendency to chill that free play of the spirit which all teachers ought especially to cultivate and practice; it makes for caution and timidity in their associations by potential teachers.

If one were to assess the events at Berkeley in the light of these sentiments—where, one asks, will one find the "openmindedness" and "the critical inquiry" that make for "responsible citizens"? In the lawlessness of the students who refused to continue the process of negotiations? In their failure to appeal to the faculty? In their threats to close down the university? Do not such actions inhibit "the free spirit of teachers"?

Professor ten Broek and his colleagues escape from drawing the proper conclusions from the above passage by professing to believe that "the academic freedom" of the students has been violated.

In order to make the notion of academic freedom applicable to students, they overlook the fact that the students' freedom to learn presupposes but is not presupposed by the teacher's freedom to teach. Where teachers have no freedom to teach, students have no freedom to learn, but even where teachers have freedom to teach, students may be deprived of freedom to learn by poverty or other social evils that as citizens we must abolish. But where students are deprived of freedom to learn because of poverty or discrimination of various kinds, it is an abuse of language to say that they are being deprived of their academic freedom. They are being deprived of their human rights.

The faculty friends of the FSM seize upon the phrase, "potential teachers," and argue that since students are "potential teachers," they are also part of the academic community, "scholars-in-training." As "scholars-in-training," they are "apprentice or junior members of the scholarly community," and therefore are entitled to the rights and privileges of academic freedom, which must be enjoyed by the educational community as a whole.

Every step in the argument is a non sequitur. And even if it were not contested on logical and factual grounds, all it would show is that students as "junior" members would be entitled not to "academic freedom" in its proper sense but, so to speak, to a "junior" kind of academic freedom.

The view that because students are *potential* teachers, they enjoy or should enjoy the academic freedom of teachers is absurd on its face. As well argue that because children are potentially parents, they already enjoy or should enjoy parental or conjugal rights of a sort. Proper parental guidance and education will someday, we hope, make it possible for children to live better lives as parents than if they are given bad education and bad examples, but it would be ridiculous to recognize their claim to parental authority now. More children will become parents than students professors, but in any case their functions, duties, and privileges are distinct.

Academic freedom may not be appreciated by teachers; it may not even be properly used: it may sometimes be abused in order to teach objectionable things or not to teach true or useful things. Nonetheless, it does not affect the validity of the ideals of academic freedom. Just as the best remedy for the abuses of a democracy is a better democracy, so the best remedy for the weaknesses of academic freedom is the strengthening of its safeguards.

In the twentieth century, academic freedom at different times in different countries is endangered not only by capitalists, politicians, and commissars but by students, too. In any university worthy of the name, students can have no academic freedom to violate the academic freedom of their teachers.

Another false cry is that the university wishes to isolate the students from the life of the community. Of course, the university is part of the social order, and the broad struggle for civil rights, equality, and human welfare will catch up students and teachers both, in its surge and sweep. On the other hand, the leaders of the FSM are highly critical of the university's existing relations to the rest of society—to business, to government, to labor, defense, medicine, and other social groups.

It is not hypocrisy to assert that the FSM wishes to take the ideas and ideals it has acquired at the university to the community and yet, at one and the same time, to condemn the multiple ways in which the university now functions in serving and criticizing society? No, the apparent hypocrisy is resolved by the leaders of the FSM in the expectations that the universities will not merely get into the social struggle—they are already in it!—but that they can be made to get in on the right side of the class struggle on which they firmly believe social progress mainly depends.

*The fact that the university today functions as the source of more criticism and dissent of the reigning orthodoxies and confusions than any other segment of society is ignored by the leaders of the FSM or interpreted as a carefully tolerated activity to channel off peacefully the discontent endemic to a capitalist society.* They confuse the legitimate concern with political issues, their discussion and study, which should be an important part of the curriculum of the university, with the politicalization of the university, which would spell its ultimate death.

The views, arguments, and positions of the leaders of the FSM would hardly be worth the effort involved in analyzing them, if they were alone in holding them. But, as the *amicus curiae* brief or statement presented to the municipal court of the Berkeley-Albany Judicial District indicates, they are also held by 25 percent of the voting faculty of the University of California at Berkeley. A still larger number, although not wholly in agreement, probably supports the major beliefs and actions of the FSM. Having declared itself on December 8, the faculty is not likely to reverse itself and condemn the lawlessness of the FSM, thereby repeating the blunder of the administration in refusing to acknowledge error.

On the contrary, the attitude will harden. Original doubts of the wisdom of the position among many members of the faculty will disappear as the necessity to justify their actions to their colleagues on other campuses arises. In time even the history of the events will be transformed. Already legends are springing up not only at Berkeley but elsewhere. It is not likely that there will be additional disturbances at Berkeley.

In the next period, the faculty will shut its eyes and ears to almost anything the students will say or do. The leaders of the FSM know that they have milked the operation for all it is worth politically. They, their friends, and congeners will seek greener campuses to widen their sphere of activity. No matter what the cause of student discontent, whether justified or not, the memory of Berkeley will be invoked.

More important than the events at Berkeley are the issues they pose. I am convinced that on the proper answers to them depend the future relations between faculties and student bodies of American universities. The primary purpose of the university is to pursue the truth and to teach it, subject only to the discipline of the rational methods of achieving the truth. It may have other moral and social purposes, too, but none incompatible with this basic ideal of liberal education from Socrates to John Dewey. All the other legitimate goals of university education are peripheral and can be achieved by indirection. However exalted, they cannot justify the betrayal of the basic ideal.

# THE TROJAN HORSE
# IN AMERICAN EDUCATION

I am here reproducing an article that appeared in the *Saturday Review* of April 19, 1969, a periodical that has consistently held the view that the student rebellion, despite its violence, "has sprung from valid causes and might not be without positive effects," to quote from the editorial disclaimer that prefaced the article. The article ties together a number of points by way of summary in presenting a liberal's "dissenting view" (as the editors put it) from the ritualistic liberalism that accepts with a kind of sadism the degradation of liberal values because it assumes there are no enemies on the left or no real enmity among those who *call* themselves "left."

Wherever American educators meet today, there is one theme of overriding concern that shadows their deliberations even when it is not on the agenda of discussion. This is the mounting wave of lawlessness, often cresting into violence, that has swept to many campuses.

Shortly after the riotous events at the University of California at Berkeley in 1964, I predicted that in consequence of the faculty's refusal to condemn the student seizure of Sproul Hall, the administration building, American higher education would never be the same again . . . I confess, however, to surprise at the rapidity of the change, if not its direction, and by the escalation of the violence accompanying it.

Equally significant in determining the changing intellectual

climate of our universities are some of the secondary consequences of the accelerating disorders. Among them are infectious,
sometimes paralyzing, fear in administrative ranks lest their campuses erupt; confusion, bewilderment, and divided loyalties among
faculties, together with some *Schadenfreude* over the humiliation of their administrations at the hands of disrespectful student
militants; outright encouragement of student violence by disaffected younger members of teaching staffs; sustained apathy
among the majority of students whose education has been interrupted by radical activists; and the mixture of rage and disgust
among the general public, whose political repercussions already
have been damaging to the cause of higher education.

In California, the indignation of citizens over campus violence
has brought Governor Reagan to the peak of his popularity.
More alarming, proposed bonds for educational expansion have
been voted down. Of approximately 186,000 communications
received to date by the trustees and colleges in the state system
more than 98 percent were against campus disruption. More than
seventy separate bills, some of dubious wisdom, have been introduced in the Senate and Assembly to deal with disruption of
campus activities by students and faculty. Similar bills are in the
hoppers of other state legislatures, twenty in Wisconsin alone.

The situation in the East, although not marked by the same
degree of physical violence (arson, bombings, beatings), educationally is equally grave. Some recent incidents at New York
University, and its sister institution in New York City, Columbia,
mark the extent to which violence has invaded the university
and rational disciplinary restraints have been eroded.

Last December, Nguyen Huu Chi, the Ambassador of South
Vietnam, visited New York University as an invited guest
speaker. At a given signal, members of the Students for a Democratic Society from N.Y.U. and Columbia invaded the hall,
stormed the stage, physically assaulted the ambassador, and completely disrupted the meeting.

Thereupon, they proceeded to another floor, battered down
the doors leading to the podium of a meeting hall where James
Reston, executive editor of the *New York Times*, was about to
deliver the annual Homer Watts Lecture before an audience of
six hundred under the auspices of the Alumni Association. The

rampaging students spurned an invitation from Mr. Reston to state their objections to what they thought he was going to say, and by threats of violence forced the cancellation of the meeting.

Two students were suspended pending action by the University Senate, and after a careful hearing, at which they refused to appear, were expelled in March. The leaders of the SDS publicly applauded the disruptions, declaring that they disapproved of the positions of the government of South Vietnam and the *New York Times* on the Vietnam War. Most shocking of all, nine members of the faculty at Washington Square in a letter to the student paper endorsed the breaking-up of the meeting of the South Vietnamese ambassador. Although they called the disruption of Mr. Reston's meeting "unfortunate" (as if it were an accident!), they strongly condemned President James M. Hester on the ground that "we do not believe that the disruption of the Reston speech warrants suspension of the students." They had not a single word of forthright or vigorous criticism of the SDS attack on Chi. The effect of their letter can only be to incite further student violence.

It is noteworthy that many meetings and rallies *in support* of the Vietcong and North Vietnam have been held without incident.

At Columbia, Acting President Andrew W. Cordier had petitioned the courts through the dean of the Law School to dismiss the criminal charges against the Columbia students arrested for serious offenses last spring. The court was assured that the university would apply appropriate disciplinary measures to those guilty. The cases were therefore dismissed.

In December, a Columbia College disciplinary tribunal of two teachers—one of them an instructor serving as chairman—two students, and an administrator decided to impose no penalties on the students whatsoever, despite the fact that the students proudly admitted violating university regulations and, to boot, denied the authority of the tribunal to judge them. This incredible decision was taken in order "to reestablish student relationship to the university."

These students had won complete amnesty for actions that had been deemed worthy of criminal prosecution when they had occurred. Twice, hearings in the Law School were violently disrupted by invading SDS students, and the faculty members of the panel were insulted with gutter obscenities. No one even dared to suggest that disciplinary action be taken against this new wave of disruption. The administrators and many of the faculty of Columbia University for months were deeply distraught.

It appears to some observers as if the university petition to have the criminal charges dropped against the students was a ruse by the administration to ingratiate itself with the militant students, to prove its "goodwill" toward them and, in this way, buy some campus peace. If so, the strategy failed. It provoked only contempt, jeers, and a stream of foul, four-letter epithets from the militants who held out for complete amnesty from the outset.

Encouraged by the amnesty, the Columbia SDS, with aid from outsiders, began to disrupt classes; a leaflet was distributed to justify such "classroom intervention." In some instances, students tore the notes out of their teachers' hands; in others, they shouted them down. By December, according to one source, as many as thirteen "interventions" had been perpetrated.

No action was taken either by the faculty or by the administration. An inquiry from an education editor, who had gotten wind of the situation, went unanswered. No one on campus would talk for publication.

Their appetites whetted by the complaisance or timidity of their victims, the students of the SDS escalated the scale of their disruptions. *The Columbia Spectator* of February 27 reported that "Members of the SDS yesterday interrupted nearly forty classes in six University buildings."

Finally, on March 10, a public statement in response to these outrages was issued by a hundred, mostly senior, professors. In it they declared that the university had an obligation to defend itself against hooliganism. Referring to the policy of amnesty, they criticized the abandonment of disciplinary proceedings for previous serious infractions.

President Cordier immediately rushed to endorse the statement, taking care at the same time to minimize the number of class disruptions, but failing to explain why he had remained silent about the breaking-up of classes in December, although he was aware of it, and why he had welcomed the abandonment of disciplinary proceedings.

Punitive legislation, either federal or state, would be undesirable in this situation for many reasons. It would tie the government too closely to campus events and discipline at a time when a section of the academic community believes that governmental presence is already too obtrusive. Further, the effectiveness of such legislation would depend upon the cooperation of administration and faculty in enforcing it. Most important, existing statutes of the university, and the criminal law, already provide sufficient penalties (suspension, expulsion, fines, and jail for trespassing and assault) to meet disruption, if they were enforced.

Why have they not been enforced? Why has the defense of faculties against these brazen attempts to violate their academic freedom, not only by disruption, but by demands to control the content and personnel of instruction, been so feeble and long delayed? Why, as one professor observed who had helped the Berkeley rebels triumph in 1964, have administrations and faculties behaved like buffalo being shot, "looking on with interest when another of their number goes down, without seriously thinking, that they may be next"?

Although the major causes of student unrest are outside the universities (Vietnam, the urban crisis, the black revolution) and cannot be solved by them alone, the way in which unrest is expressed, whether creatively or violently, can be influenced by the ideas and attitudes brought to it. This is particularly true today. For although comparatively few institutions have been the scene of violent demonstrations as serious as those at Columbia, Berkeley, and San Francisco State, there is hardly a college or university in the country in which there is not some marked uneasiness, some movement among students toward direct action on the verge of exploding into sit-downs, sit-ins, and other forms of mass violations of rules and regulations suddenly discovered to be as silly, anachronistic, or authoritarian—as some of them undoubtedly are.

But what struck me about the mood of the students in scores of colleges I visited is that even when these rules and regulations were *not* being enforced, and student conduct was as free and uninhibited as on campuses not subject to these objectionable rules, there was an insistence on their abolition—despite evidence that the formal abolition was likely to stir up a hornet's nest among alumni or townsfolk or state legislatures.

This testified partly to student impatience with the "hypocrisy" of tolerating laws that were not being enforced, but even more to the presence of a desire to precipate a showdown with authority, to be where the action is, to have the nation's television cameras focused on the local scene and on the local leaders of dissent.

One of the undoubted effects of the kind of coverage given campus disorders by the mass media in their alleged desire merely to report these occurrences is to encourage them by exaggerating their scope and glorifying the heroes of the moment.

Frenzy and excitement among student bodies have always been contagious. Last year, events on some campuses, even chants and slogans, broadcast at once, had a direct influence on happenings on other campuses. That is why the universities of this country are in this "all together," and why capitulation to extremism anywhere weakens resistance to extremism everywhere.

To an already volatile situation must be added the Students for a Democratic Society, an explosive element that claims tens of thousands of militant activists in hundreds of chapters. The SDS is an openly social-revolutionary organization, dedicated not to educational reform wherever needed, but to a strategy of politicalization of a university by the tactics of physically violent confrontation. Its operating maxim could well be: "The bloodier the confrontation, the better for our cause, and the worse for the Establishment." Its presence is sufficient to convert a situation in which problems exist into a permanent educational crisis.

The members of the SDS are ideologically confused but they constitute a hard, fanatical core of highly politicalized individuals among student bodies, extremely skillful in the arts of generating conflicts and disruption through agitation and manipulation of mass organizations. They and their congeners among the New Left, including their faculty allies, would be hard to contain by wise and enlightened administrators and faculties.

Unfortunately, these traits have not been conspicuously in evidence even in places where one would expect them. This is suggested by the fact that the worst excesses on our campuses have occurred at the most liberal institutions. The University of California, San Francisco State College, the University of Colorado, Roosevelt College, Columbia University, and New York University—these read like the beginning of a roll call of the centers of intellectual dissent, experiment, and even educational permissiveness in American life. Events on these campuses, as well as at Swarthmore and Oberlin, reveal the absurdity of the claim that the student revolution has been the consequence of dissatisfaction with the educational curriculum.

Educational changes are often desirable, but it was not a failure to introduce them that provoked the recent outbreaks of student violence, or encouraged continuance of these outbreaks. Much more warranted, as an explanation of the failure to meet the initial challenge of student disruption and to stem its growth, is a mistaken theory of liberalism, a reliance upon what I call *ritualistic* rather than realistic liberalism—a doctrinaire view that does not recognize the difference between belief or doctrine and behavior, and that refuses to grasp the fact, obvious in law and common sense, that incitement to violence is a form of behavior. It is a view that does not realize that although order is possible without justice, justice is impossible without order.

The realistic liberal outlook in education cannot be strictly identified with the liberal outlook in politics because the academic community cannot be equated with the political community. Although we may recognize the autonomy of the academic community, such autonomy cannot be complete since the political community in many ways underwrites its operation. But what both communities have in common is the centrality of the notion of due process.

Due process in the political community is spelled out in terms of specific mechanisms through which, out of the clash of public opinions, public policy is forged. Where due process is violated, consent is coerced, and cannot be freely given. The unlimited spectrum of ideas remains unabridged in the political community up to the point of advocacy, but not to the point of violent action or the incitement of violence. The forces of the state, the whole apparatus of restraint and punishment, enter the scene where the freedom of choice of the citizenry is threatened by extralegal activity.

Due process in the academic community is reliant upon the

process of rationality. It cannot be the same as due process in the political community as far as the *mechanisms* of determining the outcome of rational activity. For what controls the nature and direction of due process in the academic community is derived from its educational goal—the effective pursuit, discovery, publication, and teaching of the truth. In the political community all men are equal as citizens not only as participants in, and contributors to, the political process, but as voters and decision-makers on the primary level. Not so in the academic community. What qualifies a man to enjoy equal human or political rights does not qualify him to teach equally with others or even to study equally on every level.

There is an authoritative, *not* authoritarian, aspect of the process of teaching and learning that depends not upon the person or power of the teacher, but upon the authority of his knowledge, the cogency of his method, the scope and depth of his experience. But whatever the differences in the power of making decisions flowing from legitimate differences in educational authority, there is an equality of learners, whether of teachers or students, in the rational processes by which knowledge is won, methods developed, and experience enriched.

In a liberal educational regimen, everything is subject to the rule of reason, and all are equals as questioners and participants. Whoever interferes with academic due process either by violence or threat of violence places himself outside the academic community, and incurs the sanctions appropriate to the gravity of his offense from censure to suspension to expulsion.

The peculiar deficiency of the ritualistic liberal educational establishments is the failure to meet violations of rational due process with appropriate sanctions or to meet them in a timely and intelligent manner. There is a tendency to close an eye to expressions of lawless behavior on the part of students who, in the name of freedom, deprive their fellow students of the freedom to pursue their studies. It is as if the liberal administration sought to appease the challenge to its continued existence by treating such incidents as if they had never happened.

There is no panacea that can be applied to all situations. It is not a question of a hard line or a soft line, but of an intelligent line. It is easy to give advice from hindsight, to be wise and cocksure after the event. But it is always helpful for the faculty to promulgate in advance fair guidelines for action, so that students will know what to expect. In general, no negotiations should be conducted under threat of coercion, or when administrators or faculty are held captive. In general, no amnesty for lawlessness or violence should be offered. In general, organizations refuse to accept disciplinary principles worked out by official representatives of the student body and faculty should be denied recognition and the use of university facilities.

As a rule, it is the first step that is *not* taken that costs so much. Both at Berkeley and Columbia, failure to act decisively at the first disruption of university functions undoubtedly contributed to the students' expectation that they could escalate their lawlessness with impunity. Sometimes the attempt to retrieve a failure to meet student disruption promptly and fairly results in a greater failure.

When student defiance of reasonable rules and regulations is pointedly and continuously ignored, and then subsequently disciplined, the consequence may be worse than if the first infraction had been totally amnestied. Unnecessary delay in initiating the disciplinary measures—however mild—incurred by the infraction of rules can make it appear to large numbers of the uninformed that these students are the innocent victims of vindictive and gratuitous punishment.

The fourth and largest illegal trespass at Berkeley—the seizure of Sproul Hall—came as a consequence of the summons to four student leaders to appear before the Disciplinary Committee several weeks after they had committed the violations for which they were being called to account. There was a similar situation at Columbia. The first action that presaged the events of 1968 occurred in 1965 when students forcibly prevented the N.R.O.T.C. award ceremony. In 1967, "the administration canceled the ceremony citing insufficient time to prepare against violence." ("The Cox Report".) Violence seemed to pay off. A handful of students had forced their will on the university at the cost of seven letters of censure. After the ban on indoor demonstrations had been promulgated at Columbia—both because it interfered with the teaching of classes and because of the dangers of violence between opposing groups of demonstrating students—it was not enforced on three important occasions where it was clearly violated.

When the ban was finally invoked, it seemed to many who were unaware of the past history of student provocation and university restraint that the disciplinary action, even if feeble, was arbitrary. It is widely believed, even by some of the SDS members, that if the Columbia University authorities had moved vigorously to enforce existing regulations against the lawless trespass and destruction of property by the small group that sparked the seizure of buildings on the first day, subsequent developments would have been avoided. For campus sentiment was overwhelmingly hostile to the student rebels at the outset.

The ironical aspect of the situation is that despite the liberal character of the institutions in question, a false view of what it means to be liberal seems to provoke or to exacerbate disturbances on the campus. In certain faculty quarters especially, it is believed that the very nature of a liberal educational community necessitates, independent of any student action, an absolute taboo against physical or police sanctions. At a large metropolitan university during a student strike called by a small and rabidly fanatical minority to protest the dismissal of an administrator guilty of vicious anti-Semitic incitement, a faculty group tried to get a resolution adopted pledging the university "not to call upon the police *under any circumstances.*" Had such a resolution been adopted it would have given those who made a cult of violence assurances in advance that they could carry on as they pleased, no matter what the cost to life, limb, and university property. It would have encouraged the very violence those who favored the resolution professed to deplore.

"What's so tragic about the destruction of a little property?" one professor inquired.

He only shrugged when a colleague sardonically added, "Or a little fire?"

In the academy as elsewhere, there is no substitute for common sense. As it was, fire hoses were cut, elevators jammed to a point where their operation was dangerous to life and limb and their operation temporarily suspended, and the auditorium in the student center set afire.

Some faculty members see truly, in the words of a perceptive member of the Columbia staff, that "the authority of a university is not a civil authority, but a moral one." But he mistakenly concludes that the disruptive activities of students "can only be contained by faculty and by other students, not by the police." This is morality not of this world but of the hand-wringing, ineffectual spirit that leaves this world and its universities in possession of callow, ruthless fanatics prepared to threaten or use violence.

"Confrontation politics" in the moral academic community "is inadmissible," we are assured by those who love everybody and want to be loved by everybody. Excellent! But what if some students do what is inadmissable? What if they resort to pillage, vandalism, personal assault? What if the torch of learning in some hands becomes a torch of arson? To say that only other students can contain them, and not the police, is to forget that once we leave the world of the spirit, this is an invitation to civil war.

Wars of containment, as we know, can be quite bloody. The police may have to be called in to prevent students from containing (and maiming) each other. And like all sentimentalizing in this cruel world, the fear of relying on the police in *any* circumstances to resist the militant politics of confrontation, which brutally scorns the rationalities of academic due process, is to rely upon the politics of capitulation. It is administrative and/or faculty cowardice masquerading as educational statesmanship. It receives and deserves the contempt with which the storm troopers of the SDS greet it as they prepare for the next phase in the escalating cycle of disruption and violence.

In the light of recent events on campuses and the reactions they have inspired, it should be obvious that the SDS is *not* a Trojan horse in American higher education. It is today the "armed warrior" of antieducation. It makes no secret of its desire to destroy American democracy and the universities that it considers as a faithful replica of that iniquitous society. No, the Trojan horse in American higher education is the rickety structure of doctrinaire thought that shelters the SDS even when it takes official responsibility for violent actions, gives it a free field for operation, retreats before the politics of confrontation, and either shrinks from applying fairly and firmly the rules of reason that

THE TROJAN HORSE IN AMERICAN EDUCATION 243

should bind the academic community, or interprets them as if they had no more restraining force in times of crisis than ropes of sand.

The facts about the SDS are well known. It has the virtues of openness as well as courage. It takes public responsibility for its action of violence, and promises more to come. For it, the campuses are the front-line barricades in total war against American society. Persistent refusal to recognize these facts has prevented administrators and faculties from preparing proper defensive measures to keep the universities free. This refusal is sometimes undergirded by the odd belief that disciplinary action against an organization that officially organizes violence on campus is incompatible with the concept of a university as a "free marketplace of ideas."

The conjunction of attitude and belief is a forerunner of educational disaster. This is illustrated by the pattern of events within the last two years at the University of Colorado. It culminated early this March in the most violent outbreak in the history of the university, when a guest of the university, President S. I. Hayakawa of San Francisco State College, was almost mobbed by bottle-throwing members of the SDS and their Black Nationalist allies to prevent him from speaking.

Despite its previous actions of violence and the absence of any pledge to forswear violence in the future, the SDS had been reinstated on the campus on the ground that the university must serve "as a free market of ideas." The SDS promptly showed that its purpose was precisely to destroy the university as a free market of ideas.

The detailed story is too long to relate here,* but it can serve as a paradigm case of high-minded blunder, panicky ineptitude, and self-righteous obtuseness on the part of some regents, administrators, and faculty members who are convinced that true tolerance requires that we tolerate the actively intolerant.

In the last analysis, it is the faculties who are responsible for the present state of American universities—responsible because of their apathy for what has developed in the past, and for missed educational opportunities. Despite what is said by outsiders, the

* See Appendix III, pp. 246 ff. for the details.

faculties of most universities possess great powers that they have so far been reluctant to use. No policy in education can succeed without their support. Theirs is the primary responsibility for upholding academic freedom. Now that American higher education is at bay, challenged as it has never been before by forces *within* the academic community, the faculties must marshal the courage to put freedom first, and to defend it accordingly.

At the same time, as they move to safeguard the integrity of the educational process, faculties should, wherever they are not already doing so, undertake a critical review of all aspects of the curriculum and university life. Provisions should be made for the airing and public discussion of all student grievances. Students should be invited to assess existing courses, methods of teaching, the effectiveness of their teachers, and to make proposals for new courses.

It is a libel on American educators to imply that they are hostile to educational change. Most part criticism has inveighed against them for making curricular revisions too readily at the first cries of "relevance" by pressure groups. Educational crackpots are now rushing to claim that had their curricular panaceas been adopted, student violence would have been avoided. They assiduously ignore the fact that the extremist student groups are trying to bring down bigger game.

John Dewey was fond of saying that in the modern world there is no such thing as the *status quo*. Change in education, as in society, is inescapable. The only questions are whether the direction and content of change are sound, and what the rate and magnitude of change should be. Men of goodwill may differ about the answers. But no matter how profound the differences, they do not justify the resort to violence and the threat of violence to impose solutions. In a secular society, the places where human beings assemble to inquire and to reason together should be regarded as sacred ground. Whoever desecrates it should feel the disapproval of the entire community.

APPENDIX III

# LIBERALISM AND COMMON SENSE
# The Case of the
# University of Colorado

One of the saddest aspects of the student rebellion has been the scorn, contumely, and abuse poured on the heads of men of intelligence and goodwill who have found themselves at the head of educational institutions when the tactics of confrontation have erupted into lawlessness and violence. Anything they do or fail to do is sure to be denounced by some highly articulate group. Almost invariably they become the objects of rage and hate by radical student militants and their following unless they unceremoniously capitulate. The Puseys, the Kerrs, the Levis, the Trumans, the Hayakawas, and Kirks become sinister figures in the demonology of the academic "Resistance," whose myths gradually find some credence—strange as that may be—in circles not so emotional. In the university today, an administrator's lifework and career can tumble into ruins within a few months.

One does not have to agree with the educational philosophy of these men or their administrative decisions in times of crisis to repudiate the slanders, the caricatures, and the willful unfairness of the charge of illiberalism against them. There are very few administrators of the well-known colleges and universities of the country who are not liberal in both their educational and political outlook. It is a safe generalization that educationally administrators as a group are more liberal, more experimental minded than faculties.

Where administrators have been high-handed, reactionary, and autocratic, one could say they have brought their troubles on themselves. But the pity is that there have been administrators, intensely desirous of being liberal, and of proclaiming their liberalism, who have brought disaster on themselves and their institutions because of their failure to understand the principles of liberalism. In many instances they have mechanically repeated slogans and formulae instead of using their intelligence to make relevant distinctions.

For pedagogic purposes, perhaps the best illustration of how misconceptions of liberalism can feed the fires of disorder is provided by developments at the University of Colorado during the last few years. What Tolstoy said of families is roughly true of universities, too. Every happy university is like every other happy university, but every unhappy university is unhappy in its own unique way. Nonetheless, as different as they are, universities can learn from each other—especially in a world where some problems are common—what to avoid, what to expect, and the likely sources of trouble. The University of Colorado unfortunately did not learn from others' experience nor from its own.

What happened there is particularly instructive because at first glance this was one of the places least expected to experience the bizarre events I shall recount. Nestling at the foot of the Rockies, its campus provides comfortable and modern facilities for study and living against a physical background of great beauty. Educationally, it is one of the most liberal institutions in the country, with an impressive record of academic freedom, all the more noteworthy because it flourishes in a politically conservative state—although some caustic liberal observers contend that events on the campus during the last ten years have helped to keep the state conservative.

During this period the university has been in almost continuous turmoil, with the faculty and administration, including some members of the Board of Regents, leaning over backward in their avowals of liberalism. At crucial moments, their judgments and decisions have been self-consciously derived from what they imagined the principles of liberalism to be. It should also be noted that the Board of Regents is an elected body of six members who serve without pay for their onerous duties. They cannot plausibly be charged as a body with representing the so-called "military-industrial complex." The fact that they are elected and that issues of university policy are subjects of intense public discussion justify referring to the system as one of "community involvement" in higher education.

The intellectual climate of the university may be inferred from the fact that during the fifties it bravely withstood attacks against several teachers who had formerly been active members of the Communist party. One of the teachers, in fact, by his own avowal, resigned from the party, not because he was disillusioned with its objectives but because it was not struggling hard enough to realize them. But this tolerance apparently was not extended to liberals who were outspoken opponents of communism.

For years, charges and countercharges had circulated concerning discriminatory practices in some departments against individuals who were too militantly anti-Communist, resulting in the loss to other universities of talented scholars and teachers. The situation came to a head in 1967 when the Regents appointed a special committee to investigate explicit charges that at least two departments of the university had persistently harassed scholars of high professional standing because of their anti-Communist views by delaying their promotions, denying them salary increases commensurate with their achievementss—while rewarding collegues disproportionately whose political views were more acceptable—and subjecting them to the galling tyrannies of academic vindictiveness, which seem so petty to the layman but which can exhaust the strongest of spirits.

The members of the Committee of Investigation were Dr. Eugene Dawson, president of Temple Buell College, Dr. Ben H. Parker, former president of the Colorado School of Mines, and the Hon. Albert T. Frantz, former chief justice of the Colorado Supreme Court. After prolonged hearings in which all parties were heard, this distinguished commission filed its report with the Board of Regents in May, 1969. It makes depressing reading. Among other things, the committee reported:

> Testimony offered and evidence submitted during the . . . hearings would lead members of the panel to conclude that the climate of the department under review has, at times, been less than desirable, and on numerous occasions shocking . . . Discrimination based on ideological differences result-

ing in repressive measures against younger faculty members
is exercised within the Department of Political Science.
This can only exist because sanctioned by the majority of
the departmental faculty. (P. 9 of the official report.)

A month after the report of the special investigating committee
was filed with the Board of Regents, it appointed as the new
chairman of the Department of Political Science, Richard Wilson
one of the leading spirits of this majority by a vote of four to
two.

Whatever one can say about the background of developments
at the University of Colorado, it certainly cannot be characterized fairly as one of hostility to left-wing views and causes,
as charged by the SDS, or as anything but liberal in the conventional sense of that term.


On October 25, 1967, a group of SDS activists forcibly
blocked the placement office of the university, preventing entrance and egress, and prohibited office personnel from properly
maintaining services. They deprived other students of their rights
to use the placement services. They repeatedly refused to obey
orders of university officials to cease and desist. On November
7, 1967, they were charged with five specific counts of violation of university regulations.

On November 9, hearings were begun before the University
Discipline Committee (UDC). The students were represented
by counsel. To accommodate them further, sessions of the committee that formerly had been closed were opened to the public.
The hearing room was specially selected at the request of the
students to accommodate all the students and their many sympathizers, who functioned as a claque, applauding the students
and booing and jeering at witnesses who testified against them.

Every student charged was given unlimited leeway to testify
as he pleased, and even persons who were not members of the
academic community and not present when the acts were committed were allowed to present ideological support and praise for
the students charged.

At the conclusion of the hearings, the counsel for the students thanked the committee profusely for its "eminently cor-

rect procedure by any standard of fairness." ("Transcript of Hearings," Part I, p. 94.) The evidence showed that the dean and some members of the faculty prevented students, outraged by the SDS refusal to permit them access to the placement office, from assaulting the lawless demonstrators—narrowly averting a riot.

The University Discipline Committee unanimously found the members of the SDS guilty as charged.

Whereupon they and their counsel appealed to the appellate Subcommittee of the Administrative Council, which held open hearings on December 13, 1967. On December 19, after reading and considering the entire transcript of 225 pages before the UDC and a forty-eight page brief on behalf of the students and listening to oral argument by all three counsel for the students, it affirmed the findings of the UDC as correct. It upheld the comparatively mild punishment of suspension and probation.

The students then appealed to the Regents of the University of Colorado, which held open hearings at its regular meeting of January 13, 1968. At this hearing, students were represented by new counsel from the Colorado Civil Liberties Union. After a stormy and disorderly meeting, the Regents unaimously upheld the decision of the subcommittee of the Administrative Council of December 19, 1967.

Thereupon the students and their counsel appealed to the Federal Court for the District of Colorado for an injunction against the president and Regents of the University of Colorado on the ground that the students' Constitutional rights had been violated because of a failure of due process, arbitrary punishment, etc.

Judge Alfred A. Arraj, Chief Judge of the U.S. District Court, in a verbal ruling on February 2 and a written opinion of February 14, 1968, dismissed the appeal for an injunction and upheld the university in an unusually strong and eloquent declaration. He found absolutely no merit in the SDS contentions, and praised particularly the character of the due process they had received, which was far and beyond what was necessary. The judge declared that the University Discipline Committee "acted fairly and justly in this case. They were patient. They were deliberate. Their decision was unanimous."

In passing, one should point out that due process does not

require this overelaborate procedure. Thirty students of the SDS committing individual, unrelated, acts of lawlessness could tie up the university for years by making appeals from appeals from appeals. So long as an appeal can be taken from the University Discipline Committee to the courts, the students have adequate constitutional protection. Liberalism is not incompatible with common sense.

But the significant thing to observe is the behavior of the students at the open hearings before the meeting of the Regents on January 13. The official record (p. 28) of events after the unanimous vote was cast upholding the decision of the subcommittee of the Administrative Council—reads:

Voice (from the audience)—BASTARDS!

After this decision, a motion was made and seconded that if if any of the suspended students (only eight of the twenty two charged were punished with suspension for one term), at any time prior to the expiration of their period of suspension. promised not to repeat the actions for which they had been found guilty, they could file special petitions for readmission. (Counsel for the Students reported that none of the students would promise to refrain from acting in the same way again.) The motion was then defeated. President Smiley announced, "The motion is lost."

I read again from the official record page 31.

Voice (from the audience)—Fuck you, all of you!

Pres. Smiley—We will now have a five minute recess.

(Whereupon a five-minute recess was had, after which the board returned to the room and the following proceedings were had [sic!]:

Pres. Smiley—Gentlemen, if you are ready . . .

(Whereupon a number of students converged upon the table of the board and flung their student cards at the board members; then withdrew and threw a coin at the table from across the room. . . .)

No action apparently was taken by the Regents or the president in the face of these indecent, obscene and insulting epithets, and deliberately offensive personal misconduct, which was tantamount to physical assault. By no stretch of the imagination, even of the students' own counsel, who condemned these actions, could this behavior be regarded as constitutionally privileged. Indeed, such actions were subject to both criminal arrest and university discipline. They were ignored by the president and Regents, although I can find nothing in the philosophy of liberalism, or in the ethics of self-respect and respect for others or the principles of academic freedom that requires that such misconduct be tolerated.

This whole scene, and others like it at other institutions, have no precedents in the entire history of American higher education. No reasonable person could be blind to the character of the individuals and movement that had been given every benefit of academic due process. What happened subsequently at the judicial hearings of Columbia University was much worse. It indicated a general pattern of behavior by the SDS.

During the period of their suspension, several leaders of the SDS, although barred from classes, remained on campus and were very active in SDS affairs. Nonetheless, although they refused to give any assurances that they would refrain from further acts of lawlessness of the kind they had been found guilty of, and although the statutes of the university clearly warrant denial of admission for "serious failure to observe the standards of conduct which are prescribed by the regulations of the university or implied by membership in the university community," they were readmitted by the administration in June, 1968.

Emboldened by this treatment, the SDS applied for permission to use the facilities of the university to act as host to the national organization at Boulder. The ultimate goal of the SDS may be to destroy the existing university but, meanwhile, it must have some house room to plan the strategy and tactics of the demolition. The request set off a tragi-comic process of doubt, discussion, and action that revealed as clearly as anything could that some members of the administration had made a fetish of the words "academic freedom" without grasping the substance of the concept.

The subordinates of the president in charge of the student affairs had recommended that the request of the national organization of the SDS be granted, apparently because they feared the confrontation or disorder by the SDS students if the request were denied. The president, fearful of the responsibility of saying "Yes" or "No" passed the decision on to the Regents, who split evenly on the issue. The president then broke the tie with his statement that "the university must be a marketplace for ideas."

Actually, the question whether an outside organization should be permitted the use of university property for nonuniversity use has nothing to do either with academic freedom or free speech. This question arises only when the rights of teachers and students to teach and learn are involved, or when it is a question of permitting representatives of different political views to present them on the campus. In this respect the University of Colorado permits the widest freedom. A Socialist, a Fascist, racist, or Communist may present his ideas if the students wish to hear him. But it is utterly ridiculous to assert that, because the Communist position or the SDS position is permitted to be presented, therefore a request of the national Communist party or of the national SDS for the use of university facilities for organizational purposes must be granted, lest the university lapse into a violation of academic freedom or free speech.

A request of this kind has nothing to do with academic freedom or free speech as long as the expression of the position in other ways is normally permitted. Such a request is really a cheeky and mocking demand, backed up by threats of making trouble otherwise, for the use of the university's good name. There is a prestige in meeting on university grounds and in university rooms that helps the cause. But why should the university become a party to it, even an unwilling party, and what in the world has it to do with the university being "a marketplace for ideas"? The SDS was not selling ideas but planning an assault on the integrity of American educational institutions, including the University of Colorado.

The confusion arose in the minds of the president and the Regents because they were troubled by a seeming inconsistency in denying the request of the national organization of the SDS to use university facilities whereas the request of other organizations was granted. One regent actually said, "If use of the facilities were denied, the validity of the arguments made to students who demonstrated against the CIA last fall would be destroyed. . . . To be consistent the university must make its facilities open to all, regardless of whether the news of those who appear coincide with our views." (P. 23 from the official minutes of September 20, 1968.)

This is clearly absurd. Because some students are willing to band together for some reason as a group affiliated with some national organization, does not give that organization the right to use university facilities. If the university were to act on this silly kind of consistency, the next conventon of the Communist party or the Black Panthers or the American Nazis would be held at Boulder. All it would require would be for a few students to call themselves a branch.

Actually the reference to the case of the SDS disruption of the CIA recruiting visit underscores the fact that no question of academic freedom is involved. The CIA was not holding a national convention at Boulder. It was not selling any "ideas in the marketplace." It was there to give students at the University of Colorado a chance to interview the CIA representative for jobs on the same terms as representatives of other agencies, private and public. It was not the academic freedom of the CIA that was being defended against the SDS—*one might even argue that no recruiting agency has a legitimate place on the campus!*—but only the rights of students to be free of harassment by the SDS as they sought to interview the representatives of employing firms; their right to come and go freely; and their right to be served by university personnel. The rights of the SDS students *to protest* the presence of the CIA was not being denied. They were punished not for their dissent but for their lawlessness.

Does it follow that if any nonuniversity group is permitted to use the university facilities, every group must be permitted to do so? Of course not! University policy adopted by the Regents on November 18, 1955, laid down two generic conditions for the use of university facilities by nonuniversity groups:

A. The event may not conflict with the functions, activities, or regular operations of university agencies.

B. The provision of facilities or services to nonuniversity activities must be in accord with the best interests of the community and state.

(The language of these conditions leaves something to be desired. To be enforceable, B. must be read to mean "must be compatible with the educational and public-service objectives of the university.")

It is quite clear that these directives solve the question of consistency. There is no inconsistency in permitting the Modern Language Association to use the facilities of this university and barring them to the American Nazi party or the Ku Klux Klan or the Communist party, even if the latter were to plead that all they wanted to do was to sell their ideological goods in President Smiley's "marketplace of ideas."

Similarly there is no inconsistency in leasing university facilities to a hiking club but refusing to do so to a nudist colony; in allowing Young Democrats, Young Republicans, and Young Socialists to use facilities—and *in the light of its program and history of organizing violent confrontations*—denying their use to the national SDS. For, in the first case, the goals and activities of the organizations in question are comparable with the educational objectives of the university; and in the second case, not. This is no arbitrary distinction, and the courts will uphold it,

Some ritualistic liberals will see and applaud the distinction when one points out that although students have a right to hear a racist speaker if they wish to invite one to address them, this does not mean that the university must recognize the existence of a student organization based on principles of racist discrimination or invite the national organization of racists to use campus facilities. This is incompatible with the educational objectives of the university. However, just as soon as the same principles are applied to the SDS, these ritualistic liberals will cry that "the free marketplace of ideas" is being violated—whereas in both cases the more legitimate claim is that it is being protected.

The University (of Colorado) offers a clear case in which failure to understand the true meaning of liberalism led to an awful blunder that weakened the defense of academic freedom despite the unctuous rhetoric about preserving it. But worse was to come as the unhappy consequences of this decision unfolded. One of the regents, fearful that the SDS convention might be used to plan for confrontations that were illegal on their face—something forbidden by the laws of the regents on the policies of university—moved as a substitute motion "that the SDS National Council be allowed to use University facilities for its meetings, providing all sessions are open to the press and the public."

Needless to say, the SDS was jubilant about the decision, gave all the required assurances, and then proceeded to violate them by barring all tapes and television cameras—the tool of the modern press—from meetings.

(The SDS knew what it was doing when it barred tapes. Their language is extreme and frightening. Penciled notes can be impunged as inaccurate but the voice on the tape is damning, and for obvious political reasons the SDS felt it could not permit the permanent record to be made.)

At first university officials insisted that TV cameras and tapes be admitted since this was part of the bargain. The SDS leaders in rejoinder "pointed out that four hundred to five hundred young radicals were already on their way to Boulder, that some were potentially violent and beyond their leader's control, and that violence might result if the CU forced a confrontation on this issue." (*Denver Post*, October 16, 1968.) This, of course, is a typical stratagem. It is not the SDS that initiates the violence or seeks the confrontation. The SDS only defends itself against violence when steps are taken to meet its lawless action. In this way it seeks to put the odium on its victims.

The university, or rather the president, yielded to this threat and at the first meeting the SDS barred the presence of any cameras and tapes. When infuriated TV, radio, and press men broadcast the decision, Regent Danial Lynch, who had moved the substitute motion that granted the request of the SDS, subject to the condition of a completely open and public meeting, got in touch with the president and informed him that the sense or intent of the motion was that cameras and tape recorders should be permitted—that open and public meant open and public. The president reversed himself and withdrew his earlier capitulation.

But when an attempt was made to introduce the cameras and tape recorders, the SDS forcibly prevented it, by blocking and seizing instruments, and violently ejecting cameramen, their police escort, and Regent Lynch himself.

At a press conference held by President Smiley and Regent Lynch they confessed that the members of the press "would have to choose between covering the SDS convention or covering a riot." After further consultation the university officials reversed themselves again and decided not to use police either to force the admission of cameramen or to clear the hall.

The SDS had scored a great triumph by its threat to riot. Both the president of the institution and the regents who suported him not only revealed themselves as hopelessly confused about the nature of academic freedom, but also as lacking the courage to stand on the principles they themselves had laid down. It was a sad day for the University of Colorado and for American higher education, for it only emboldened the SDS and its allies to continue their policies of confrontation and educational demoralization.

There is no space here to outline a counterstrategy to combat by educational and other means, within the framework of liberalism and academic freedom, the program of the SDS and of its allies among the junior faculty. Both administrators and faculties must see the SDS as it is, and disabuse themselves of the pitiful illusion that it wishes to take its place side by side with other student organizations in the university, conceived as free marketplace of ideas.

Where there is a record of SDS-inspired violence, particularly when it takes official responsibility for the action, it should be treated like any other organization that foments disorder. If found guilty after a formal hearing before the appropriate disciplinary bodies, university recognition should be withdrawn and the use of campus facilities denied. Here, too, the persistent confusion of the political community and the academic community crops up again in the position of those who demand that procedural safeguards available to defendants in a *criminal* trial be accorded to students in *administrative procedures* involving probation or suspension or expulsion.

All the relevant court cases, and notably the most recent decision, *Grossner v. Trustees of Columbia University* (287 F. Supp. 535 [1968]), make abundantly clear that the very function of the university renders this unnecessary when reasonable regulations governing student behavior exist. To insist that a full common law trial must take place whenever any disciplinary proceedings are undertaken against students or their organizations is almost as absurd as to assert that when a teacher fails a student for giving wrong answers in an oral examination he is denying him his constitutional right of free speech. The activities of organizations on the campus must always be evaluated in the light of the central purposes of the university.

The public reaction to the arrogance of the SDS, its failure to honor its promises, its manhandling of those who were exercising their rights was overwhelmingly hostile, and the Regents called upon the Joint Board on Student Organizations and Social Life, composed of three faculty members and three students, to report on the activities of the SDS chapter. On November 22, 1968, the Regents, because of the illness of one of its members who had previously voted to open the campus to the national organization, withdrew the affiliate status of the SDS by a vote of three to two. This action denied the organization the use of university facilities and services although, as individuals, members of the SDS were left free to do almost everything the SDS could do as a group. The action of the Regents actually had very little effect on the behavior (or language!) of the SDS, which was more wounded in its sensibilities than in its power.

But sensing an issue that could radicalize the campus, the SDS portrayed itself as an outraged victim of arbitrary administrative tyranny. In this claim, it was eloquently aided by some members of the faculty. One of them at a rally protesting the decision declared: "I cannot urge you to obey the order they [the Regents] made on Friday. They have disaffiliated themselves from the university."

It was also aided by the dissenting Regents, one of whom, Daniel Lynch, asserted that the SDS was being hanged without a trial. It was true that the action, long delayed, was in some respects precipitate; that the procedure would have been improved if it had been more deliberate. Not satisfied with contesting the wisdom of the action, Rent Lynch charged that the basic civil rights of the SDS members were being violated—a very serious charge.

In a letter to the *Boulder Daily Camera* (November 20) he said:

I took an oath to uphold the Constitution of the United
States, which in turn requires that, each person, good and
evil, be given due process of law before being deprived of
rights and privileges accorded by the state.

In other words, Regent Lynch considered the action of disaffiliation to be illegal. So did the SDS, which filed a suit with
the Denver U.S. District Court against the Board of Regents.
However, it did not wait for the judicial judgment as to whether
the dissaffiliation violated the accepted standards of either administrative or criminal law—which would have clarified the
whole situation.

Assured by the public statement of three regents (including
the one whose absence had resulted in the 3-to-2 vote for disaffiliation) that if it reapplied, it would be reaffiliated, and fearful that the judicial decision would go against it, the SDS withdrew its legal suit a few minutes before a motion to reaffiliate
the organization was introduced at the December meeting of the
board. The SDS was acting in apparent concert with some of the
regents, who pleaded with them to avoid "extralegal or disorderly means of protest" on the strength of the renewed assurance of support.

To a disinterested observer it would seem that if it was
wrong to disaffiliate the SDS without hearings about the nature
and program of its activities, it was just as wrong to reaffiliate
it without the same due process, especially since there was a
prima facie case against it on the basis of its previous actions.

The motion to reaffiliate resulted in the expected tie vote,
and once more, President Smiley voted affirmatively, in favor of
the SDS. He justified his vote, once again, on the ground that
he believed the university should be "a free market of ideas"—
as if it were the *ideas* of the SDS that were at issue, ideas its members had always been free to propagate, rather than its *actions*.
This declaration played nicely into the hands of the SDS, which
in the meantime had launched a broad-gauged campaign in
behalf of "free speech," which it maintained was the only
issue at stake.

As if to teach the president and the regents voting in its favor
a lesson as to what it really meant by "free speech," the SDS,
in conjunction with the Black Nationalist students, proceeded

to stage one of the most violent and disgraceful riots in the history of American education on March 3, 1969. In an attempt to prevent Dr. S. I. Hayakawa from speaking at the Mackay Auditorium, its members first set up a clamor to make him inaudible, then hurled steel chairs and glass bottles at him, tossed burning cigarettes onto the platform, and at the critical moment stormed the podium, only to be beaten back by a force of security guards and local policemen. A panic in the audience with a possible great loss of life was narrowly averted.

The complete details of this incredible episode were described by a group of staff members of the *Denver Post* in the March 23, 1969 issue. (A copy is available in pamphlet form from that newspaper.) The following day, the leader of the SDS, speaking at another university campus in the state, confessed that disruptive actions of the magniture launched at Boulder, could not have taken place without careful advance preparation. When word of this came out, with its obviously damaging implications of planned disruption, the public reaction—already high—was intensified. Characteristically, the SDS leader denied that he had said any such thing. He was then confronted with a tape recording of his remarks. This led to an indignant attack by spokesmen of the SDS on "the capitalist press" for tape-recording his speech. The response pointed up the reason for the SDS allergy to tapes at its meetings.

No single event, according to some long-time residents, ever stirred up the state of Colorado as much as this attempt to lynch an invited guest of the university. Its repercussions are bound to be felt for a long time to come, both educationally and politically. At a subsequent meeting of the Board of Regents, after painstaking hearings before two judicial panels, the board finally voted to disaffiliate the SDS from the University of Colorado by a vote of five to one. Regent Daniel Lynch held out to the last, protesting not his sympathy for the SDS but his belief that such an action would win greater support for it, something much more problematic than its clear violation of every principle of academic civility and freedom. The minutes of the meeting do not reveal any reference to the necessity of preserving the university as a "free market of ideas" as a ground for opposing disaffiliation. This was the reason, it will be recalled, that had moved some of the Regents, notably Regent

Lynch and the president, to approve the invitation of the national organization of the SDS to the campus the previous fall.

By the summer of 1969, more than four hundred universities had refused to permit the national SDS to convene on their campuses. It was reduced to the necessity of hiring a hall in Chicago, where its feuding factions met in turbulent and disorderly meetings. According to Regent Lynch's view, this refusal to give house room to the SDS would constitute evidence that a large sector of American higher education had abandoned belief in the "free market of ideas" and therefore judged deficient in its liberalism. There are much stronger grounds for condemning those who would make such judgments as deficient in their understanding of liberalism.

Happily, the administration or most of the regents, and hopefully, most of the faculty of the University of Colorado, are now aware that the SDS is selling goods other than ideas. But at what a cost! The pity of it is that the evidence was there for all to read. Long before the SDS applied for the use of the facilities of the University of Colorado, Tom Hayden, the thirty-year-old *eminence grise* of the SDS, in his article, "Two, Three, Many Columbias," wrote:

> Columbia University opened a new tactical stage in the resistance movement which began last fall: from overnight occupation of buildings to permanent occupation; from mill-ins to the creation of revolutionary committees; from symbolic civil disobedience to barricaded resistance. Not only are these tactics already being duplicated on other campuses, but they are sure to be surpassed by even more militant tactics. In the future it is conceivable that students will threaten destruction of buildings as a last deterrent to police attacks. Many of the tactics learned can also be applied to smaller hit-and-run operations between strikes: raids on the offices of professors doing weapons research could win substantial support among students while making the university more blatantly repressive. (*Ramparts*, June 15, 1968, p. 40.)

Here the armed enemy of American education is out in the open. Educators should not build a Trojan horse of questionable dogma in which the enemy can hide. In the troublesome days ahead, they would do well to clear their minds of cant and empty rhetoric. They would do well to take their enemy seriously, not to underestimate him and the power of his sympathizers and allies. They should face the truth. There are some things that are worse than defeat in an honorable cause if one has fought to the limits of one's intelligence and courage. When educators are the victims of violence, they should not paralyze themselves or the defense of their institutions by invoking pious and irrelevant platitudes about the "free market of ideas". Nor should they construe student riots, in accordance with the aforementioned directives, as new and original forms of dialogue.

Firmly upholding the principles of academic freedom, both of *Lehrfreiheit* and *Lernfreiheit*, American educators should at the same time insist on the full acceptance of the responsibilities entailed by these academic rights. For without the sense and discipline of responsibility, of the mutuality of respect, academic freedom is indistinguishable from academic anarchy. Where academic anarchy prevails for long, it is followed by academic tyranny or despotism.

# INDEX